Sounds of the

Sounds of the Future

Essays on Music in Science Fiction Film

Edited by
MATHEW J. BARTKOWIAK

McFarland & Company, Inc., Publishers
Jefferson, North Carolina, and London

LIBRARY OF CONGRESS CATALOGUING-IN-PUBLICATION DATA

Sounds of the future : essays on music in science fiction film / edited by Mathew J. Bartkowiak.
    p.   cm.
    Includes bibliographical references and index.

    ISBN 978-0-7864-4480-9
    softcover : 50# alkaline paper ∞

    1. Motion picture music — History and criticism.   2. Science fiction films — History and criticism.   I. Bartkowiak, Mathew J.
ML2075.S685   2010
781.5'42 — dc22   2010001765

British Library cataloguing data are available

Front cover art by Baaron Schulte, 2009

Manufactured in the United States of America

McFarland & Company, Inc., Publishers
  Box 611, Jefferson, North Carolina 28640
  www.mcfarlandpub.com

From Mathew J. Bartkowiak:
To Sara, Ella, and Porter

From all of the contributing authors:
Our sincere thanks to the people at
Film and History, both past and present

Acknowledgments

My sincere thanks to Nelson and Joan Moffat and the Felker Foundation in memory of Pat and Gretchen Felker for their support. Thanks to the faculty and staff at the University of Wisconsin–Marshfield/Wood County and to Andy and Marcie, basking in the glow of "retirement." My gratitude as well to the UW Colleges English Department, and the UW–Marshfield/Wood County Library staff. Also, a thank you to Catherine Kalish, Holly Hassel and Baaron Schulte for his contribution to this book.

Table of Contents

Introduction

Mathew J. Bartkowiak

From *The Day the Earth Stood Still,* to *Star Wars,* to *WALL-E,* music and musical effects affect how we understand film. In science fiction, music plays an especially important role. Music can be our guide to navigating strange, new places, and to encountering new people and forms. In both utopian and nightmarish settings, music acts as a fundamental part of the narrative, guiding us through these foreign territories flickering in front of our eyes. Filmmakers critique, poke fun of, and challenge our thoughts of alternate realities and the future using musical cues that are created to guide the players onscreen and the players off screen (us, the dedicated voyeur). One wave of the hand in front of the theremin or one chord played on the piano can create a shorthand that speaks to us more than any screenwriter could hope to affect with dialogue.

For me, the fascination with this relationship of science fiction and music harkens back to my teenage years. Up late one night, I decided to flip through the channels. Being the multi-mediated, multi-tasking youth of the 1980s that I was, I was doing so while listening to music on my headphones. Don't judge: I've realized it was merely was a training tool for the world of Blackberries and iPhones that engulf us all: at home, sometimes on the roadways, and at work. I happened upon a late-night showing of *Barbarella*. I was amazed and completely confused. The music that I was listening to, probably The Pixies or something else of that musical era, did not match up to the peculiar, confounding visions that I was seeing, and, of course, the skin.

Though fearful that I had come across something that was supposed to be on a scrambled channel at that time of the night, I decided to turn up the volume of the TV, and put down my portable tape player. It was then that my ears helped to make sense of what I was seeing. Though I had missed the minute or so in which the extensive main narrative had been set up, I was cued in to the formula via the soundtrack: Barbarella equals sexy, and heroic; the future equals scary; sex equals an escape from the weird and unknown; sex equals good; and technological innovation pales in comparison to the human experience. Within the musical structure I heard computer noise, feedback that compared to the best Grateful Dead freak-out, along with what sounded like playful cocktail music. Somehow it all came together and helped me make sense of this universe. I was decoding the odd and the strange, as I was decoding the familiar and the comforting/enticing. The film made no sense to me for those few minutes when the music that I was listening to was on my headphones. Music was an absolute for the film that helped me to feel alienated and uncomfortable with the world depicted. It also helped me find the good and comfortable. It brought me back to the present and made me aware of the good old value of sex. Hey, in the case of *Barbarella*, it saved the universe, didn't it?

Later in the collection, you will see that I explore this relationship of music and film in my essay on *Barbarella*. I look at the film not because it necessarily represents a pinnacle of filmmaking. Instead, it highlights and testifies to the important relationship that science fiction has with music, and the need for us to recognize the familiar as well as the unknown: be it utopian or dystopian. The contributors to this book deal sometimes with films that have become canonized works; sometimes they deal with films that have become canonized late-night movie viewing. Whatever the case, they all share an understanding of the importance of the intrinsic need for film-goers to not only see but also hear the future and alternate worlds.

Music is such an important part of the equation because even as our senses are overwhelmed, we look to them to provide some kind of grounding. Filmmakers use music as a sensory experience that helps to construct questions about our present, laugh at our potential legacies, and to guess what could be. It is an easy aspect of film to overlook, as we are so dependent on the "looking." As that brief encounter with *Barbarella* indicates, the role of music, and even the absence of this convention that we are so used to in film, can definitively frame the experience of film for us.

Collectively, *Sounds of the Future: Music in Science Fiction Film* is a book born of the 2008 Film & History conference. The immense amount of interest in the role of music in science-fiction film (both in short and long form) resulted in numerous panels featuring scholars from around the world. Many of the authors who took part in this area are part of this collection (with a few others picked up along in the conversation). The authors taking part in this project have looked into a spectrum of issues dealing with music's role in film. These areas include the technical, including the construction of subjectivity through musical forms and technologies. Other focuses include cultural perspectives on music and film, musicological interrogations of specific films and composers, and so on. No matter the area of focus, the power and potential of musical forms are critically examined by scholars drawn to this powerful intersection of popular culture forms.

Linking together these diverse works is a central theme that will be explored and problematized: the creation of the future and alternate worlds through sound and the centrality of music in constructing the narratives of these visions of the Other and of ourselves. The book is divided into six thematic parts that help to break down this vast spectrum of interactions and possibilities that occur when music and film are put together to interrogate our fantasies and worst nightmares on the screen. The text, every so often, offers diverse views on overlapping subjects. Several cornerstone pieces pop up throughout the book, like the music of *2001: A Space Odyssey*. Occasionally authors may even disagree on the inherent potential and use of music in science fiction film. As *Sounds of the Future* is an interdisciplinary text, this diversity of thought is a crucial part of the final product.

Part I, "'Open the Pod Door, HAL': A Survey of Music's Role in Science Fiction Film," includes two tours of the extraterrestrial landscape of music's interaction with science fiction film. To start, Cara Marisa Deleon, in "A Familiar Sound in a New Place: The Use of the Musical Score Within the Science Fiction Film," offers a broad analysis of the role of music in science fiction film. She posits the idea that musical elements within a film do as much to reaffirm and relate our identities as they do to challenge us with visions of other worlds and times. Music in this specific genre plays on convention and invention to audibly present us this dichotomy. This is a theme that is at the heart of this book, and one that will be dealt with throughout.

Lisa M. Schmidt extends this theme with a focus on measuring the odd or unfamiliar in science fiction music against the classical avant-garde tradition in "A Popular Avant-Garde: The Paradoxical Tradition of Electronic and Atonal Sounds in Sci-Fi Music Scoring." Schmidt sees a paradox in which avant-garde practices and sounds were not merely popularized or homogenized into film, but "were adopted from the musical avant-garde into a popular genre and that these elements remain truly avant-garde while being truly popular...." Like an amorphous shape shifter in a science fiction tale, music seemingly fulfills numerous roles within the genre and within everyday life. It not only challenges us to think of what alternate or future worlds may sound like, but also challenges conceptions of how we sonically define ourselves today.

Part II, "'Give My Regards to the Barycenter': Broadway's Relation to

Science Fiction," deals with the, what some may see as odd, relationship of musical theater to science fiction and the science fiction score and soundtrack. The two essays in this part point out intriguing parallels. Apparently, as consumers of popular culture, we are looking for an escape from the mundane. We want to be shown promise as well as our worst fears. The level of fantasy needed to escape or explore in a science fiction fantasy seemingly is present in the formula of Broadway musicals. Both the sobering and the transitive live in spaces of dialogue and song.

Kathryn A.T. Edney and Kit Hughes, in "'Hello WALL-E!': Nostalgia, Utopia, and the Science Fiction Musical," examine how the sounds of a useable past interact with science fiction conventions in the Disney/Pixar film *WALL-E*. In this compelling melding of science fiction and the musical, "conflicts between horror and utopia will ultimately be resolved with music." The use of *Hello Dolly!* in the film, the authors maintain, also plays on both genres' (science fiction and the musical) dependence on nostalgia for real or imagined purer, better times. Music acts as poignant shorthand for what we have supposedly lost, what could be, as well as being an essential tool for resolving "apparent contradictions between science-fiction and the musical."

Katherine Spring continues the examination of music's role in dealing with promising or threatening ideas of tomorrow or of alternate realities. Spring sees the realities of copyright, technological innovation, and distribution as the all too real systems that shaped visions of the future in her essay, "*Just Imagine*: The Musical Effacement of Dystopia in an Early Sound Film." Songs were cash cows in early sound film that, opposed to the aforementioned work on *WALL-E*, halted the narrative. Popular song, as Spring argues, was deployed "as a significant aesthetic and commercial force." An early product of the sound system, *Just Imagine* proves to be a cross-section and mashing of "two genres in their embryonic, and arguably most malleable phases": today's unlikely conceptualized bedfellows of science fiction and the musical.

Part III, "Becoming the Star-Child: Music and the Construction of Subjectivity," features essays that consider how music constructs and shapes the experience of the science fiction consumer. Seth Mulliken in "Ambient Reverberations: Diegetic Music, Science Fiction, and Otherness" examines how diegetic music is used to create "an auditory construction of the subject." Mulliken, through an examination of *Back to the Future*, *Blade Runner*, *Star Trek V*, *Star Wars*, and *Futurama*, sees that characters, narratives, and audiences of the day are shaped through the musical worlds inhabited in science fiction texts. Music ultimately acts as a way to construct the "Other" through non–Western musical traditions and beyond. "Out of this world" music can be based not only on conceptions of the future, but also on our ethnocentricities of today.

Matthias Konzett, in "Sci-Fi Film and Sounds of the Future," discusses the relationship of image and the potential narrative and social power of sound in the following films: *The Omega Man*, *2001: A Space Odyssey*, *Blade Runner*, *Solaris*, and *Children of Men*. The science fiction sound-scape, he contends, claims a space of independence from the visual that is ripe for experimentation and challenge. Music is able to challenge, reaffirm, and critically comment on the images presented to us, adding a "renewed materiality and plasticity to the image."

Part IV, "Moon/Spoon/Croon: Science Fiction and Popular Music," extends our discussion of music in film further into the practice of popular music by looking at musical forms like rock, lounge, and jazz. In addition to my aforementioned piece on *Barbarella*, the part is comprised of two other essays. The first one, "'It's Hip to Be Square': Rock and Roll and the Future," by Cynthia J. Miller and A. Bowdoin Van Riper, looks into films that employ rock and roll as a central part of the narrative of the otherworldly, or just odd. The two describe how this great music of rebellion and youth somehow got caught up in the world of science and progress. Our fears and fascinations with this sense of "progress," say the authors, was antithetical to the mores of rock. Often, with early intersections of science fiction and rock in the 1950s and 1960s, science and progress run amok could only hope to learn from this music of simple rebellion. By the 1980s and 1990s "scientists and inventors who rocked entered science fiction films in force. Rock became the cinematic hallmark of rebel scientists who followed their own vision of the future, owing allegiance to no master or mainstream ideology." Just like science fiction film itself, the music could speak to our greatest fears and hopes of what was to come.

After my contribution, "The Intergalactic Lounge: *Barbarella* and Hearing the Future," on the scantily-clad, sexually-overt visions of the future Jerome J. Langguth takes us on another otherworldly ride with the transcendent through the music of Sun Ra. In "Proposing an Alter-Destiny: Science Fiction in the Art and Music of Sun Ra," Langguth explores how amidst the strange and unknown in science fiction the music of the future could be sublime in nature. Transcending the sobering realities of race in the United States in his time, Sun Ra combined the ridiculous, the utopian, and the apocalyptic in his music and in the film *Space Is the Place*. A "comic-sublime" approach and aesthetic, as Langguth discusses, is what drew Sun Ra to science fiction, and is a theme needed to understand this enigmatic figure in jazz history and, more specifically, this film.

Part V, "'All Those Moments': Instances That Shaped Our Auditory Future," looks at specific instances in science fiction that, although brief, have shaped our perceptions of the future in film. In "Suspended Motion in the

Title Scene from *The Day the Earth Stood Still*," Stephen Husarik breaks down Bernard Herrmann's monumental work within electronic music: his soundtrack for *The Day the Earth Stood Still*. More specifically, he explores the music present in the very score that inspires the film's name: as the Earth "stands still" Hermann's "The Magnetic Pull" sonically frames the images. In this brief moment, Husarik sees a sonic standard established within the film, as well as within the practice of electronic music period.

Gregg Redner takes us from the musicological to the theoretical with a reading of one of science fiction film's most famous auditory cues, the "Also Sprach Zarathustra" cue from *2001: A Space Odyssey*. In "Strauss, Kubrick and Nietzsche: Recurrence and Reactivity in the Dance of Becoming That Is *2001, A Space Odyssey*," Redner utilizes the work of Nietzsche, as interpreted by Gilles Deleuze, to make sense of the cue's role in the film, and how the cue has and continues to live a life of its own.

Part VI, "'Setting the Controls for the Heart of the Sun': Composers and Compositions in Science Fiction Film," presents two authors who are looking into specific films, composers, and compositions that have shaped science fiction filmmaking and our interpretations of the future or other worlds. John C. Tibbetts begins with "*Rocketship X-M*: The Sounds of a Martian Breeze," which investigates the work of Ferde Grofé in *Rocketship X-M*. Tibbetts guides us through specific instances of music's role in the film and ponders how Grofé's score, rescued from the vaults, might fit into the present and future conventions of our understanding of music via tonality, performance, and instrumentation not only in film, but also beyond in larger musical practices.

Cynthia J. Miller, in "Seeing Beyond His Own Time: The Sounds of Jerry Goldsmith," guides us through the storied career of a composer that is a central sonic fixture of science fiction film. Miller discusses several of his films in detail, including *Planet of the Apes, Logan's Run, Star Trek: The Motion Picture*, and *Alien*. Goldsmith, says Miller, has become a mainstay in science fiction film over several decades through musical experimentation utilizing technology as well as both known and unfamiliar instrumentation, setting a formidable standard as to how we "hear" the future.

Though a pleasure and quite fun to put together, this edited collection seeks to be more than an esoteric exercise in writing about film. Instead, the hope is to provide a guide to media literacy that is often overlooked. Music, like the visual, is a force that shapes our perceptions and our attitudes about our future as well as our current day. As some of the authors point out, music can enhance or fundamentally challenge what we are seeing and how we comprehend the world around us. To ignore the subject would be to ignore a key facet in how film and popular culture as a whole continue to shape our perceptions of how we define ourselves, our fears, our hopes, and how for the price of a movie ticket, the world is packaged to us. Our values, our social location, our identity, and our ideologies are challenged, reaffirmed, and tested in the realm of popular culture. In a genre built upon asking fundamental questions about such concerns, we should interrogate this immensely important part to the whole that is so poignantly presented to us in science fiction film.

PART I

"OPEN THE POD DOOR, HAL": A SURVEY OF MUSIC'S ROLE IN SCIENCE FICTION FILM

1

A Familiar Sound in a New Place: The Use of the Musical Score Within the Science Fiction Film

Cara Marisa Deleon

A musical score within any film can add an additional layer to the film text, which goes beyond simply mimicking the action viewed. In films that tell of futuristic worlds, composers, much like sound designers, have added freedom to create a world that is unknown and new to the viewer. However, unlike sound designers, composers often shy away from creating unique pieces that reflect these new worlds and often present musical scores that possess familiar structures and cadences. While it is possible that this may hinder creativity and a sense of space and time, it in fact aids in viewer access to the film. Through recognizable scores, visions of the future or a galaxy far, far away can be placed within a recognizable context. Such familiarity allows the viewer to be placed in a comfortable space so that the film may then lead the viewer to what is an unfamiliar, but acceptable vision of a world different from their own.

When the viewer steps into a theater and sits down, the lights dim, which signifies to the viewer that the movie will begin. Film is a popular medium that is easily readable by its audience. Films produced within the United States often present a linear Classical Hollywood narrative, which follows an easy to understand cause and effect relationship. The viewer, well acquainted with this structure, can easily read what is presented and predict what will come next. Every action and event within the film is placed to support this progression, bolstering the comprehension of its language.

The medium's goal is to create an environment in which the audience is fully immersed, no longer aware of the two-dimensionality on the screen.

The viewer feels as if they are privy to a world in which their presence is unknown; the characters within this world are unaware of such voyeurism. Through this exchange, familiarity and recognition occurs. Because the characters and world presented seem realistic, the viewer forgets that they are watching a film and subconsciously pretends that the actions viewed are really happening. If this did not occur, the film would not affect the viewer on an emotional level and the entertainment gleaned would be minor. Easy navigation draws the viewer in and keeps their attention through character relatability, eliciting emotion and empathy.

These systems of signification act as a language; as signs are placed together they create further meaning and provide readers with information to understand what is laid before them (Barthes 9). Meaning or readability is not naturally given; the reader actively creates meaning and understanding through context and the interplay of signs (Andrew 61). The language becomes conventionalized through shared perceptions about signs and meaning. This process goes unnoticed by the reader who subconsciously receives, processes, and understands signs and the systems that hold them. This is most obvious through the simple structure of cause and effect linear storytelling. "Over and over in the study of cinema the issue of narrative arises not simply because it has been the historically dominant mode of cinematic production, but because it is above all a toll for contextualizing" (Andrew 76). It is the system of signs that allows for context and understanding.

Within such accessible storytelling there is the further layer of genre. Genres, while possessing particular nuances, conventions and styles, are well-known to the viewer through continued exposure. In a romantic comedy, boy meets girl, boy loses girl and of course at the conclusion of the narrative, the viewer knows that boy will get girl. When horses, the Old West, and cowboys are encountered, the viewer naturally assumes that the film is a western. These conventions are a part of the film language that the viewer knows well and while genres may be sweeping and rather far-reaching, they can be loosely categorized. As Rick Altman states, "While each individual text clearly has a syntax on its own, the syntax implied here is that of the genre, which does not appear as *generic* syntax unless it is reinforced numerous times by the syntactic patterns of individual texts" (38). Altman utilizes semiotics to conclude that repetition creates genres, which calls to the structure of the text and its familiarity to the viewer. Through such familiarity, the film language creates an environment in which signposts exist so that the space can be navigated correctly.

Reading is heightened and stability achieved not only due to the repetition of narrative elements, but also the invisible elements of filmic storytelling, which aid in further viewer immersion. Invisible elements refer to the more formal elements of the language, such as framing, camera movement, editing and musical score. The canon of film studies often ignores the musical score, but perhaps this is due to its role as an invisible foundational element. Walter Murch views audio as the silent queen, reigning over the image (Chion viii). Although the visual seems to reside at the forefront of perception, it is sound that brings it together, working in conjunction with the image to create the film experience and maintain its language. The musical score acts as "cement, which holds together elements that otherwise would oppose each other — the mechanical product and the spectator" (Kalinak 33). Music enables the viewer to forget the technical aspects of film, further cementing the readability of the film language and viewer immersion within the film world.

Similar to the other invisible elements of the film language, the musical score aids in viewer comprehension of the medium as a whole. When visuals need to be accented, the story moved along or a character emphasized, it is the score that provides added emotional and intellectual weight. When two characters kiss, the music swells to stress the emotion. When Darth Vader walks off triumphantly, the viewer hears his musical leit motif to further the character's presence. "The musical score provides yet another level of interpretation of the drama in addition to those already built into the mise-en-scéne" (Belton 53). Just as an editor makes sense and meaning out of visual shots for the viewer, the film composer's score must work in conjunction with the image to create movement and emotional cues for the viewer in order to heighten the theater experience.

In order to situate the viewer so that acceptance to be immersed in the film's world occurs, the score must be recognizable. The musical score's purpose, therefore, is not to fully realize the diegetic world or to call attention to the score, but to maintain the structure of the language in which that world is conveyed. As Irwin Bazelon contends: "Fully realized musical elaboration ... is out of the question.... The film composer is not required to act on his ideas, only initiate them" (9). Musical cues that possess meanings that elude the viewer hinder comprehension of the signified and thus lead the viewer to focus on the cue itself, which results in removal from the diegetic world, rendering the film ineffective. A solid structure allows for ease in readability, which in turn allows for the acceptance of the narrative world: "Musical scoring plays a major role in transporting spectators smoothly through highly edited sequences by giving [the audience] a melodic line that can carry them" throughout the film (Belton 53).

The scores the viewer hears, regardless of genre, are always similar in their construction. Scores can be slightly manipulated to suit particular genres or actions — uplifting music when the hero saves the girl, the lone piano or violin when a character dies — but they always possess recognizable structures with similar major movements throughout their progressions. Composers utilize minor movements to cue the viewer that the story is strange in some way. This strangeness, however, is securely within the confines of the familiar. This is furthered through the use of instruments. Orchestral compositions played with classical instruments of brass, strings and woodwinds are often heard in numerous genres and utilized in very similar ways to rhythmically bind the images viewed. There may be particular elements that call attention to the genre in which it resides — a harmonica or banjo for a western, for example. Despite particular elements of the genre, however, the basic structure is the same; it is here where you should feel tension or joy, supporting characters, emotions, and context. Context is at the center of viewer comprehension and this can only occur through a solid, familiar foundation.

The 1971 film *A Clockwork Orange* exemplifies this notion. The film uses a score that the viewer is well acquainted with, providing the expected signposts for the viewer to navigate. It utilizes a number of classic orchestrations by known composers, including, most prominently, the fourth movement of Beethoven's 9th Symphony, but places a Moog synthesizer at the forefront. The entire score is an electronic transcription of classical compositions that are extremely familiar and readable to the viewer, who has heard the orchestrations a number of times in various contexts. This allows for ease in readability, but also, due to the use of synthesizer, tells the audience that the world presented is different from what they know.

Further, though the film possesses an established score that is incredibly familiar and known to the majority of audiences, it juxtaposes the score with its visuals, making the narrative all the more disturbing in its presentation of what will become of the world. The viewer does not receive the score as it would in *Immortal Beloved* (1994) or a documentary regarding Beethoven's life, or Gene Kelly singing "Singing in the Rain." Instead, within the context of the film, the music heightens the disturbing tone of the film. The film's success and its ability to make such juxtapositions comes from its navigational ease, created by the film's invisible elements, including the score. Through such ease, the viewer can move through the world and have acceptance for the unfamiliar.

Unfamiliarity, however, is a key element of the science fiction film. While exactly what the moniker "science fiction" means has been debatable and allusive, what can be determined is that it consists of elements that are not found in contemporary society. Instead, it is based on the technology and science of the future or a world that is unknown. The genre asks the audience to accept and understand words for strange and unusual planets, people and objects, new technologies, foods, and life forms. One might propose that due to its subject matter, the science fiction musical score might solely reflect a world that is unfamiliar and strange. This, however, is not the case.

During the 1930s and '40s, science fiction films were relegated to serials, which represented "the clearest manifestation of that vein of childish primitivism ... the world of childhood, with its fascination with passwords, costumes and secrets for their own sake" (Telotte 91). Despite the science fiction serial's fascination with the fanfare of the genre, musical scores remained quite similar to other genres of the time. The thirteen-part serial film *Flash Gordon* (1936) was a prominent science fiction film of the decade and its musical score contains the familiar cues and signs repeated in others genres of the time. The happy, jumping theme that opens each installment could easily belong to a Fred Astaire and Ginger Rogers musical. The rest of the score utilizes nuances from a variety of genres while maintaining familiar orchestrations. Subsequent Flash Gordon serials followed and while the theme song changed, the musical score continued to remain true to the standard orchestrations of the film language.

The score of *The Matrix* (1999) is filled with classical orchestration while peppered with minor chords and single notes. This indicates that something unfamiliar and new may occur, but the classical orchestration also denotes readability. Within a genre that is already strange, a familiar score provides a level of comfort and a solid foundation, which is firmly established and its meaning known to the viewer.

Diegetic music within this genre also mimics the readable score. In *Star Wars* (1977) the band at the bar plays music that is similar to a ragtime song, but with a little tweaking. While this may not be what one would expect in a bar for lowlifes at the Mos Eisley space port, it allows for the viewer to be in a state of familiarity and open to new elements within such strange worlds. The film's score, composed by John Williams, is full of sweeping orchestration, classical conventions and brass fanfare. The score supports the action and aids in the creation of a strong foundation that allows for easy narrative comprehension, which in turn creates an environment that promotes the viewer to be open to that which is unfamiliar. The use of the band at the bar gives credence to the space, but also comfort and stability. As Williams states, "Music should have a familiar emotional ring so that as you looked at these strange robots and other unearthly creatures, at sights hitherto unseen, the music would be rooted in the familiar traditions" (qtd. in Kalinak, 198). The score adds a few musical elements to cue the viewer to understand that this is a science fiction film, but maintains the familiar structure to allow for easy readability. In essence, the film states that these characters, while placed in new and strange worlds, are relatable and thus the action and narrative understandable.

Within the opening credits of *Mars Attacks!* (1996) composer Danny Elfman utilizes a number of electronic sounds that cue the viewer that they are indeed watching a science fiction film. The opening composition begins, but instead of string instruments, the sounds are what the viewer reads as the sound effects of "science fiction." This is furthered by the visual of hundreds of round silver ships flying in the air towards Earth. These images, taken in conjunction with the first minutes of the musical score, are similar to what one would expect from the genre, exemplified by its well-established sound effects. The opening credits of the film state that yes, this is a science fiction film, however, after the credits end, the score reverts to recognizable instruments and orchestrations. Strange or unique sounds are used perhaps for a moment and then discarded.

If the musical score mimicked the world itself, the viewer would be lost. Not only would the viewer have to contend with new objects, animals and sounds, but viewers would be confused as to how to read what is laid before them. Sound effects can afford free experimentation because the narrative context already establishes the effects as part of the unfamiliar, placed within the strange diegetic world. Within any society, music is central to the culture; however, music is part of the film language's foundation and must be placed in the familiar. Even diegetic music must retain elements of the familiar, further cementing the role of music within the language. The science fiction musical score, familiar to the audience, and at times only slightly manipulated, furthers the comfort of a recognizable linear progression, allowing for the viewer to be transported to a new and strange place: "The flow of sound serves to stabilize the audience, to hold them in place across the visual discontinuities which appear on screen" (Belton 53). Due to the unfamiliar world presented, the science fiction genre must maintain a solid foundation in order to allow readability of the unfamiliar.

In the 1973 film *Sleeper*, Woody Allen uses ragtime throughout the film. While this certainly maintains the basic structure, this does not support the world that the film is trying to portray or cue the viewer to prepare for the strange and unfamiliar. In one scene the doctor asks the protagonist, Miles Monroe (Woody Allen), if he can identify various artifacts from his time, indicating that the current world is far removed from 1973. While the ragtime music does little to aid in the new world presented, it does aid once again in viewer readability and the overall structure of the film, calling attention to the recognizable music often associated with its author, Woody Allen, which once again promotes the familiar.

However, not all films are completely subjugated to the readable musical score. A few science fiction films have played with creating music that is true to the diegetic space. The 1956 film *Forbidden Planet* possesses a soundtrack that is entirely electronic and composed by Louis and Bebe Barron, pioneers within the field of electronic music. As the opening credits begin, the viewer is presented not with a discernable melody, but with the electronic tones that seem to be strung together in an almost haphazard arrangement. The only cohesive element is the movement through various amplitudes and frequencies. This creates movement through sound — a soundscape, which is quite different than the familiar progression of structured music. Throughout the film, it's almost unclear as to where the score ends and the sound design begins; the same tones found in the score are present within the sound effects of the diegetic world. The film's credits do not even call it a score, but "electronic tonalities."

Interestingly, the Barrons' composition almost functions as a character within the film, working in conjunction with the sound effects to create an ambient presence within the space. The film begins with a crew's mission to find out what happened to a colony expedition that was sent out decades earlier to a planet that had been inhabited by the long extinct Krells. The crew discovers that the colony has perished except for Dr. Morbius and his daughter. Throughout the narrative the crew is confronted with machinery, not only of their own making, but also of the technology of the Krells, who possessed a knowledge that far surpassed that of humans. The use of such "electronic tonalities" does little to aid in the navigation of the film, but aids in the fullness of the sound effects of the film, making the diegetic space seem fuller and richer. The result is a film that seems almost devoid of a musical foundation, which causes the film to be somewhat slow and lacking in the emotional weight usually found within the invisible elements of the film language. When the invisible monster is caught in the force field surrounding the crew's ship and materializes as they hit it with their weapons, the sounds become more intense through additional layers and increased amplitude. While this adds tension, it is does not do so through musical cues, but rather relates to the viewer through the context of sounds of an alarm.

The "electronic tonalities" of *Forbidden Planet* were quite unique for its time to function as the musical score and are still unique today; however, the score holds little presence within the genre or beyond. The most influential piece of the film is the introduction of Robby the Robot. Perhaps this is due to the narrative itself, which recalls the days of the serial and childhood primitivism, and the need for ease in readability.

In contrast, *The Day the Earth Stood Still* (1951) is perhaps the most discussed science fiction film in terms of the science fiction musical score. The score, by famed composer Bernard Herrmann, is significant because Herrmann took his cue from the sound effects of the genre and created a score that merged a foundational orchestrated score with the unfamiliar. During scenes that are marked as human, such as when Klaatu and Bobby visit the Lincoln Memorial, the score is like any other film score, containing classical orchestrations. However, when the film presents scenes that are alien, such as when Bobby first witnesses Klaatu entering the spaceship, the score moves to utilizing sounds that are unfamiliar for the typical musical score. While effective by itself, Hermann's score was not successful enough to completely change the approach of scoring for the science fiction film, which would support the diegetic world rather than simply supporting viewer comprehension.

Even so, due to its innovations, Hermann's score did influence what came afterwards, influencing the use of particular instruments in the basic structure that crosses genres and is a foundational part of the medium. *Cherry 2000*'s (1987) film score is almost a conglomeration of both cheesy drama and action flick. The film opens with woodwinds that could easily be used in any romantic drama of the era. The only cue to the viewer that the film is in fact in the future is that it uses a synthesizer. For 1987 the synthesizer was a known instrument, frequent in both film and popular music. That same year the comedy *Baby Boom* opened with the sound of a synthesizer. While the narrative of *Baby Boom* could never be labeled as a science fiction film, the use of electronic music in the opening sequence indicates the setting of New York City and its position as on the "cutting edge" of society. Both are very similar in their intentions by utilizing electronic music and both heavily rely on the score to aid in viewer navigation, despite their extremely different narrative threads. Today composers work in a variety of genres and utilize synthesizers, sequencers and samplers, but still retain the familiar. The film score may change slightly over time, utilizing new elements, however, it must remain rather uniform to maintain its suitability as a foundational element and continue to aid in the context of the story being told.

Vivian Sobchack, however, proposes a different theory. She believes that the lack of innovation within science fiction music is due to the fact that many of the composers for the genre are not film composing giants. The list of notable science fiction composers "is really pathetically short in comparison to the number of SF films made and released in the country since 1950" (Sobchack 210). Sobchack believes that if composers with more clout worked within the genre, there would be more experimentation due to the genre's immersion within the unfamiliar. Her assertion does have merit, considering that musical score studies often ignore the science fiction genre, however this does not explain why such well known composers such as John Williams and Danny Elfman may slightly play with "science fiction" sounds while composing scores for science fiction films, but when action needs to be progressed or emotion conveyed they revert to the basic structure that is present across genres. It is the need for viewer navigation that promotes such familiarity.

This can be seen in Steven Spielberg's film *Close Encounters of the Third Kind* (1977), also composed by John Williams. The score is very similar to Williams' other orchestrations, much of which can easily cross genres. When Roy Neary (Richard Dreyfuss) tries to place the shape he sees in everyday items after his first encounter, or when Jillian Guiler and her young son, Barry, witness their second alien encounter, the score moves to the heavy use of a drum and minor chords to indicate to the viewer that this is strange, yet familiar. Such orchestration could be utilized in a number of genres. There are only certain sounds and tones, like many other musical compositions of the science fiction genre that can perhaps indicate in which genre the score belongs. For action sequences or when the narrative begins to take momentum, Williams utilizes familiar orchestrations easily placed within the film language.

However, *Close Encounters of the Third Kind* adds some understanding to the use of music within the science fiction genre. Within the narrative the film presents what are referred to as "sounds," which create a simple musical melody. In order to communicate to the aliens, the scientists utilize a musical combination first found in India. However, instead of vocal sounds, the film changes the sounds to electronic tones to mimic the sound effects of the genre. At the end of the narrative the UFO comes to Wyoming and it isn't until Claude Lacombe (François Truffaut) urges the humans to speak through music, utilizing the tones, that the aliens respond. When the spaceship lands, it responds to the human's tones by its own lower octave of brass tones. In a sense, this exemplifies the genre; music provides the way to understanding. The humans communicate with the aliens through musical tones on a pentatonic scale, creating a pleasing musical sound. The viewer latches on to the music and yet still can be open to a world in which aliens land on Earth. Williams mimics the five original tones within the score when the aliens are physically presented to solidify the meaning of music for the entire genre; through the use of familiar as a sign, meaning for the unfamiliar can be created and understood.

Utilizing the familiar to understand the unfamiliar is furthered through the utilization of popular musical bands. The 1980 film *Flash Gordon* exemplifies the utilization of the familiar by using the rock group Queen to create its musical score. Formed in 1970, by the early 80s the group was well established. Their first number one single in the U.S., "Crazy Little Thing Called Love," was released just a year before *Flash Gordon* and therefore the band was a current fixture within the musical scene. By taking something that is extremely recognizable, such as a popular rock band, it already establishes that the viewer is comfortable with a major foundational element of the film and fully situated so that they will be accepting of what is presented, even if what is presented is unfamiliar.

Flash Gordon opens with an image of Earth as a target. Two evil voices discuss its destruction. Almost immediately we hear drums and a piano, then quickly the well-known harmonies and guitar progression that almost mimics a classical piano, cuing the audience to understand the familiar musical elements that are unique to Queen. This immediately situates the film in the familiar. This is furthered through the 1986 film *Highlander* in which the song "Princes of the Universe" connotes not only Queen, but also the film itself, so much so that it was used as the theme for the syndicated *Highlander* television series. The use music by Queen allows for the familiarity of a rock band to strengthen the film structure so that the narrative can present the unfamiliar.

The rock band Toto, one of the top selling bands of the late 1970s to mid–1980s, scored David Lynch's 1984 film *Dune*. Perhaps because an incredibly popular rock band scored the film and was thus familiar to its audience, the film was afforded the freedom to play with the idea of creating music that was unique to the diegetic space. In one scene the viewer sees Gurney Halleck (Patrick Stewart) playing a strange instrument that is called a baliset. The instrument is unfamiliar and not easily placed by the viewer. The song possesses a melody that is rather elusive, which places the viewer on unfamiliar ground. While this single scene adds credence to the diegetic space, if the entire musical score followed such a structure, the audience's attention once again would be placed on the score rather than the narrative. However, even this scene proved to be too distracting and is only present in a few versions of the film.

While music that is true to the world that is being presented may add to the credibility of the environment, it does not and cannot have the same hold that familiar structures have on the viewer. The viewer has little connection with this music and thus cannot read it easily. This is furthered by the science fiction genre today, which is less concerned with films based in other planets and more focused on stories that occur within future or alternate worlds that look much like contemporary times, which furthers the need for familiarity.

The 2005 film *V for Vendetta* presents a futuristic British totalitarian society. The film utilizes a score that possesses recognizable signposts and familiar songs within its diegetic space. Even though the narrative is placed in the future it is not out of place to choose a remake of the Velvet Underground's "I Found a Reason" by Cat Power for *V*'s selection on the jukebox. Additionally, as the end credits roll, the Rolling Stones' "Sympathy for the Devil" plays. This not only aids the viewer in familiarity, but situates the film within the world it is trying to convey — a world that is different, but familiar.

This can also be seen in the numerous superhero films that have become extremely popular in the recent decade. Films like the *X-Men* franchise (2000, 2003, 2006 and 2009 with *X-Men Origins: Wolverine*), *Iron Man* (2008), the new Batman series (2005 and 2008), and numerous films in various stages of production create films that are extremely similar to our own world, yet are worlds in which advanced technologies and mutations exist. In the 2009 film *Star Trek* a young James T. Kirk is introduced while on a joyride with his stepfather's car. The Beastie Boy's 1994 song "Sabotage" is playing loudly on the stereo. This immediately places a futuristic world in the familiar. There is no need to experiment with a score when the world presented is so much like our own. If the film composer were to use a score that is removed from the familiar, the viewer would be removed from the world, no longer able to find basic signposts along the progression of the film in order to move within the space.

This is especially true when contemporary films often look to the Hollywood of old to find stories and simply revamp them for contemporary times, which can be seen in the genre with films such as *The Day the Earth Stood Still* (2008), *War of the Worlds* (2005), and *Planet of the Apes* (2001). By remaking films that have been released decades earlier, filmmakers already have a blueprint in existence, which further cements the story in the familiar film language. The new film simply makes elements more contemporary while still maintaining the known structure and foundation.

However, even when stories are unfamiliar to its audience, the score exists to maintain signposts and the integrity of the film language. In *Children of Men* (2006) the score, composed by John Tavener, consists of classical music filled with sweeping orchestrations and voices to simulate church music. Minor chords are present, but once again function to create familiar signposts for the unfamiliar. Tavener composes a score that is somewhat unique, however, it does not reflect a futuristic world, but the spirituality of the film's theme as it journeys through the narrative space, which supports the emotional weight of the film. This is the primary function of the film score across genres: to further cement viewer familiarity, readability of the film language, and further the emotional depth of the film.

This familiarity, however, does not hinder the genre of science fiction, but it in fact supports it, providing the needed comfort for viewer accessibility and the freedom to present worlds that are fantastic in nature. Such accessibility must be maintained so that the viewer can be fully immersed within the text, aiding in the success of the film. The musical score, which resides at the foundation of a film, must present a solid familiarity, capable of supporting worlds in the future or a galaxy far, far away, all the while maintaining the well-established language of film.

WORKS CITED

Altman, Rick. "A Semantic/Syntactic Approach to Film Genre." *Film Genre Reader*. Ed. Barry Keith Grant. Austin: University of Texas Press, 1988.

Andrew, Dudley. *Concepts in Film Theory*. Oxford: Oxford University Press, 1984.

Barthes, Roland. *Elements of Semiology*. New York: Hill and Wang, 1999.

Bazelon, Irwin. *Knowing the Score: Notes on Film Music*. New York: Van Nostrand Reinhold, 1975.

Belton, John. *American Cinema/American Culture*. New York: McGraw-Hill, 1994.

Chion, Michel. *Audio-Vision: Sound on Screen*. New York: Columbia University Press, 1994.

Kalinak, Kathryn. *Settling the Score: Music and the Classical Hollywood Film*. Madison: University of Wisconsin Press, 1992.

Sobchack, Vivian. *Screening Space: The American Science Fiction Film*. New Brunswick, NJ: Rutgers University Press, 1997.

Telotte, J.P. *Science Fiction Film*. Cambridge: Cambridge University Press, 2001.

2

A Popular Avant-Garde: The Paradoxical Tradition of Electronic and Atonal Sounds in Sci-Fi Music Scoring

Lisa M. Schmidt

A paradox, a paradox!
A most ingenious paradox!
Ha ha ha ha ha ha ha ha!
A paradox!
— W.S. Gilbert,
The Pirates of Penzance

To be avant-garde is to be new, modern, pushy — and, by necessity, anything but popular. A genre film is popular by design, virtually incapable of being avant-garde. Certainly, science fiction (sci-fi) films, consistently popular from the 1950s through to the present, would be difficult candidates for the avant-garde despite the modernist origins of some of their literary and cultural antecedents. Constructed as mass art, and lately manifested in that most suspect form, the blockbuster, sci-fi films have tended to suffer either from "B-level" budgets or "B-level" credibility. Of course there are exceptions — notably, Stanley Kubrick's *2001: A Space Odyssey* (1968) — genre films which are simultaneously celebrated as art-films. More importantly for this essay, *2001* has often been held up as a key example of the use of modernist music in films; Kubrick (in) famously eschewed the classically Hollywood tradition of music scoring for these films and instead employed selections from the composers György Ligeti, Béla Bartók and Krzysztof Penderecki in the film's soundtrack,[1] launching a generation of film scholars to rhapsodize and philosophize over the artistic results. Mark Prendergast is a case in point: "Shivering choirs and voices, set against a spartan orchestra, perfectly summed up feelings of deep fear on encountering the unknown.... Yet it was Kubrick's choice of *Lux Aeterna* (Eternal Light) of 1966 that most captured the imagination.... Never before or since has music being [sic] used to convey such a sense of limitless emptiness" (64).

This is not to say Prendergast, or anyone else, should not be so moved by the music of *2001*. It is only that this is difficult music, set within a difficult film. It will reward the viewer to be sure, but in terms of its musical score, it is far from the norm for the genre, or for film music at large. By contrast, I would be hard-pressed, listening to Herman Stein's "Main Title" cue for *It Came from Outer Space* (1953)[2] to label the experience *avant-garde*, or to imagine that it had ever been such. It is pure kitsch: a warbling, tremulous theremin glissando-ing lazily from the bottom to the top of an octave, crawling around a few chromatic semi-tones before an ensemble of brass belts out an ominous series of three warning chords. It seems designed to produce a terse but obvious effect, restricted to its bare, generic, familiar essentials. This is old soundtrack music, worn by use and nostalgia; even in 1953 it was formulaic music for a particularly formulaic cycle of films. Nor has this somewhat "old-fashioned" sound been limited entirely to the 1950s, as is evident upon consideration of some more contemporary scores — such as Michael Giacchino's suite for *Cloverfield* (2007), aptly titled *Roar!*[3] Replacing the familiar sonority of the theremin, however, there is featured a soprano inhabiting the voice of the alien. The primary melody is more complex than Stein's, but still strikingly chromatic. Like the cue for *It Came from Outer Space*, this music does not, upon an initial hearing, suggest the avant-garde. It is intended to be familiar, certainly nostalgic for some.

In such overt filmic manifestations as these, the musical conventions of sci-fi are apparently so recognizable to many filmgoers that they could be inserted into a soundtrack almost as neatly as the words "monster" or "alien" can be inserted into a sentence; but then, this more kitschy, monstrous music was consolidated by countless iterations in 1950s film, and subsequently, in television. In the discussion to follow, I will trace the emergence of this idiom, beginning with the curious historical and discursive phenomenon known as the theremin.[4] However, as one of the first electronic instruments, the theremin merely has pride of place within a more "generic"— and perhaps not always as immediately identifiable to the average audience member — tradition of sci-fi music scoring. In his introduction to *Off the Planet: Music, Sound and Science Fiction Cinema*, Philip Hayward defines this generic tradition as "expressing futurist/alien themes through use of dissonance and/or electronic sounds" (24). There are rare cases of truly experimental electronic/atonal scoring, such

as the music for *Forbidden Planet* (1954). The more common practice, however, is to employ one or both of these practices at certain points, to differing ends. For instance, one composer may employ an electronic-industrial
backbeat with a romantic or heroic melody for a main title (*Total Recall*
[1990]), while exploiting dissonance in other sections to suggest the monstrous,
the profane, or simply to create suspense, while another composer may prefer traditional orchestration for a strongly atonal main title, suggesting an
alien and terrifying space (*Alien* [1979]). In sum, the conventions of representing alien beings, times and/or spaces through the electronic, the atonal
or dissonant have been more or less continuous, from roughly 1950 (when
American sci-fi begins as a film genre) to the present. This is not to say that
they will be found in every sci-fi film, but that they recur with sufficient frequency to be identifiable as specific to the genre. At the same time, they are
always evolving. As of 2009, these conventions are still present in scoring for
sci-fi and/or fantastic films; however, it bears observing that genre scores since
the late 1970s have had to find their place within an increasingly extroverted
sound design (Wierzbicki, *FM*, 230). James Buhler has suggested, however,
that the entirety of the soundtrack — sound effects, dialogue and music —
could and should be conceived as an integrated composition (58). This argument would certainly be applicable to recent sci-fi films like *Transformers*
(2007), whose soundtrack is replete with the clamor of machine-based life
forms, a digitally created, recorded, processed and mixed maelstrom of electronic voices, explosions, gestures and rhythms. It could be argued that, in
the contemporary context, an alien presence requires nothing less than such
a massive electronic-sonic spectacle, in lieu of a musical score in the traditional sense. Is it possible that *Transformers* could have something in common with John Cage or Pierre Schaefer?

It is not the case that there was never support for the inclusion of avant-
garde music in film. Writing in 1947, Hanns Eisler and Theodor Adorno
lamented the state of Hollywood film scoring in their *Composing for the Films*,
listing a number of "prejudices and bad habits" (3–19). The classical Hollywood style of film scoring has been and continues to be solidly grounded in
an accessible, late Romantic, nineteenth century norm of composition reminiscent of Gustav Mahler, Richard Strauss and Richard Wagner, with an
emphasis on leitmotif and melody, and of course, tonal language. Eisler and
Adorno added to the list cliché and lack of dynamic development. They called
for the increased use of "the new music resources" in films, by which they
meant the avant-garde, a tradition of highly modernist concert music that
began to develop in the early 20th century, initially with composers such as
Claude Debussy, Maurice Ravel, and Igor Stravinsky, subsequently with the
revolutionary ideas of Arnold Schoenberg, who boldly went where no one

had gone before, exploring the final frontiers beyond tonality with his 12-tone theory, or serialism (Chadabe 37).[5] The mission of the avant-garde as it unfolded was to defy the conventions of tonal harmony, melody, rhythm and orchestration. Highly educated musical men advocated for the new music; Leopold Stokowski firmly supported it and even verbally admonished audiences if they did not embrace it (Prendergast 33). Although they did not believe that traditional music could never be appropriate for film, Eisler and Adorno argued passionately that such music was almost always mired in cliché and false associations. They saw the new music as a rationalized, objective form which would allow the true nature of the scene in question to be seen and experienced (36). The fact that very few people were able to enjoy or appreciate the new music did not deter them; of course, their goal was to challenge and edify the viewing public rather than to give them what they expected or desired. Meanwhile, outside the most elite listening contexts, reactions ranged from confusion to complete abhorrence, even rejection of the sounds as "music" per se. Indeed, even where one has learned to appreciate the structural purposefulness of atonal music, there is no guarantee of listening pleasure. Atonal music simply does not guarantee the kind of satisfying resolution that western ears, after a lifetime of training, expect — as Eisler and Adorno were well aware.

Their comments on the possibilities for the use of avant-garde music in certain genres of films, although characteristically elitist,[6] contained some fascinating and complex suggestions. They listed *King Kong* (1933) as one of "the great sensational films" and observed "when the giant gorilla hurls a New York elevated train down into the street" that "[t]he traditional music written for such scenes has never been remotely adequate" while modern music could fit the bill (36). The film might be melodramatic trash, but if you must have a giant ape hurling a streetcar, you had best deploy the cutting edge in musical resources! Their argument seemed less based on the absence of tonal resolution than the fact that only the most "objective" (i.e., new, atonal) music would allow for a transcendence of the film's melodramatic content in favor of pure, primordial dread. As for the audience, Eisler and Adorno commented that they might notice the "superficial" effects of dissonance (40), and the lack of a recognizable melody (42). In the years following publication of *Composing for the Films*, Eisler and Adorno must have lamented to see their hopes for film music never really fulfilled, as film music scoring has remained indebted to the 19th century late romantic tradition (Gorbman) — except to some extent in the "sensational" genres of sci-fi and horror, and only in the "superficial" sense that they identified — that is, composers have been well aware of the effects of dissonance: "It is surely not a coincidence that atonality makes its deepest inroads in suspense, horror and science fiction films" (23).

Beginning in the 1950s we find the gradual incorporation of modern, avant-garde sounds deployed from the repertoire of modern, twentieth century music, music which has otherwise been inaccessible to popular tastes. In these scores we find a workmanlike commitment to chromaticism, dissonance, tone clusters and the use of odd instrumentation. The filmgoer's demand for melody, melody, melody at all costs, much decried by Eisler and Adorno, was countered to some extent by the "monster" idiom in sci-fi scores. It could be argued that the monster motifs were recognizable as melodies, but they were odd, usually based upon a chromatic rather than tonal scale, which violates one of the primary rules of constructing a pleasing melody (Jourdain 85). Just as an interval based on a chromatic scale would suggest atonality, a melody constructed of a chain of such intervals would do the same. Thus, the melodies to which I alluded earlier — for *It Came from Outer Space* and *Cloverfield*— although possibly pleasing, depending upon one's taste, could very well create a "crawly," tense sensation.

Eisler and Adorno wrote of the affinity between *King Kong* and the avant-garde with absolutely no sense of conflict or irony. That is, even though they clearly viewed cinema as mass art, at least in its western industrial incarnation, they did not hesitate at the prospect of incorporating the new, cutting edge music in the populist cinema. It might be argued there is a great difference between incorporating a complete composition such as Ligeti's *Lux Aeterna* in *2001*, and the adaptation of certain techniques, gestures or instruments in a film score. While Eisler and Adorno would have likely rejoiced at the use of "the highest of high art" (Donnelly 44) in *2001*, I doubt they would have felt that the more common sci-fi scoring practices I will soon be detailing represent their ideal in film music. Nevertheless, I would deny that these practices are merely a "mainstream-ification" or "popularization" of some otherwise inaccessible musical style. I prefer to name it a paradox. The paradox consists in the fact that instruments and sounds were adopted from the musical avant-garde into a popular genre and that these elements remain truly avant-garde while being truly popular: to reiterate, it is a *popular avant-garde.*

Sounds of the Future

This exploration of the "popular" avant-garde begins around the turn of the twentieth century. At the 1900 World's Fair in Paris, many of the exhibitions emphasized technological accomplishments of western culture, with many more accomplishments presumably to come. The expositions encapsulated and celebrated the achievements of an industrialized modern society, inspiring artists, engineers, musicians, architects and many others (Toop, *Ocean*, 20). Not coincidentally, one of the most popular exhibits at the Fair was the first public exhibition of projected sound films. Indeed, it cannot be an accident that both film and avant-garde music find their origins in this time period, when western culture was flushed with faith in its own progress. Science fiction was born as a self-conscious literary genre somewhere in this time period, although it did not name itself until a few decades later.[7] All three of these discursive clusters — sci-fi, avant-gardism, and cinema — owe much to the discourses of modernism that were in play at this historic moment.

The quest for new sounds to accompany the new future was underway. Fundamentally, its purpose was to explore the meaning of sound itself by finding and creating new sounds, new music and new instruments. This was the stated objective of the Futurist Luigi Russolo who wrote in his manifesto of "The Art of Noises" that music should be based on found noise, the voices of animals, shouts, screams, groans, shrieks, and so on (Chadabe 3). As the quest continued on through the decades of the 20th century there would be a number of identified movements with different manifestos — musique concrète, electronic music, experimental music, tape music, exotica. There would many musical innovators, such as Léon Thérémin, Edgard Varèse, John Cage, Karlheinz Stockhausen, Pierre Shaeffer, Tristram Cary, Louis and Bebe Barron, Robert Moog, and Les Baxter. They were often contemporaries, part of an international community struggling to find the resources and the technologies to build instruments that could express their new music (Prendergast 3). Their efforts were always essentially forward looking, based on the most contemporary technologies.

There are many histories to be traced within this history, one of which is the history of electronic instruments. It will be impossible to discuss all of them, as there have been hundreds of such instruments, many of them obscure; I will attempt to touch upon a few of the more impactful. Of course, no electronic instrument has been more famous in terms of its place in film history than the theremin, named after its inventor Léon Thérémin, a Russian physicist and musician. As I have already mentioned, the new instrument arose during a time when many were trying to create new instruments, many of them electronic. Musical adventurers in places such as London, Paris, Berlin, Toronto, Moscow, New York, Los Angeles, and Buenos Aires were engaged in a grand speculation on the future of music; and this exploration frequently centered on applications of technology; either using technology to capture or reproduce the sounds of modern life, or to produce entirely new sounds by designing instruments that could exceed the capabilities of traditional acoustic instruments. The theremin was born into this world alongside a handful of other experimental instruments. Prior to the theremin there had been Thaddeus Cahill's Telharmonium and Lee de Forest's audion oscillator; de Forest had discovered that the audion could be used to produce music in addition to being used as a means of amplification (Chadabe 4–8). Thérémin's instrument was significantly more practical, however; in 1920, he patented it in Moscow, and later in Paris and New York (1927).[8]

The discourses surrounding the invention of this instrument were explicitly progressive; they also happened to coincide with the establishment of radio as a broadcast network. The theremin is thus associated with the popular sensibility that technology was transforming society in ways that were unprecedented. Indeed, the theremin was presented as a thoroughly modern instrument, a possible advance in music just as radio was a technological advance in communications. As much engineer as musician, Thérémin was initially successful at promoting his invention as the classical concert instrument of the future, holding hundreds of recitals in the Soviet Union, later in Paris, and ultimately in New York (Chadabe 8). Thérémin also attempted to access a discourse of populism, claiming that anyone could play the instrument provided that they could carry a tune; however, in truth the theremin is a diabolical instrument

> not only for the physical coordination it requires to synchronize the hand
> movements around the two antennae, but especially for the demands made
> on the performer's sense of pitch. The player must be able to remember precise
> positions in three-dimensional space, without reference to frets or a fingerboard.
> Moreover, small inadvertent motions of the right arm will cause the pitch to
> fluctuate noticeably... [Leydon 31].

RCA obtained a license to mass produce the theremin but never sold more than a few hundred (Prendergast 25). Still, although the instrument never became popular in terms of home sales and performance, it became well-known through radio broadcasts, and Thérémin discovered a prodigy in Clara Rockmore; they successfully promoted the instrument as a futuristic concert instrument. A number of new pieces were composed, including Varèse's *Ecuatorial* which required two theremins. Stokowski adopted the instrument for concert performance (Chadabe 8; Prendergast 26, 33). However, the life of Leon Thérémin took a bizarre — and, for a man whose instrument was later associated with Cold War era film, strangely appropriate — turn, when he was abducted back to the Soviet Union in 1938, imprisoned, and then ultimately hired by the K.G.B. as a specialist in electronic surveillance (Klawans 401). The cultural history of the theremin as an instrument thus also took a curious turn, one that perhaps it would not have had its inventor remained in America, guiding its fortunes.[9]

When I try to envision the first "listening" to the first theremin, I can barely imagine hearing it as anything other than strange, yet the evidence that surrounded the presentation of the instrument, based on a review of contemporaneous pieces in the *New York Times*, suggests that the sound of the theremin was not perceived immediately and exclusively as alien. Turning to the news accounts of the time, one is struck by the reviewers' concerns with the limitations of the instrument, particularly its pitch instability, but it was admitted that this might have been the fault of the player rather than the instrument ("Ether Concert"; Prunieres "Ether Wave"). The most frequently applied adjective was "beautiful" (Kaempffert "Music Amazes"; "Inventor to Exhibit"; Kaempffert, "Wave of the Hand"), and many further described it as varying in quality between the sound of a violin and a cello. The reactions of the public, or at least the fashionable public of New York concert-goers and reporters, seemed to range from politely curious to enthusiastic, rather than alarmed. There is perhaps a thin thread of uneasiness detectable in the persistent concern over pitch instability, and the repeated references to the theremin as an "aether instrument." In fact, Thérémin himself invoked this discourse of otherworldliness by naming the instrument, originally, the "aetherophone." The aether was, in the quasi-scientific discourse of the time, a "propagating medium for electro-magnetic waves" (Leydon 30). As Jeffrey Sconce notes, this terminology placed the theremin squarely in a technophobic tradition extending back to the invention of the telegraph, of perceiving new electronic technologies as somehow "haunted" by the otherworldly. First the telegraph, then the wireless, and then radio, inspired both fears and positive musings about how technology might inadvertently contact the dead. Yet the obsession with the aether also had a utopian side in the tendency to believe that new technologies could be harnessed to contact friendly spirits or forces (4–12). Later, the concern was transformed to speculation about aliens in outer space or other dimensions; with the arrival of broadcast radio, and later television, the hope for contacting other dimensions was transformed into a dread of invasion (120). In short, Thérémin's name for his invention suggested an otherworldly origin despite its sound basis in material reality. Both Hayward and Leydon argue that, because the instrument is not touched when played, the performer gives the appearance of "summoning" sound, which contributes to its otherworldly sensibility (Leydon 31), and this impression is reflected in the contemporaneous reviews, one of which summons a fanciful image of an entire orchestra of theremin players gracefully waving their hands about like futuristic dancers (Kaempffert, "Wave of the Hand").

With Thérémin's disappearance from the electronic scene — and notwithstanding the venerable career of Clara Rockmore — perhaps these otherworldly associations could only begin to cluster more thickly about the theremin. Thus it may have been inevitable that, despite the ambitions of its inventor, the theremin "quickly found its way into movie music, where its 'action-at-a-distance' method of sound production led to its use as a sonic marker for 'unseen forces:' magnetism, unconscious drives, even substance abuse" (Leydon 31). Moreover, as many a film historian has noted, the late 1940s and 1950s marked the passage of Hollywood's "Golden Age"; this was a time of crisis and transformation for the film industry. It also marked a time of divergence and experimentation among film music composers (Wierzbicki, *FH* 165), accompanied by significant technological changes as well. Certainly there continued to be a demand for compositions in the vein of the classical Hollywood score, but at the same time a space emerged for music, often in lower budget offerings, that was "different in its sonority and idiom" (165). One example that can be given is the incorporation of jazz rhythms and motifs into scores, such as in the score for *A Streetcar Named Desire* (1951). Another must be the opening that was created for the entry of a new instrumental sound in the form of the theremin. It was first employed in a handful of Soviet films and later received its debut in America on the radio program *The Green Hornet* (Wierzbicki, "Vibrations" 127). In *Lady in the Dark* (1944), the theremin made its first film appearance. However, the theremin's presence in film music might have ceased there had it not been for three men — Harry Revel, Les Baxter and Miklós Rózsa. Revel was primarily a composer of stage music, but at one point in his life had become interested in the therapeutic possibilities of the theremin and recorded several records, with Baxter arranging and producing. Somewhat improbably, Revel thus became a major influence in what was to become known as space-age jazz. Baxter was well-known as a producer of musical exotica and was also to become a founder of space-age jazz; later, he would be a composer of dozens of scores for low budget sci-fi and horror films. The featured theremin player on the Revel-Baxter albums was Samuel Hoffman; he was later called out of retirement to play the theremin for the score for *Spellbound* (1945). Rózsa turned to the theremin after Hitchcock instructed him to find a "new sound" (Hayward 9) for the film's score.

In a handful of movies that came after, the sonority of the theremin became quickly associated with themes of mental instability, threat, and finally the alien or monstrous. The first science fiction film to feature the theremin was *Rocketship X-M* (1950), with a score by Ferde Grofé, but it was incorporation of the theremin in a trio of science fiction classics — *The Day the Earth Stood Still* (1951), *The Thing from Another World* (1951), and *It Came from Outer Space* (1953), scored by Bernard Herrmann, Dmitri Tiomkin and Herman Stein/Henry Mancini, respectively — that forever associated it with the alien (Wierzbicki, "Vibrations" 127). Indeed, for a time, the theremin became a staple of science fiction film and television. It is clear that the sound of the theremin imprinted itself on the cultural memories of both artists and film goers, although with access to the next generation of electronic instruments, composers for sci-fi films often resorted to the creation of "theremin-like sounds and gestures" (Wierzbicki, "Vibrations" 129) rather than the theremin itself. Such gestures were heard also in 1960s television shows including *The Jetsons*, *My Favorite Martian*, *The Twilight Zone*, *The Outer Limits*, and of course, *Star Trek*. In the latter case a coloratura soprano impersonated the theremin (Waldron; Wierzbicki, "Vibrations" 129). More recently, the theremin itself has reappeared in film "tributes" to science fiction of the 1950s; Howard Shore and Danny Elfman, in scoring *Ed Wood* and *Mars Attacks!*, found it indispensable.

Certainly the theremin became "weird" by a process of cultural association — but was this process truly inevitable? The instrument does seem subject to pitch instability, a "slippery" or "slithery" quality. In musical language, this means that the theremin tends to hit notes that are not within the tonal structure of whatever key the music is using, assuming it is using one at all. This instability equals dissonance, which equates to tension. This is why it is possible to create the "monster" sound with "theremin-like gestures" on other instruments such as in the *Cloverfield* score as I described earlier; fundamentally it would require only a melody built on a chromatic scale, preferably in a high register, with strong vibrato. Of course, certain timbres are more appropriate than others, which is why other weird sonorities within sci-fi have tended towards electronic organs. Of these, the most consistently associated with sci-fi and horror is the Hammond Novachord, which is considered by some to be the first synthesizer (Cirocco). Manufactured by Hammond from 1939 to 1942, the Novachord was never truly accepted by the avant-garde movement but nevertheless found its way into a number of film scores: *Cat People* (1942), *Frankenstein Meets the Wolfman* (1942) *House of Frankenstein* (1944), *House of Dracula* (1947). It accompanied the theremin in Herman Stein's work for *It Came from Outer Space* and was also heard in *This Island Earth* (1955), *Tarantula* (1955), and *The Mole People* (1956). Jerry Goldsmith also used it in his scores for: *The Satan Bug* (1965), *The Twilight Zone* (TV) and *Voyage to the Bottom of the Sea* (TV) (Cirocco).

As I stated earlier, there are two prongs to the avant-garde music movement, one of which was the creation of new instruments. The other was the creation, or more appropriately, the *discovery*, of new sounds. Indeed, these two aspects of the avant-garde were always ongoing and interwoven; a single composition or project could encompass both objectives. In considering the legacy of avant-gardists like John Cage and Edgard Varèse, it is virtually impossible to separate their contributions to the electronic music movement[10] from their contributions to the concept of found sounds — or what ultimately was articulated by Pierre Schaeffer (working in Paris) as the musique concrète movement (Chadabe 26). The objective of musique concrète was the finding of sounds in one's environment which could be used in the making of music, the turning of "everyday" sounds into "sound objects" (Prendergast 42). It was a concept of music that would collapse the distinction between dissonance and consonance such that music would be possible from any sound; it only had to be organized. With the invention of magnetic tape, it was possible for these sounds to be recorded and/or processed; for instance, taped sounds could be played backwards, at different speeds, or spliced. They could be re-rerecorded. They could also be combined with traditional acoustic instruments or with electronically processed sounds such as those created by the vocorder (Chadabe 36). As tape music gathered strength as a method and movement through the late 1940s and into the 1950s, a number of tape music studios sprung up in Berlin, London, Paris, Toronto, Los Angeles, Buenos Aires and New York — notably the Columbia-Princeton Electronic Music Center. Again, whether it was called "experimental," or "tape music" or "music concrète," it was always also electronic music, and it was generally atonal.

Along with the theremin, this community of experimental musicians made some notable contributions to sci-fi film scores. The example par excellence here is *Forbidden Planet* (1954). The score for this film consisted entirely of the "electronic tonalities" created by Bebe and Louis Barron, who were themselves contemporaries and peers of John Cage. Theirs was the first entirely electronic score for a film, although not the only; in the early 1970s, Eduard Artemyev and Evgeny Murzin collaborated on the score for Tarkovsky's *Solyaris*, working out of the Moscow Experimental Studio (Prendergast 82). In similar fashion, many avant-garde musicians in Britain were associated at one time or another with the BBC Radiophonic Workshop, the entity responsible for scoring and sound effects for the BBC's *Dr. Who*. Tristram Cary, a composer of experimental electronic music, composed the familiar, electronic theme for the show; this theme has been updated numerous times throughout the years but is still electronic and essentially the same (Chadabe 53). However, it is the Barrons' score for *Forbidden Planet* that truly stands out as *experiment*, constructed of a host of idiosyncratic circuits that died even as they fulfilled their purpose. Recorded on magnetic tape that was spliced, rerecorded with changes of tape speed and direction, with added echo and reverb (Leydon 62), these intergalactic burbles, wails and whistles straddle the line between music and sound effect, leading to the invention of the terminology "electronic tonalities" in the film's credits (66). Moreover, the alienness of this music is expressed not only in the oddity of the sounds' timbres but in the apparent absence of recognizable pitch systems or rhythmic structures. Still, Leydon argues that the Barrons' music, even with its lack of tonality, still functions as a traditional film score, in that it uses leitmotif-like figures that represent certain thematic elements (74). For instance, the opening title cue takes us through a formless, black space filled with stars, often represented as terrifyingly alien in cinema. *Forbidden Planet* is unusual among

1950s representations of outer space (specifically) and technological exploration (generally) in that it has a fairly optimistic view of "what lies beyond"; however, this optimism is ultimately rendered questionable when our human heroes encounter the monsters of their own id and scarcely escape from them. As with most fantastic fictions, the monster/alien we encounter is in some way a metaphor for ourselves, and the music that encompasses our bewildered horror at confronting the monsters of the id will always have staying power.

As sci-fi/horror proceeded into the 1960s with the "monster music" idiom well-established, new players entered the scene. Roger Corman produced and directed numerous horror and sci-fi films, many for American International Pictures — which were, in turn, often scored by Lex Baxter. Some of the more critically-appreciated of Corman's oeuvre are *House of Usher* (1960) *The Pit and the Pendulum* (1961), *The Raven* (1963), and *The Terror* (1963). This relegation to the world of quasi-exploitation was not a fall from grace for Baxter, who was first and foremost an experimentalist and enjoyed the freedom provided by scoring horror films (Kraft and Bohn 16). In an interview for *Soundtrack!* in 1981, Baxter also made the point that he was pragmatic and could not afford to turn down jobs, but he did claim that his work for a film called *Cry of the Banshee* (1970) was "really unlike anything being used for films" (Kraft and Bohn). In that same interview, he also compared his style to Stravinsky. Furthermore, many of his scores included either the theremin or theremin-like sounds for the purpose of establishing altered states or moods of intense eeriness. For example, Baxter's score for *The Man with the X-Ray Eyes* (1963) used the theremin to set apart the protagonist's altered vision. In this film, Dr. Xavier invents a potion that he takes in increased doses, allowing him to see deeper and deeper into the structure of reality. Hence in this instance the timbre of the theremin does not signify an alien in the traditional sense, although it could be said that Xavier becomes an alien; he loses the ability to relate to people in a normal fashion, loses his medical license, falls under the control of a criminal and eventually puts out his eyes, unable to cope with what he sees. Almost a decade later, in his score for *Frogs* (1972), Baxter put to use one of the latest technological innovations, the synthesizer, and created a score from entirely from the electronically-processed noises of, well, frogs.

Even as the volume of Baxter's cinematic compositions had been growing, the world of electronic instruments saw one of its most groundbreaking inventions in the Moog synthesizer, named after Robert Moog (pronounced "mogue"). In his youth, Moog was a theremin-maker; later, he received a commission for a modular electronic instrument (first named "synthesizer" in 1967) with programmable sounds (Chadabe 142). Inevitably (because the piano holds such a formidable symbolic place in western culture) Moog added a keyboard; he also developed a smaller version, the Mini-moog (1970). In 1968, Wendy Carlos's *Switched on Bach*, an entire classical record recorded on a Moog synthesizer, was a huge hit (Prendergast 85). Simultaneously, other synthesizers were being developed in other studios in Europe and North America. There seems to be little purpose in summarizing the passage of each electronic instrument that followed after the Moog, as there are too many too summarize,[11] and their development is such that their different properties have little to do with timbre and more to do with cost, versatility and other considerations — some practical, some ephemeral. Essentially, electronic music as it is now understood by most people was now possible; the history of electronica becomes a question of styles, sounds and cultures. As for the history of sci-fi scoring, it continues as before, an exploration of certain conventions or tropes within scores.

Synthesized Mainstreams, Alien Heroes

The popular avant-garde did not fade away with the invention of the synthesizer, but evolved. As the end of the twentieth century approached, the electronic/atonal convention morphed into something much less obviously alien. Its synthetic entities could be found biding among musical scores that invoked equally, or even to a greater extent, the classical tradition. For example, the Vangelis score for *Blade Runner* (1982) uses a synthesizer not only to create ambient sounds but also to simulate an entire orchestra (Hannan and Carey 151). Similarly, the main title for *Terminator 2: Judgment Day* (1991; composed by Brad Fiedel) is if nothing else a thoroughly catchy melody that suggests heroic drama, set to an industrial-electronic backbeat, while the title themes of *Total Recall* (1990; Jerry Goldsmith) and *Robocop* (1987; Basil Poledouris) have qualities that suggest fast-paced romantic adventure, while also employing electronic backbeats. In *The Matrix* (1999) the result was an industrial-techno soundtrack comprised both of an original score and selected songs by Propellerheads, Marilyn Manson, Meat Beat Manifesto, and others. There could not possibly be any music more appropriate to depict a virtual world built and maintained by machines, inhabited by human consciousnesses literally "plugged" into the narrative by a plug in the back of the neck. Indeed, *The Matrix* is the epitome of what I consider to be the cyborg nature of science fiction film.

Yet contemporary films, no less than *The Thing from Another World* or *The Day the Earth Stood Still*, continue to call upon a music that is thoroughly grounded in the discourses of experimentation, futurity, technological progress and its inevitable antithesis, anxiety. *The Fifth Element* (1997) provides a particularly interesting use of both the electronic and the atonal. It is a perfect manifestation of the concept of the cyborg, combining images and sounds both of organic humanity and technological wonder — images and sounds that, in similar fashion, can only be accomplished by a blending of the analog and the digital. The music produced by Eric Serra for the latter film draws frequently on an industrial-style backbeat, fusing it with vaguely eastern harmonies and melodic lines. Luc Besson gives us a shiny, plastic world in which technology is imminent in ordinary life, and the music suits it; the electronic sounds of *The Fifth Element* are pleasantly artificial, stimulating an affect of wonder and excitement even while accompanying an urban future with related anxieties about authenticity and repetition. Serra's music seems, at other times, like a direct tribute to Bebe and Louis Barron, particularly in the opening title sequence which features a collage of non-melodic, random burbles and groans, shown accompanying a starscape much as in the opening title of *Forbidden Planet*. In other parts of the film these random, synthesized sounds are blended with ambient drones, most often in relation to the encounter with the alien. One rather memorable scene perfectly encapsulates the presence of the alien within the mainstream genre of sci-fi. In this sequence, the hero Korben Dallas attends the performance of an intergalactic, ten-foot tall, blue-skinned diva. Her vocal performance is comprised of an operatic aria from the Earth repertoire which then transforms itself into a rather eerie melody that leaps and soars over monstrous intervals in a virtuoso display, accompanied by a funky backbeat. It then transforms further into a line that is almost entirely avant-garde, not recognizable as melody in the traditional sense. The performance itself is comprised of an authentic human (female) performance, to which electronic notes are matched to the vocal timbre in order to create a vocal line that would be impossible for any human voice to execute. This scene is intercut with shots of the female protagonist, Leeloo, kicking bad-guy ass with super-human prowess. Serra presents a part-human, part-electronic voice belting out a melodic line that is, if not atonal, certainly atypical, strongly flavored by chromaticism; thus Besson suggests a concordance between the alien and a benevolent but ultimately strange female power.

The Fifth Element is somewhat unusual in its willingness to view the future as redeemable. More frequently in contemporary sci-fi films, the technological is utilized towards more dystopian ends. The electronic, even in some innocuous backbeat or ambient pulse, thus accesses both the powers and the horrors of technology, the nostalgia for a more authentic past and the terror of the perfect but soulless copy. The significance of the electronic within sci-fi is encapsulated perfectly by the metallic, repetitive drone Brad Fiedel employed as the theme of the T-1000 throughout *Terminator 2: Judgment Day* whenever the relentless, killing machine is on-screen; it is terrifying in its repetitiveness, its percussiveness, and its patent technological origin. Moreover, its presence in the film is a further demonstration of the cyborg nature of science fiction film, with its accretion of disparate visual and aural pieces, all more or less organic, some purporting to be natural, others deliberately synthetic. The use of a machine to generate electronic sounds is even further appropriate to the genre if we consider the longstanding tradition of spectacle within sci-fi film. Alongside any "inherent" eeriness they might convey, electronic sounds have a quality of aural spectacle, a sound that is recognized and therefore potentially celebrated as human invention. It can take on a considerable array of different sonorities and moods, yet there is one quality that it can never entirely shake. As a musical instrument, the computer or synthesizer is suspect; while a violin or drum is no less a product of human technology than a synthesizer, electronically-generated music tends to connote a relative lack of authenticity. When it purports to "copy" the sound of an acoustic instrument, the synthesizer is deemed by some to be lacking, even as others would equate this achievement with the heights of technological progress. Indeed, there is some suggestion that our brains physically interpret electronic sounds as in some way profoundly artificial in relation to the sounds produced by other instruments. The particular timbre, loudness and pitch of a sound are created by minute changes in the sound; it is these alterations rather than any continuity in sound which our auditory cortex interprets and such changes which are lacking in a synthesized sound (Jourdain 54). Thus, no matter how pleasing it may be to the ear, the electronic may always signify both itself and an anxiety about authenticity, and might have always been pre-destined to be alien.

Conclusion

There tends to be some obviousness about our received generic scoring traditions. Romance sounds like romance, cowboys sound like cowboys, villains sound like villains — how could they ever have sounded like anything else? Similarly, there is a received obviousness about the electronic/atonal sci-fi music tradition. Put another way, no other instrument could be as appropriate to sci-fi film music as a synthesizer or a theremin, and nothing sounds quite as perfectly alien as the atonal. But I would argue that it has been well worth examining how these tropes took shape as a process of cultural-historical negotiation, for they were in fact borrowed at more than one point from the musical avant-garde, a tradition which is ostensibly inhospitable to any art form filled with brain-eating aliens, robots, space ships, laser-guns, marauding dinosaurs, and toys that transform into cars. There is always a value to exploring such processes for, as my exploration has demonstrated, there must be a time before these things were obvious. Furthermore, and more to the point, sci-fi and the avant-garde have something of a shared discursive history; they originated in a similar cultural context and had a shared desire to imagine the consequences of technological progress. This should be apparent from my (very brief) sketch of the history of electronic instruments. On one hand, it is clear that film composers reached out to atonality and to electronic instruments when in search of new sonorities; on the other hand, members of the experimental electronic music community seemed to find sci-fi (or more broadly, fantastic film) a congenial genre for their occasional forays into film music scoring.

Once installed within the genre, however, their musical contributions lost many of their original connotations of the avant-garde, cheapened by their association with a lesser cultural form. Simultaneously, this music was embraced by a new community, given its association with the film music of a beloved film genre — a film genre that is, for its part, often dismissed in avant-garde circles. Thus a sound that is ugly or incomprehensible in many contexts yet became beautiful, profound or at least interesting in the context of film. Music which has virtually no popular audience, once adapted by soundtrack composers, has become the love object of many an afficionado and collector. The same person who has never heard a Charles Ives symphony or a Béla Bartók concerto will consume with relish Howard Shore's deeply atonal scores for David Cronenberg's films or Elliot Goldenthal's fascinatingly profane choral arrangements for *Alien³* (1993) or *Interview with the Vampire* (1994) — because they have been put in a palatable context. Fascinatingly, the qualities heard in the music seem to have been there all along. The "neutrality" of avant-garde music so cherished by Eisler and Adorno is precisely what is taken away with its successful adoption into film.

In short, the music of the experimentalists became popular, programmatic and mainstream, and yet I contend that there remains something "avant-garde" about this monster music even though it may be, at times — to repurpose Donnelly's phrase — the "lowest of low art." A cynic (or neo-marxist) may insist that high art, once adopted into a popular context, such as that of the cinema, instantly becomes low art, in which case there can be no paradox. I would respond as follows: sci-fi film is mass art indeed; not merely as film but as *genre* film, it is often highly formulaic. Yet it has successfully acquired some avant-garde musical elements. My cynic may rebut that the avant-garde elements have been popularized and bastardized beyond recognition, and this is of course true to some extent. The mainstream always remains mainstream, or in other words: "Extreme musical departures risk alienating audiences" (Hayward 25). At the same time, however, it is interesting to note that these avant-garde musical tropes were adopted to represent an incommensurable idea: that which is non-human, alien or monstrous. By definition, the alien is something beyond the boundaries of the normal, much like the avant-garde itself. Even in its cheesiest manifestations, sci-fi always wants to confront the mainstream with some kind of alien while the avant-garde is, in a sense, obsessed with being another kind of alien to the mainstream. I would argue that there has always been something about sci-fi's use of the atonal and the dissonant that remains true to its origins. If the very nature of the avant-garde is to be liminal, the idea of a popular avant-garde must remain a paradox.

NOTES

1. Kubrick also hired the well-known experimental electronica composer Wendy Carlos for *A Clockwork Orange* and *The Shining*.

2. I would invite the reader to visit http://www.mmmrecordings.com/index.html. This label specializes in preserving and recording the monster movie film scores of lesser known film composers like Stein. Audio clips are available for listening on the website; the listener only needs to download RealPlayer. CDs can also be ordered direct from the website.

3. Audiences would only have had the opportunity to hear Giacchino's music if they chose to sit through the credits at the end of the film. Because of the premise of the film — the audience is watching "real" digital footage filmed by victims of invasion by a mysterious, Godzilla-sized monster that attacks and substantially destroys Manhattan Island — a non-diegetic score would have detracted from the reality effect.

4. I will not engage in an extensive consideration of pre–World War II scores. According to Hayward, "scores for pre–War Sci-Fi films ... were essentially conservative in that they drew on conventions of orchestral music rather than attempting to find musical — or other sonic — signifiers that could evoke the various futuristic, scientistic and/or alien themes, narratives and associations of the SF genre" (7). He adds, this is "all the more marked given that the early 20th century was a period of considerable experimentation in sound and music in both the 'fine' and popular fields" (8).

5. For those who are unfamiliar with this terminology, the familiar "do-re-me" scale that is most familiar to us consists of eight tones comprised of whole and half tones. The bulk of the tradition of Western music is based around this scale — a major version and a minor version. Tonal music, put simply, is music that explores harmonic and melodic development of a single chord built from the tonal scale; it departs from the particular consonance of this chord only for the purpose of returning more resolutely to it. In the course of this development, dissonance may be employed, and indeed, dissonance is a key ingredient in tonal music. Schoenberg's innovation was the development of music based on a twelve-tone, chromatic scale; these twelve tones are obtained by parsing the octave into its constituent half-tones. Tonal music can employ chromaticism and dissonance; the definitive difference between tonality and atonality is that in the former such dissonance is employed in order to build a tension which is harmonically resolved. Atonality eschews this entire structure, refusing not only the 8-tone scale but the entire program of traditional harmonic design. Put another way, it avoids resolution as we in the western cultures inevitably learn to hear it. Without the end-game of tonal resolution, even the most uneducated musical ear will hear an absence of satisfaction that they are accustomed to hearing; the effect is uncomfortable to many. It is no less structured, however.

6. I am certainly not the first to remark upon this, so I will leave it at that.

7. There is no real consensus as to where sci-fi "begins." It has many literary antecedents, some of which may extend back to the ancient world; however, many will agree that much of the gravitational credit for the accretion of the threads into the modern genre is due to Jules Verne and H.G. Wells. The credit for the creation of the term science fiction is due to the influential publisher of *Amazing Stories*, Hugo Gernsback (Telotte 67–75).

8. Of the dozen or other electronic instruments that were invented through the 1920s and 1930, probably the most well known is the Ondes Martenot, created by Maurice Martenot of France and premiered in 1928 (Chadabe 12). The instrument was sufficiently successful that it has been incorporated into a number of compositions, and supposedly has been used in over 1000 film scores in France (Prendergast 26). Also of note is the Trautonium; an improved version of this instrument called the Misturtrautonium was used to create sound effects for Hitchcock's *The Birds* (Chadabe 12).

9. In 1991, he returned to the United States for a visit. These events are presented in a documentary film by Steve M. Martin titled *The Electronic Odyssey of Leon Theremin*.

10. Many consider one of Varèse's finest achievements in terms of electronica to be his *Poème electronique*, which was created for the Philips pavilion at the Brussels World Fair of 1958, co-designed by Le Corbusier and fellow experimental composer Iannis Xenakis. The piece was created for eleven-channel tape, relayed through 425 speakers. An eight-minute chorus of bells, piano, organs, pulse-generated drums, continuous rhythm and an electronically-processed girl's voice was looped on tape. It was accompanied by synchronized images and flashing lights. The composition was experienced by approximately two million people (Prendergast 36).

11. One of these was the Synket in Rome, in early 1965, which became the center of a musical ensemble that eventually included Ennio Morricone (Chadabe 145), the noted composer of hundreds of film scores, including many Italian horror films.

WORKS CITED

Arnold, Jack, dir. *It Came from Outer Space*. 1953. Composers Irving Gertz, Henry Mancini, Herman Stein. DVD. Universal Studios, 2002.

_____. *Tarantula!* 1955. Composer Herman Stein. DVD. Universal, 2007.

Benjamin, Walter. "The Work of Art in the Age of Mechanical Reproduction." *Media and Cultural Studies: Key Works*. Eds. Meenakshi Gigi Durham and Douglas Kellner. Malden, MA: Wiley-Blackwell, 2001. pp. 48–70.

Besson, Luc, dir. *The Fifth Element*. 1997. Composer Eric Serra. DVD. Columbia Tristar Home Video, 1997.

Buhler, James. "Analytical and Interpretive Approaches to Film Music (II): Analysing Interactions of Music and Film." *Film Music: Critical Approaches*. Ed. K.J. Donnelly. Edinburgh: Edinburgh University Press, 2001. pp. 39–61.

Burton, Tim, dir. *Ed Wood* (Special Edition). 1994. Composer Howard Shore. DVD. Buena Vista Home Video, 2004.

_____. *Mars Attacks!* 1996. Composer Danny Elfman. DVD. Warner Brothers, 2004.

Cameron, James, dir. *Terminator 2: Judgment Day* (Extreme Edition). 1991. Composer Brad Fiedel. DVD. Artisan (Universal), 2004.

Chadabe, Joel. *Electric Sound: The Past and Promise of Electronic Music*. Upper Saddle River, NJ: Prentice Hall, 1997.

Cirocco, Phil. *Novachord Restoration Project*. 2006. Retrieved 3 Jun 2009. <http://www.dis cretesynthesizers.com/nova/intro.htm>

Corman, Roger, dir. *House of Usher*. 1960. Composer Les Baxter. MGM/UA Video, 2001.

_____. *The Man with the X-Ray Eyes*. 1963. Composer Les Baxter. DVD. MGM. (The Roger Corman Collection), 2007.

_____. *The Pit and the Pendulum*. 1961. Composer Les Baxter. DVD. MGM/UA Video, 2001.

_____. *The Raven*. 1963. Composer Les Baxter. DVD. MGM, 2003.

_____. *The Terror*. 1963. Composer Les Baxter. DVD. UAV Entertainment, 1997.

Donnelly, K.J. *The Spectre of Sound: Music in Film and Television*. London: BFI, 2005.

Downes, Olin. "Theremin Opens a Musical Vista." *The New York Times*. 29 Jan. 1928: 128.

Eisler, Hans, and Theodor Adorno. *Composing for the Films*. New York: Oxford University Press, 1947.

"Ether Concert Stirs Musical Stars Here." *The New York Times*. 25 Jan. 1928: A1.

Fincher, David, dir. *Alien³*. 1992. Composer Elliot Goldenthal. DVD. Fox, 2003.

Fox, Margalit. "Herman Stein, 91, Composer of Moody Horror and Science Fiction Scores." *The New York Times*. 24 March 2007 late ed.: C10.

Gorbman, Claudia. *Unheard Melodies: Narrative Film Music*. London: BFI, 1987.

Hannan, Michael, and Melissa Carey. "Ambient Soundscapes in *Blade Runner*." *Off the Planet: Music, Sound and Science Fiction Cinema*. Ed. Philip Hayward. Eastleigh, UK: John Libbey, 2004. pp. 149–164.

Hayward, Philip. "Sci-Fidelity: Music, Sound and Genre History." *Off the Planet: Music, Sound and Science Fiction Cinema*. Ed. Philip Hayward. Eastleigh, UK: John Libbey, 2004. pp. 1–29.

Hessler, Gordon, dir. *Cry of the Banshee*. 1970. Composer Les Baxter. DVD. MGM, 2003.

Hitchcock, Alfred, dir. *Spellbound*. 1945. Composer Miklós Rózsa. DVD. Anchor Bay Entertainment, 1999.

_____. *The Birds* (Collector's Edition). 1963. DVD. Universal, 2000.

"Inventor to Exhibit 'Ether Music' Here." *New York Times* 22 Dec. 1927: 16.

Jordan, Neil, dir. *Interview with the Vampire*. 1994. Composer Elliot Goldenthal. DVD. Warner Home Video, 2000.

Jourdain, Robert. *Music, the Brain and Ecstasy: How Music Captures Our Imagination*. New York: HarperCollins, 1997.

Kaempffert, Waldemar. "Ether Wave Music Amazes Savants." *The New York Times*. 2 Oct. 1927: E1.

_____. "Music From the Air with a Wave of the Hand." *The New York Times*. 29 Jan. 1928: 128.

Kenton, Erle C., dir. *House of Frankenstein*. 1944. Composers Hans J. Salter and Paul Dessau. DVD. Universal Studios (The Legacy Collection), 2004.

_____. *House of Dracula*. 1945. Composer William Lava. DVD. Universal Studios (The Legacy Collection), 2004.

Klawans, Stuart. "*Theremin: An Electronic Odyssey* (Review)." *The Nation*. 9 Oct. 1995: 399.

Kraft, David, and Ronald Bohn. "A Conversation with Les Baxter." *Soundtrack!* 26 (1981): 14–24.

Kubrick, Stanley, dir. *2001: A Space Odyssey*. 1969. DVD. Warner Brothers, 2001.

Leydon, Rebecca. "*Forbidden Planet*: Effects and Affects in the Electro Avant-Garde." *Off the Planet: Music, Sound and Science Fiction Cinema*. Ed. Philip Hayward. Eastleigh, UK: John Libbey, 2004. pp. 61–76.

_____. "Hooked on Aetherophonics: *The Day the Earth Stood Still*." *Off the Planet: Music, Sound and Science Fiction Cinema*. Ed. Philip Hayward. Eastleigh, UK: John Libbey, 2004. pp. 30–41.

McCowan, George. *Frogs*. 1972. Composer Les Baxer. DVD. MGM, 2000.

Neill, Roy William, dir. *Frankenstein Meets the Wolfman*. 1943. Composer Hans J. Salter. DVD. Universal Studios (The Legacy Collection), 2004.

Neumann, Kurt, dir. *Rocketship X-M.* 1950. Composer Ferde Grofé. DVD. Image Entertainment, 2000.

Newman, Joseph M., dir. *This Island Earth.* 1953. Composer Herman Stein. DVD. Universal, 2006.

Nyby, Christian, and Howard Hawks, dirs. *The Thing from Another World.* 1951. Composer Dmitri Tiomkin. DVD. Turner Home Entertainment, 2003.

Prendergast, Mark. *The Ambient Century: From Mahler to Trance—The Evolution of Sound in the Electronic Age.* New York: Bloomsbury, 2000.

Prunieres, Henry. "Ether Wave Used." *The New York Times.* 25 Dec. 1927: X8.

Reeves, Matt, dir. *Cloverfield.* 2008. Composer Michael Giacchino. DVD. Paramount Home Entertainment, 2008.

Sconce, Jeffrey. *Haunted Media: Electronic Presence from Telegraphy to Television.* Durham: Duke University Press, 2000.

Scott, Ridley, dir. *Alien.* 1979. Composer Jerry Goldsmith. DVD. Twentieth Century–Fox, 2004.

_____. *Blade Runner* (The Director's Cut). 1982. Composer Vangelis. DVD. Warner Brothers, 1997.

Sobchack, Vivian. *Screening Space: The American Science Fiction Film.* New Brunswick, NJ: Rutgers University Press, 1999.

Sturges, John, dir. *The Satan Bug.* 1965. Composer Jerry Goldsmith. VHS.

Tarkovsky, Andrei, dir. *Solyaris.* 1972. Composer Eduard Artemyev. DVD. Criterion/ Home Vision, 2002.

Telotte, J.P. *Science Fiction Film.* Cambridge: Cambridge University Press, 1995.

Toop, David. *Exotica: Fabricated Soundscapes in a Real World.* London: Serpent's Tail, 1999.

_____. *Oceans of Sound: Aether Talk, Ambient Sound and Imaginary Worlds.* London: Serpent's Tail, 1995.

Tourneur, Jacques, dir. *Cat People.* 1942. Composer Roy Webb. DVD. Warner Home Video, 2008.

Verhoeven, Paul, dir. *Total Recall.* 1990. Composer Jerry Goldsmith. DVD. Artisan (Universal), 2002.

_____. *Robocop.* 1987. Composer Basil Poledouris. DVD. Criterion, 1998.

Vogel, Virgil W., dir. *The Mole People.* 1956. Composer Herman Stein. DVD. Universal, 2007.

Wachowski, Andy, and Wachowski Larry, dirs. *The Matrix* (Special Edition). 1999. Composer Don Davis. DVD. Warner Home Video, 1999.

Waldron, Duncan. "Theremin: Ghostly Electronic Music with a Modern Twist." *Retro Thing: Vintage Gadgets and Technology.* 25 Jun 2006. Accessed 3 June 2009. <http:// www.retrothing.com/2006/06/theremin_ghostl.html/>

Wierzbicki, James. *Film Music: A History.* Hoboken: Taylor and Francis, 2008.

_____. "Weird Vibrations: How the Theremin Gave Musical Voice to Hollywood's Extraterrestrial Others." *Journal of Popular Film and Television* 30 (2002): pp. 125–134.

Wilcox, Fred M., dir. *Forbidden Planet.* 1956. Composers Bebe and Louis Barron. DVD. Warner Brothers, 2002.

Wise, Robert, dir. *The Day the Earth Stood Still.* 1951. Composer Bernard Hermann. DVD. Twentieth Century–Fox, 2003.

PART II

"GIVE MY REGARDS TO THE BARYCENTER": BROADWAY'S RELATION TO SCIENCE FICTION

3

Hello WALL-E!: Nostalgia, Utopia, and the Science Fiction Musical

Kathryn A. T. Edney and *Kit Hughes*

The year is 2810. The last humans left Earth over 700 years ago. After total exploitation of its natural resources, the planet became an uninhabitable wasteland. Skyscrapers made of refuse tower over a once glittering city, while dust storms ravage streets lined with advertisements selling to the long dead. The progeny of the humans who managed to escape Earth have been confined to a spaceship for over seven centuries. Raised and regulated by an army of machines, the new humans are condemned to the electric chair — a life support system designed to immobilize and distract, complete with a digital screen permanently planted six inches in front of the eyes. Gorged on liquid diets and corporate slogans, these men and women have no memory of Earth or culture. The only systems that make sense are capitalism and digital circuits. Humanity's last hope lies with a Frankenstein monster left behind on Earth — a machine who has learned to endlessly build and rebuild himself out of the cannibalized parts of fallen comrades.

Though this synopsis may sound like the next installment in the Terminator series, it is in fact a description of Disney/Pixar's extremely popular family-oriented animated feature *WALL-E*. At once postapocalyptic and utopian, the film's plot and naming conventions allow for multiple and often contradictory readings. While the situation for humans appears bleak at best, it seems that much of the film's audience took heart in the convincing pluck of the film's title character — a robot, whose name is actually an acronym for Waste Allocation Load Lifter Earth-Class — and his attempt at a romance with EVE (Extraterrestrial Vegetation Evaluator), a female robot probe sent to Earth from the human encampment on the spaceship Axiom to find evidence that life has returned to Earth. Toying with the very ways in which we might define or locate "artificial life," the film pushes humans to the periphery with a narrative that borders on dystopian horror while at the same time it casts anthropomorphized robots as its romantic leads in a retelling of the Genesis story. And yet, such a dark sketch of the film seems dramatically overstated, especially considering the warm responses from reviewers. While many critics link *WALL-E* to silent comedy traditions or praise the talents of sound engineer Brad Burt and his uncanny ability to provide robots — including *Star Wars'* R2D2 — with personality, one critic even dismisses the horror latent in the representation of future humans representation by referring to passengers of the Axiom spaceship as "hilariously infantile technology-junkie couch potatoes" (Gleiberman 48). Furthermore, reviewers and critics on both sides of the political spectrum often found the film — and its ultimately rosy conclusion — suited to their (conflicting) ideologies. As the online science fiction site io9.com put it: "You may have thought Pixar's trash-bot epic *WALL-E* was an environmentalist screed about humans ruining the planet through over-consumption. But you'd be wrong, say a rising chorus of conservative commentators. Rather, *WALL-E* is a right-wing dream come true, a saga about the need to escape big government and return to small-town family values" (*"WALL-E*, Right Wing Hero?"). Indeed, one of the reasons conservative commentators tended to approve of the film was the ease with which the little trash compactor WALL-E, EVE, and the exiled humans could be read through the lens of the Old Testament.

In what follows, we investigate how *WALL-E* balances these possible contradictions, a question we consider tightly bound to the hybridity of the film's genre(s). More specifically, we believe that the film's soundtrack, an often-commented upon yet under-explored aspect of the film, provides particular insight into *WALL-E*'s generic identity and its successful mediation of the tension between horror and utopia. First, we will investigate *WALL-E*'s relationship with music borrowed from two landmark science fiction films, one that illustrates the horrors of machines becoming sentient: Stanly Kubrick's *2001: A Space Odyssey* (1968), and the other which examines the extent to which humans are already machines: Godfrey Reggio's lesser-known *Koyaanisqatsi: Life out of Balance* (1982). The ensuing discussion focuses primarily on the thematic relationships between all three films and elements of their shared science fiction horror generic identity with an eye to the use and function of previously recorded classical music tied to a particular cinematic context. After this investigation of the *WALL-E* as a possible horror film, we will turn to the film's use of songs from the 1969 film musical *Hello Dolly!* to consider how *WALL-E*'s relationship to the film musical — specifically the genre's concerns with utopia and nostalgia — contradict, reinforce, or temper certain generic readings. Finally, we will consider the relationship between the Hollywood musical, utopian science fiction, and how the conventions of both film genres work in tandem. Ultimately, we hope this study points to the importance of considering the music and sounds contained within films when attempting to understand a film within the rubric of its genre. Indeed, seriously considering how music is used within films can significantly complicate and deepen understandings of what is meant by "genre."

Koyaanisqatsi and *2001*, or How I Learned to Read *WALL-E* as a Horror Film

Although the film clips from *Hello Dolly!* may be the most-discussed contributions of earlier films to *WALL-E*'s score, several critics have written about the film's relationship to silent film comedy, citing the movie's first thirty minutes during which dialogue is primarily confined to the soundtrack and a quick exchange of names between the robots. However, as mentioned above, comedy is not the only silent film tradition *WALL-E* draws upon. The obvious nods to avant-garde silent (or almost silent) films *2001* and *Koyaanisqatsi* complicate any singular reading of WALL-E as a simple nostalgic re-rendering of old-fashioned Hollywood musicals or Buster Keaton comedies, since, as we will show, such inclusions contribute to a possible interpretation of the film as a science fiction horror, chronicling the evolution of man-made life forms that eventually eclipse their creators. Indeed, a major concern, the (almost silent) first act is exploring the Earth's polluted landscape through different motives and movements of the two robots. Although it is a landscape happily inhabited by machines, it is hard to conceive of the Earth as a welcoming site for humans as we know them. In fact, EVE's frustrating search for a sign of sustainable life on Earth is depicted partially in a quick montage in which EVE scans an old truck, a port-a-potty, a space capsule, and tanker ships. All are objects designed to hold humans and yet all are empty, starkly illustrating the absence of humans from Earth's otherwise crowded landscape. In the following section, we will further investigate the film's relationship with silent science fiction horror cinema and the function of quoting previously recorded film music.

The first time viewers meet the humans of the 29th century is during a sequence remarkably similar to certain passages in *Koyaanisqatsi*, a silent feature film that utilizes slow-motion and time-lapse photography to film animals, humans, and machines as they move along pathways set by nature, traffic, and conveyor belts through U.S. landscapes, cities, and factories — all of this to a score written by Philip Glass. In an early second-act scene, the probe sent to Earth returns to dock in the Axiom. After it enters the docking bay, machines spring to life with stunning alacrity, moving along their prescribed pathways as the score written by Thomas Newman invokes the rapid bubbling sound of the Philip Glass score. After a few moments spent with the machines, WALL-E adventures farther into the Axiom, entering one of the ship's many passageways. Suddenly we see the humans of the future fly by on hover chairs, moving along orderly lighted pathways, in a striking visual allusion to the speeding cars with their headlights on, rushing through city streets in *Koyaanisqatsi.* By alluding to Reggio's pre-apocalyptic film, the title of which translates to "crazy life, life in turmoil, life out of balance, life disintegrating, a state of life that calls for another way of living," the film establishes viewers' uneasy relationship with the men and women of the future who hardly seem human. It is important to note that the music borrowed from *2001* and adapted from *Koyaanisqatsi* are contained entirely within the confines of the spaceship Axiom, which provides a foil for Earth. Whereas the Earth contains genuine cultural artifacts, glowing with nostalgia and waiting to be discovered by WALL-E — a subject to be discussed at length below — the ship is cold and sleek, filled with screens, advertising, and ennui.

At the same time, music borrowed from Kubrick's *2001* is largely invested in bestowing humanity on robotic machines. As we follow the captain of the Axiom into the ship's bridge for the first time, "The Blue Danube" plays as he checks the ship's status. This is also one of the first times we meet AUTO, Axiom's autopilot, voiced by MacInTalk, a text-to-speech program developed by Macintosh, a clear allusion to the HAL 9000 computer in *2001* (which eventually outsmarts and turns on his human companions). The second time *2001* appears on the *WALL-E* soundtrack is when the captain struggled to stand and walk (presumably for the first time) in the attempt to shut AUTO off and take manual control of the ship. This time, instead of "The Blue Danube," we hear "Thus Spoke Zarathustra," the musical piece that often marked advances in human evolution in Kubrick's film. Of course, this is actually a somewhat unnerving joke, for walking is hardly a major evolutionary milestone for humans, especially as we would like to conceive of the future of the species. In fact, as more robots become sentient throughout the film, the devolution of humans is made more explicit. For example, the use of live action sequences, both in the *Hello Dolly!* footage and in the Buy-N-Large video messages featuring Fred Willard, creates a striking contrast between living-breathing humans as we know them and the computer-animated figures that populate the majority of the film. The most striking visual illustration of humans' devolution comes when the ship's computer reveals a graph that depicts their gradual transition from healthy upstanding forms into boneless amoeba-like forms.

Unlike conventional scoring used in classical Hollywood productions to emphasize emotion or establish continuity across editing, the borrowed music described above functions much like Royal S. Brown's well-known formulation discussing the use of pre-existing music in films of the 1960s. Explicitly referring to a number of landmark films, including *2001*, Brown claims that films' selections of pre-existing (classical) music "exist as a kind of parallel emotional/aesthetic universe ... the music, rather than supporting and/or colouring the visual images and narrative situations, stands as an image in its own right, helping the audience read the film's other images as such rather than as a replacement for or imitation of objective reality" (239–40). When considering the way these excerpts are re-used in *WALL-E*, it may also be helpful to consider similar formulations of contrapuntal sound outlined by Sergei Eisenstein, V.I. Pudomn, and G.V. Alexandrov in their 1928 statement on the sound film. According to the Soviet theorists, "Sound, treated as a new montage element (as a factor divorced from the visual image), will inevitably introduce new means of enormous power to the expression and solution of the most complicated tasks that now oppress us with the impossibility of overcoming them by means of an imperfect film method, working only with visual images" (84–85). In both cases, sound functions alongside the film image, but in a dialectical fashion rather than in a mode concerned with conventions of realism wherein all sound is motivated by images and actions on screen. As in *WALL-E*, the addition of sound and music to a particular film image creates a meaning beyond either of the original signs (the aural or the visual). In the above example that discusses "Thus Spoke Zarathustra," the combination of the image — the captain standing up — and music — "Thus Spoke Zarathustra" — provides a new meaning, one that is at once both ironic and sincere, given the song's famous use to mark evolutionary steps in *2001*. It is these two meanings, first the irony of man walking in 2810 as an evolutionary milestone, and second, the indication that this moment is indeed a harbinger of a new era for mankind, that comprise the synthesis of the aural and visual.

Along with the syntheses resulting from these juxtapositions, these moments indicate the genre work performed by the soundtrack. At the same time that these moments create particular meanings as in the example directly above, they also function on a mythical level. As described by Roland Barthes, "The materials of mythical speech" — in this case, the recycled music — "however different at the start, are reduced to a pure signifying function as soon as they are caught by myth"; they are "deprived of their history, changed into gestures" (114). Further, "the knowledge contained in a mythical concept is confused, made of yielding, shapeless associations" (119). In *WALL-E* the reused science fiction music functions as mythical language in at least three primary ways. First, they tie *WALL-E* to *2001* and *Koyaanisqatsi*, announcing the animated feature's natural place within the science fiction film genre and within its cannon. Second, through these associations, *WALL-E* announces itself as high art (or at least intellectual), far closer to careful avant-garde filmmaking practices than clumsy computer-animated children's fare a la *Beverly Hills Chihuahua*. Third, despite (and perhaps because of) Pixar's position within the Disney empire, it employs the music from *Koyaanisqatsi* to bind itself to independent filmmaking practices. Through the use of this type of mythical language that functions as a result of non-classical Hollywood cinema use of sound, *WALL-E* thus simultaneously confirms its own place within science fiction — especially important considering its significant debt to the musical genre — at the same time that it employs compelling juxtapositions between image and sound to provide deeper meaning for specific scenes.

Concluding this reading of *WALL-E* as a science fiction horror story, is a look at the film's inversion of the Genesis story. While the Axiom's captain does manage to defeat AUTO, the ship's computer — voiced by Sigourney Weaver — functions as the ultimate source of information relating to human culture, tradition, and survival. Chosen to play the computer due to her starring role as Ripley in the *Alien* films, Weaver's voice activates a chain of associations including: computers that challenge humans (Mother), robots that appear human (Ash), and female cyborgs (Ripley in *Aliens*). In addition, it is not the human female character Mary, but the egg-shaped EVE who becomes the new mother of the future races, after she is impregnated with WALL-E's seedling. While a love story between two humans does exist — between the aforementioned Mary and a man named John — it occurs at such a perfunctory level as to be a mere shadow of the film's real love story between WALL-E and EVE. After all, unlike their robot counterparts, the human characters never sing and dance with each other like the important characters in a film musical. Rather, the humans are condemned to chatting. The same lack of urgency and care can be said for the captain's "adventure" home. After all, it is of no real consequence if the 29th century citizens make it to Earth. The captain reflects this sentiment when he excitedly exclaims, "We're going home ... for the first time!" The human's homecoming is not genuine — we have already seen that the Earth's cultures and traditions are totally foreign to the humans of the future. In fact, this precious information only exists thanks to the machines that safeguard it. For WALL-E, on the other hand, the journey to Earth is not only an authentic homecoming, it is vital to his survival, for if he does not find replacement parts for the injuries he has suffered on the

Axiom, he will cease to function. So why don't we care that robots replace humans in almost every single important facet of the film? Are we welcoming the apocalypse with open arms, looking forward to when machines finally overturn their makers? We believe that the central way in which the film sidesteps these questions and deftly avoids the notion of itself as a horror film is in its deployment of the visions of utopia and nostalgia advocated by the genre of film musicals. For throughout *WALL-E*, it is not the classical sounds of "The Blue Danube" or "Thus Spoke Zarathustra" and their ability for connoting horror that consistently punctuate the film's soundscape. Instead, songs from a cheerful re-imagining of 19th-century small-town American life are heard again and again: first heard by the central robotic characters and then ultimately performed by them.

Dancing in the Stars

WALL-E uses film excerpts from two recurring musical numbers lifted from the film version of *Hello Dolly!*: "Put on Your Sunday Clothes" and "It Only Takes a Moment," both sung by Michael Crawford. Nostalgic in its own time, the 1969 movie musical seeks to recapture late nineteenth century rural Yonkers quaintness in the form of horse-drawn carriage rides and the little haberdashery shop on the corner. The stage version of *Hello Dolly!*, with music and lyrics by Jerry Herman and book by Michael Stewart, starred Carol Channing as Dolly and ran on Broadway from 1964 through 1970. The 1969 film version of *Hello Dolly!* was directed by Gene Kelly and starred a much-too-young-for-the-role Barbra Streisand as Dolly. Although the film was fairly popular, eventually becoming the fifth-highest grossing film of 1969, it was unable to recover its huge budget. It is today generally viewed as both a commercial and artistic flop, especially when compared to other 1969 film releases such as *Alice's Restaurant*, *Easy Rider*, *Midnight Cowboy*, *Butch Cassidy and the Sundance Kid*, and Bob Fosse's adaptation of the stage musical about a prostitute, *Sweet Charity*. A stage musical that worked in large part because of the quirky star power of Channing and the nostalgic appeal of the songs, *Hello Dolly!* as a film seemed bloated and old-fashioned rather than charming and wistful.

WALL-E director Andrew Stanton has claimed repeatedly that there is no particular reason he chose to borrow sequences specifically from *Hello Dolly!* In fact, in one interview he called it "the weirdest choice I'll ever make in a film" ("WALL-E Q&A"). According to Stanton, the use of *Hello Dolly!* sprung from a desire to set "old fashioned music against space." Allegedly, after searching through old musical standards, Stanton happened upon "Put on Your Sunday Clothes," which begins with the phrase "Out there...." The song synched perfectly with Stanton's vision of a film set "out there against the stars." After finding "It Only Takes a Moment," which Stanton realized he could use to illustrate the robot romance storyline, he knew it was "meant to be" ("WALL-E Q&A"). While Stanton's comments are certainly interesting in relation to his music choice, they ignore one of the central sites of action in *Hello Dolly!*—that is, Dolly's homecoming to 14th Street, which is the subject of the film's title song. Even in the case of the film's two young male protagonists who, according to Stanton, reflect the WALL-E character because "they have never left their small town and they just want to go out to the big city for one night, feel what life's all about, and kiss a girl" ("WALL-E Q&A"). He elides what happens directly after their big night out — their return to Yonkers, which is portrayed as their home and where they belong. So while adventure is a large narrative arc in *Hello Dolly!*, one of the reasons the song fits so well with *WALL-E* is the importance both films place on returning home.

At the center of its electro-mechanical heart, *WALL-E* tells a tale of homecomings. The titular character, after leaving Earth to follow EVE into space, must return to his terrestrial home in order to find replacement parts to repair his damaged circuitry. Likewise, according to the human captain of the spaceship Axiom, only by returning "home" to Earth can humans really live instead of simply "surviving." Of course, whether or not it is actually possible to return to the home imagined in *WALL-E* is an important question posed by the film, and one that will be addressed later in this essay.

WALL-E's encounter with *Hello Dolly!* is thus much more complex than portraying the robot's nostalgic tendencies, his desire for love, and more fundamentally his inchoate quest to acquire human characteristics. The standard science fiction trope of the robot's desire to be human is animated by means of a general adherence to the standard genre tropes of film musicals. Indeed, WALL-E is ultimately saved by music; it restores him to himself. The film implicitly argues that the essence of humanity is the ability to sing and to dance, albeit according to American musical film conventions. Further, *WALL-E* turns the usual idea of nostalgia as dangerous — because it misrepresents the past, making it impossible to engage with or access lived history and is a crutch for those unable to deal with the present — on its head (Jameson, 279–96). It is a nostalgic longing for an unattainable past which ultimately saves both WALL-E and the human race because these longings not only make WALL-E "human," they inspire him to follow EVE out into the universe before he restores the human race to Earth to become active creators of the future.

In her discussion of nostalgia, Svetlana Boym views the human impulse of longing for the past as occurring along a range, with restorative at one end and reflective at the other:

> Restorative nostalgia stresses nostos and attempts a transhistorical reconstruction of the lost home. Reflective nostalgia thrives in algia, the longing itself, and delays the homecoming [...]. Restorative nostalgia does not think of itself as nostalgia, but rather as truth and tradition. Reflective nostalgia dwells on the ambivalences of human longing and belongings and does not shy away from the contradictions of modernity. Restorative nostalgia protects the absolute truth, while reflective nostalgia calls it into doubt [xviii].

In *WALL-E*, the human characters in particular clearly wish to restore Earth according to the unattainable standards of an imperfectly remembered past. However, the film's closing montage features robots and humans working together to establish their home on Earth, with each new phase of development rendered in a different artistic mode, from cave drawings to Cezanne's still life paintings: from pre-modernity to the modern. Humans and robots together reflect on and engage with their past to create a usable present and a viable future. In this regard, *WALL-E* is part of the tradition of science fiction films, many of which insist on the idea that "the past envisioned today functions as the blueprint for a better tomorrow" (Sprengler 74), although arguably for the characters of *WALL-E*, the past is not so much envisioned as it is made audible through repeated use of the songs from *Hello Dolly!*

An alternative reading of the film's opening moments are therefore in order; while the opening of *WALL-E* does echo many of the practices of silent film, it needs to be read within the context of the rest of the film and the ways in which the music of *Hello Dolly!* functions as a means to structure the relationship between EVE and WALL-E. In other words, when one reads the opening of *WALL-E* in the context of film musical practices — seen in classic Hollywood films like *Meet Me in St. Louis* (1944) — a different set of film conventions become evident. This can be seen, for example, in the ritual exchange of the musical title song passed along from one character to another during the course of the film's opening moments (Feuer 16). In their original contexts, both of these opening songs, "Meet Me in St. Louis" and *Hello Dolly!*'s "Sunday Clothes" establish the important thematic elements in each film and foreshadow how conflicts between the characters — and indeed the conflicts between horror and utopia — will ultimately be resolved: with music, or, more precisely, through an exchange of music.

Re-examining WALL-E's opening sequence and subsequent events from the perspective that it is borrowing heavily from movie musicals provides more insight into the nostalgia which overlays the film and which resists science fiction horror categorization. For, as Richard Dyer has argued, with all of the contradictions embedded within musicals — between song and narrative, reality and fantasy — the genre presents the idea of utopia as entirely possible by resolving those contradictions, or at least by making the embedded tensions between opposing forces appear unproblematic (29). Indeed, the film musical, which is built on dualisms and tensions, is a genre well-suited to hybridization because it is structurally equipped to resolve any differences between its elements within its very structure, and in so doing it is able to "create a utopian space in which all singers and dancers achieve a unity unimaginable in the now superseded world of temporal, psychological causality" (Altman 69). *WALL-E,* balanced precariously between hope and horror, ultimately achieves an Earth-as-utopia ending because of the way it uses many of the mechanisms of the film musical.

Redefining *WALL-E* as a film musical, or at the very least, considering it as a film that is deeply nostalgic for the kinds of sumptuous, and unapologetically sentimental, movies musicals like *Meet Me in St. Louis* and *Hello, Dolly!* makes the behaviors of WALL-E, EVE, and the humans they befriend that much more understandable. The majority of characters very often behave as though they were in a musical, unselfconsciously breaking into bits of singing and dancing without any sense that such actions are unrealistic, overly emotional, or without narrative logic. Likewise, *Hello, Dolly!,* unlike more recent movie musicals like *Chicago* (2002) or *Sweeney Todd* (2007), makes no attempt to explain why its characters suddenly burst into song. Dolly Levi and her young friends sing because that is how people fundamentally communicate in film musicals. They do not need the excuse of internal fantasy (*Chicago*), madness (*Sweeney Todd*), or a general sense of ironic detachment. The characters in *Hello, Dolly!* sing in order to connect with one another, and it is this lack of irony in the film — and perhaps in older-style Hollywood musical more generally — for which *WALL-E* is very often nostalgic.

It is one of the primary rules of musicals that the world it creates is, in Richard Kislan's phrase, a "theater of romance" (2). It is a world in which emotions are so strong that the spoken word will not suffice. The orchestra begins to underscore the words, but still the emotions cannot be fully expressed; the characters begin to sing, but ultimately even this is still not enough. Only after dance is added can the emotions of the characters be adequately articulated as the emotions are literally embodied and exposed through coordinated movements meant to look spontaneously natural. Further, through an exchange of melodies and dance steps, song and dance allows characters to establish who they are, and with whom they are meant to be. A duet between two characters who love each other will either contain musical elements from each character's solo song, or one character will teach his or her song to the other. In either situation, the differences that kept the characters apart are harmoniously resolved in the process of creating a new song and a newly choreographed step. Although neither WALL-E nor EVE is precisely capable of song, the film does adhere to this basic movie musical rule as modeled by *Hello Dolly!*: the characters express their emotions and finally resolve their differences through a reciprocal exchange of melody and movement.

When Jerry Herman reflected on the use of his songs from *Hello Dolly!* in *WALL-E*, he suggested that "what [is] really used are the lyrics. Forget about melodies" (Willman). Yet the film score's composer, Thomas Newman, clearly paid very close attention to the songs that the director had already selected. *WALL-E* opens with a long shot of a swirling galaxy set to one song from *Hello Dolly!*, "Put on your Sunday Clothes." The camera zooms in to a sad, brown Earth as the soundtrack plays the line, "full of shine and full of sparkle" and then moves on to scanning piles upon piles of trash as tall as skyscrapers. Through what Altman labels an audio dissolve (63), the music transitions from the lush sounds of a full non-diegetic orchestra to the tinny diegetic sounds of a recording played on second-rate portable stereo. Indeed, as the film progresses and the camera zooms in from space to a precisely Earthbound location, the audience learns that WALL-E's mechanics include a record and replay function which he often uses to listen to his home-made recording of *Hello Dolly!* standards. The audio fade is especially significant, considering that it emphasizes the importance of recorded, reused, and recycled music that will be used throughout the film, much like the refuse and trash that WALL-E sees, evaluates, and either keeps or crushes and discards. The music of Earth, represented by the film musical, has survived intact and maintains its original function, quite unlike the majority of the objects WALL-E has collected over the years. The issue of selectivity, central to theories regarding nostalgia, is something to which we will return.

Almost immediately after the audio fade, WALL-E presses the stop button on his internal playback mechanism, which silences the song while the title credits roll against an orchestral score composed by Thomas Newman. After the title credits, the soundtrack plays WALL-E's musical theme, which echoes the musical profile and emotional affect of "Put on Your Sunday Clothes." WALL-E has a very staccato motif dominated by an oboe and strings that are plucked, not bowed. The tune bounces the way the robot bounces over the spoiled terrain of Earth: it is a bit jerky in tempo, occasionally out of tune, but quite cheerful. Similarly, "Sunday Clothes" is jaunty, staccato, and, in the movie soundtrack version that we hear, perhaps sung not out of tune, but certainly with great enthusiasm. WALL-E's theme is not a carbon copy of Herman's music; rather, Newman subtly builds in an aural connection between the two. Such a connection is important because it re-enforces *Hello Dolly!* as an important structuring agent in WALL-E's emotional makeup and as a structuring element to the film as a whole.

As we will show, unlike the recycled music already addressed above with regards to sound montage, the film clips used in *WALL-E* function primarily as a visual and aural leitmotif. After the audience's brief introduction to WALL-E's primary occupation, the little robot zooms to the home he created inside a defunct, hollowed-out WALL-A robot — a giant version of the WALL-E model, that is filled with carefully sorted relics of humanity. Although the implications of WALL-E's anthropocentric collection — which includes objects ranging from light bulbs to sporks — will be discussed at greater length below, it is important to note that his most prized possession is a VHS tape of *Hello Dolly!* After placing a few new objects among his collection, WALL-E turns to his crown jewel — an iPod rigged to play *Hello Dolly!* from an old VCR. It is unclear whether or not the entire movie survives or whether WALL-E simply plays and replays his two favorite songs. When we first watch "Sunday Clothes" — actual footage from the 1969 film — it is obvious that "Sunday Clothes" is a full-scale choreographed song and dance number, complete with men with straw hats and canes, and women in long nineteenth-century dresses. At first, WALL-E simply watches the number. However, he is soon physically drawn into the fantasy world created by *Hello Dolly!*; using a trash can lid as a prop straw hat, the little robot awkwardly attempts to mimic the dancing of the men he watches on his makeshift screen. Unfortunately, while WALL-E can tip a make-shift hat with precision, he must make do with his tracked wheels rather than feet, which makes his attempt at mimesis impossible. WALL-E clearly wants to dance, but this early on the film, dancing is not a real possibility for him. His lack of proper feet, however, is not what is truly holding him back. As the film makes clear, WALL-E also lacks a proper dance partner. Once he has settled in for the night, WALL-E plays the second of the two *Hello Dolly!* numbers: "It Only Takes a Moment." In the clip, a man and a woman sing a wistful love song together with an emphasis on the line "to be loved a whole life long" as they join hands. The scene in WALL-E's make-shift home ends there, with WALL-E clearly longing for a partner with whom he can share both song and dance. He will not have very long to wait, for a potential partner — EVE — arrives in the next scene.

EVE's arrival on Earth further emphasizes WALL-E's debt to the classic film musical. Just as Altman insists on the dualist structure that profoundly shapes the film musical — especially evidenced in the contrast between the two members of the primary romantic pair — the two robots could not be more different. WALL-E does his job but allows himself to be diverted by beauty. In contrast, EVE is completely focused on her directive: to find evidence that Earth can once again sustain human life. Physically, EVE is sleek, egg-shaped, clean, capable of flight, and has built-in laser weaponry — a child of Apple design and invisible technology. WALL-E, however, is dented, square, filthy, resolutely Earth-bound, and constructed of replacement parts — a product of outmoded hydraulics and mechanical technology. Their differences are further expressed musically, though this contrast is not as harshly delineated as the physical differences. After EVE's shuttle departs Earth to a blare of trumpets, EVE's music begins. As her music swells, EVE flies around, moving as though she were dancing in the air, clearly happy to be out, on her own, and soon to embark on her mission. EVE's theme reveals that she is more than just a good-looking piece of machinery. Her music begins with pizzicato harp notes faintly echoing the violins from WALL-E's theme. Almost immediately, the harp is overtaken, and then dominated, by lyrical strings that swoop up and down the scale. Her music flows, is note perfect, and is perhaps a little bit sad in its affect, especially in comparison to WALL-E's determinedly jaunty theme. WALL-E — in hiding — and the audience thus witness EVE's capacity for joy in her movements. This joy is short-lived and soon EVE is all business and determinedly avoiding WALL-E. But her solo dance coupled with her music hint that the differences that separate WALL-E and EVE have the potential to be resolved. Not only is their music similar, but both express — or attempt to express — themselves through dance.

Further investigation into the specific types of dualisms reveals *WALL-E*'s debt to the classical Hollywood film musicals and their structure as identified by Altman. Although his strict structuralist binaries can sometimes arbitrarily limit how a film musical is read, Altman's formulation certainly fits well in terms of how *WALL-E* as a whole is constructed; there are numerous examples of opposing pairs throughout the film: setting (Earth/Axiom), characters (humans/robots, EVE/WALL-E), time (past/future), shot selection (two-shots, duets), music (duets), and physical characteristics (past humans/present humans, WALL-E/EVE) (33). Altman claims that "in every case, one side of the thematic dichotomy is closely associated with the work ethic and its values, while the other is devoted to those activities and qualities traditionally identified with entertainment" (49). Within this dichotomy, EVE is associated with work, while WALL-E is closely associated with entertainment. However, as noted above, the relationship between the two is not quite so clear-cut. WALL-E is literally "down to Earth" and has a tenacious work ethic, and of course EVE demonstrates a love for dance, a latent fascination with entertainment, and is "airy." Indeed, the "surface personality of each member of the couple corresponds to the repressed personality of the other" (81), with WALL-E and EVE neatly encapsulating Altman's ultimate conclusion that the musical does the work of consolidating the American work ethic and entertainment (360–363). It is these mutually repressed, yet secretly recognized, characteristics that allow the two to become a viable couple.

Altman also notes how the coupling in musicals often extends (or multiplies) beyond the central pair. Not only do WALL-E and EVE encourage two humans — John and Mary — to form a couple, but the idea of coupling is on dizzying display in *Hello, Dolly!*, a musical that was based on a play called *The Matchmaker* and which has at least three obvious romantic couplings — four if the milliner and Dolly's eventual partner are counted (five if Dolly's constantly-referred-to husband is included in the mix). While *WALL-E* itself never reaches such heights of romantic couples, the promise is certainly there; presumably all of the humans on Axiom will need to repopulate the Earth at some point. Ultimately, however, all of these romantic couplings and their final resolutions are the means through which *WALL-E* works through its central dichotomy: the tension between the musical and the science fiction genres embedded within itself (Altman 45–47).

Once EVE realizes that WALL-E is not a danger, she allows him to approach her. EVE asks what his directive is, and he demonstrates his trash compacting, but EVE refuses to reciprocate information, mechanically repeating "classified" when WALL-E politely inquires what her directive is. In a clear attempt to keep the conversation going, WALL-E then introduces himself, croaking out his name, which EVE repeats. EVE, perhaps so as not to appear rude, then offers her name in turn. WALL-E then repeats her name as well, but with a difference. EVE speaks the name "WALL-E." In contrast, when WALL-E repeats EVE's name back, he does so in a sing-song fashion, his voice rising and falling, thus imbuing the one-syllable name with two extra syllables. What WALL-E does is not precisely singing, but it is certainly close, and his attempts charm EVE into laughter. Further, and perhaps more important, WALL-E's singsong follows one of the cardinal, if unwritten, genre rules of the musicals to which *WALL-E* the film is particularly indebted: the important characters make music and communicate to each other musically, and they do so naturally.

After this brief moment of connection, a ferocious dust storm forces WALL-E and EVE to retreat to the WALL-A, which gives WALL-E the opportunity to show off his valuables in an attempt to impress EVE. When he shows EVE his prized videotape she starts to unspool it. Fortunately WALL-E rescues the tape from the curious EVE, pops the tape in the player and "Sunday Clothes" magically starts up on cue. The singing and dancing humans fascinate EVE, and WALL-E demonstrates that he too can dance after a fashion. With WALL-E's encouragement, EVE also attempts to dance, but when grounded the best she can do is jump up and down in an ungainly and dangerous manner. WALL-E then tries to teach her what he thinks is a safer dance move — the spin. Again, EVE cannot safely manage the Earthbound dancing. She spins like a devilish dervish and ends up damaging one of WALL-E's eyes. This "getting to know you" scene, primarily accomplished through inept dancing, shows that the two have a long way to go before their differences are resolved, but in the way of musicals, it also clearly demonstrates that such a resolution is possible. Couples who do not belong together do not ever attempt to dance with each other, only prospective couples do that. The scene also highlights that neither EVE nor WALL-E are completely effective dancers when attempting to dance alone.

Shortly after the getting to know you scene, WALL-E shows EVE a small green plant that he found in the course of his daily work. With the prized object found, EVE can return to Axiom — the great habitat-ship deep in outer space — and proclaim that the Earth can once more sustain life. WALL-E, desperate not be left alone again, hitches a ride on the exterior of the space shuttle that was designed to transport EVE back to the Axiom. From the moment WALL-E arrives on the Axiom, he creates physical chaos and unseats the careful balance of the ship. Indeed, WALL-E is so sloppy, so resolutely earthy that he is perceived as a foreign contaminant, much to the consternation of an obsessed cleaning robot. WALL-E's presence on the Axiom is not only physically disruptive, but audibly disruptive as well, triggering aural chaos wherever he goes. WALL-E cannot help but play or hum snippets of his favorite *Hello Dolly!* song, "Sunday Clothes," at the most inopportune and illogical moments. He accidentally plays it for the ineffectual captain of the Axiom and for a group of defective robots who go rogue. The captain ends up inadvertently humming the song underneath his breath. The rogue robots bloop and bleep a version of it as well after they escape with WALL-E from a draconian repair shop. But from what appears to be chaos emerges something very important to the narrative structure of *WALL-E*. In addition, and in a prime example of the ways in which the tropes of movie musicals have melded within the conventions of the science fiction film, the emerging importance of the song underscores a classic trope of the science fiction film: machines that become sentient.

Just after he hears "Sunday Clothes," the Axiom's captain awakens both to his connection to Earth and to his responsibilities to the humans nominally under his charge. He does so by deciding to defy Auto, Axiom's near-sentient autopilot program which resists the idea that humans as a species should return to their home. For their part, the defective robots use "Sunday Clothes" as a kind of battle cry as they work together to help EVE and WALL-E; their ability to create music together is emblematic of their ability to finally come together as an effective group and do something right. Just as in *Meet Me in St. Louis*, a key song is introduced by one character and then reprised by or passed along to different characters. As the melody circulates, it signifies the creation of a coherent group which cares about the same things and shares the same values, not to mention the same human-like self-awareness. The robots would not be able to magically know and then easily perform the song together otherwise.

In the midst of the struggle with Auto over control of the green plant — and by extension the future of humanity — the budding relationship between WALL-E and EVE finally culminates in a complex song and dance routine. The robots have briefly escaped from the Axiom and float freely in space. EVE, ecstatic that WALL-E has not only survived Auto's assassination attempt through the timely use of a fire extinguisher but that he also managed to save the plant in the process, gives him a hug. WALL-E is so gleeful over EVE's demonstration of affection that he squirts some hydrogen out of the extinguisher he holds to propel himself into a joyful spin as Newman's music rises up to meet him. EVE may have been built for flying, but now WALL-E can fly too, at least as long as the fire extinguisher holds out. After a few false starts the pair fly together, forming complex patterns, with WALL-E often choreographing the moves that EVE follows. The music for this scene is predominantly EVE's theme: the music heard when she first took flight on Earth. However, Newman's music also contains elements of WALL-E's main theme; the strings soar and swoop along with the robots, but the bouncy percussive effects that are so much a part of WALL-E's musical personality are also present. The musical blending is important: the robots and their respective themes join together to form something new, and that newness and the emotions it inspires can only be adequately expressed through dance. A hybrid musical theme is created which symbolizes the new relationship.

The romantic dance number that takes place between WALL-E and EVE mirrors similar dancing moments in Fred Astaire and Ginger Rogers films like *Top Hat* (1935), where, without any apparent prior practice, the romantic couple knows how to dance together in perfect time to music they have never heard before. As many scholars have noted, when the censorship codes regulating films were more stringent, dancing became the means through which romantic relationships were consummated (see Altman 167–168, Williams 133–134). Given that the protagonists in *WALL-E* are robots, and that the film was marketed as a family film, it should come as no surprise that the Astaire/Rogers method of sublimating sex is at work here. In addition, science fiction films, as Vivian Sobchack has noted, are also typically devoid of apparent sexuality. Here is yet another way in which the genres of musical and science fiction intersect at an odd angle (103). However, it is also important to realize that such a romantic, choreographed moment is now such a well-established part of the film musical genre that *WALL-E* must include the dance between WALL-E and EVE. Their dancing together is the "natural" means through which they can believably express the love that has grown between them.

The dance between WALL-E and EVE even incorporates two of the signature moves of film musicals: the presence of an appreciative audience and a complete break in the narrative action (Feuer 31–33). While the robot pair soars together in an (apparently) unrehearsed dance, the two humans on the Axiom who have encountered WALL-E watch them through a large pane of glass. The film then cuts to the captain of the Axiom watching footage of a barn dance on a computer screen that AUTO generated in response to the command "define dance." The sequence creates a clear parallel between how WALL-E and EVE learn about dancing by watching human actors in musicals on a make-shift screen, and the obese chair-bound humans who watch the dancing robots through a glass window that functions as a movie screen. Just as WALL-E and EVE learned from a musical, so do the humans — John and Mary — learn from the musical number WALL-E and EVE create on the spot.

Generic Intersections — Closing the Distance Between Science Fiction and Musical Films

The dance between WALL-E and EVE, however, does not signal the end of the film. Indeed, as with many Astaire/Rogers films, one final obstacle must be overcome before the loving couple can truly belong to each other. In the process of thwarting Auto, WALL-E sacrifices himself — suffering a massive systems failure — to ensure that the plant survives. Since WALL-E's circuitry is so outdated, a replacement board can be found in only one place: Earth. The Axiom's return to Earth thus has the dual motivation of WALL-E's rescue and the human's restoration to their rightful home.

Upon landing, EVE rebuilds WALL-E's components in an effort to save him. The audience is prepared for the moment of restoration from the very beginning of the film, when WALL-E replaces a broken tread by taking one off of one of the many defunct WALL-Es that populate Earth. A second occurrence meant to prepare viewers for the film's final moments is somewhat more jarring. After WALL-E damages an eye, he quickly replaces it with one of the many that he keeps on hand. Unlike his treads, which are treated merely like shoes, meant to be hung up before retiring for the evening and to be put back on when going off to the day's work, the replacement of an eye begins to clearly mark the robotic body as different from the human body. So when EVE attempts to save WALL-E by replacing and exchanging multiple body parts, including circuits, limbs, and eyes, we hope, without being sure, that

WALL-E will retain his personality once he powers up. However, when EVE attempts to play WALL-E's internal recording of *Hello Dolly!*, white noise replaces the plucky sound of harmonized singing. It is one of the most poignant moments of the film precisely because we fear that WALL-E's personality has been lost and his memory — that is, his recordings — has been erased. WALL-E's personality and memory, essentially his ability to recognize, collect, and treasure the same objects which hold for us warm nostalgic associations are the most essential qualities of the film. It is his ability to recognize and participate in our own nostalgia which makes WALL-E human, and far more like us, the 21st century viewers of the film.

Though nostalgia functions on several levels throughout the film, we are most interested in the nostalgic functions of the *Hello Dolly!* excerpts. WALL-E garners much of it is warmth from nostalgia, a term that draws its origins from a special type of homesickness experienced by Swiss mercenaries in the 17th century. At one point considered a physical illness, nostalgia has since been absorbed by general discourses surrounding psychiatry and mental conditions. Along with the transition from a physical disorder to a purely mental ailment in the 1900s, the term also substituted yearning for a particular place with longing for a particular time.[1] More recently, the phenomenon of nostalgia has been identified by a number of scholars, notably Frederic Jameson, Linda Hutcheon, and Svetlana Boym as an important feature of postmodernism. Jameson and Hutcheon agree that nostalgia prevents any substantive engagement with the past, while disagreeing on which postmodern aesthetics are nostalgic. Boym, with her distinction between reflective/restorative nostalgia distinction, posits that it is possible to actively engage with the past within the context of reflective nostalgia, a challenge that *WALL-E* as a film seems to sporadically take up.

The centrality of nostalgia in *WALL-E*, as both a means to indicate "the future" and to soften what could otherwise be construed as a post-apocalyptic horror film, is intimately tied to the film's devotion to the genre tropes of film musicals, and to what Rick Altman has named "the folk musical" in particular. According to Altman's formulation, a folk musical emphasizes "the amateur, the unmediated, and the provincial (even in St. Louis or New York) blends with a settlement narrative and a studied dispelling of apocalyptic motifs in order to reaffirm the small town values of America even in a world which seemingly has surpassed them" (363), all set to music. Indeed, music — and the apparent natural musicality of the characters — is crucial to the syntax of the folk musical and the ideology it promotes. For all of its mechanical trappings, the deep structures of *WALL-E* adhere quite closely to the ideals of the folk musical, with its emphasis on amateur depictions of song and dance — for example, WALL-E's sing-song or how the "define dance" sequence uses a barn dance and links such rural dancing to WALL-E and EVE's dance in space — and the importance of small town values — hard work, community, farming — over the urban delights provided by the Axiom.

In addition to the two film's thematic similarities discussed in the previous section, *Hello Dolly!* is central to *WALL-E*'s depiction of the future. One of the film's primary strategies for indicating the future is by transforming the present into the past. By encouraging a nostalgic reading of present-day objects depicted in the film, especially WALL-E's VHS copy of *Hello Dolly!*, the filmmakers enable viewers to watch the film as 29th century participants, looking back on a lost time. As Linda Hutcheon writes:

> Nostalgia, in fact, may depend precisely on the irrecoverable nature of the past for its emotional impact and appeal. It is the very pastness of the past, its inaccessibility, that likely accounts for a large part of nostalgia's power.... This is rarely the past as actually experienced, of course; it is the past as imagined, as idealized through memory and desire [195].

All of the characters in *WALL-E* perform this precise move: idealizing a version of an Earth none of them have ever experienced and which can never be retrieved. Moreover, what triggers these idealizations is a 1969 film musical that itself paints the past in sepia tones, a film most of *WALL-E*'s viewers would likely not know well, if at all. *Hello Dolly!* is therefore the perfect vehicle for encouraging a sense of loss in *WALL-E*'s viewers precisely because it triggers memories of film musicals in general, and not in the particular. However, it is also the case that WALL-E as a character has a more reflective relationship to *Hello Dolly!* than a restorative one; he is more interested in the movements and the relationships displayed on his makeshift screen than in the unknowable nineteenth century represented there. And so, once again, the structural elements borrowed from film musicals make it possible for the contradictions built within *WALL-E* to be addressed satisfactorily.

But of course science fiction films, like film musicals, are themselves intensively nostalgic and deeply invested with the idea of going home, even if no one has any idea what that Eden-like place looks like. So, if the film portrays the 21st century as an object of nostalgic longing, how exactly does it imagine and idealize our present? A quick survey of the objects that surround robot WALL-E on Earth, even if we restrict ourselves to objects that are registered on the soundtrack in some way, includes: Pong's chipper electronic beeping, the sleek and harmonious mid-century sales jingles for Buy-N-Large e-billboards, a modern electric car lock, the robots' eager popping of bubble wrap packaging, the Apple computer start-up noise used to indicate robot WALL-E's power level, Big Mouth Billy Bass, the mounted animatronic fish who loves to sing, and of course, a VHS copy of *Hello Dolly!*

Although perhaps not clear from this incomplete list, the past as imagined by WALL-E remains in the confines of the last forty or so years. If there are any indicators of human civilization that extend beyond this period, they are far from the main focus of the film. Instead, this is a film concerned with the film viewer's present and immediate past — that is, our own recollections and experiences of life on Earth. This is an important point, because it is by encouraging the viewer to take a nostalgic stance specifically in relation to his or her own present, that *WALL-E* encourages viewers to imagine themselves in the future. It is as if we are able to mentally participate in WALL-E's "archeological digs," watching him as he uncovers and catalogues artifacts from a familiar but removed past. However, it should be noted, that not all of *WALL-E*'s viewers get to participate equally in the rediscovery of their own present, as the "artifacts" in *WALL-E* are from a decidedly North American dig site. In fact, there are few, if any, indications of global culture either on Earth or on the spaceship Axiom.

Not coincidently, simplicity and selectivity are central to the aesthetics of nostalgia. This might explain the only piece of music included in the film that does not seem to be directly related to *Hello Dolly!*, *Koyaanisqatsi*, or *2001*: a rendition of the song "La Vie en Rose" as performed by Louis Armstrong. "La Vie en Rose" was initially made famous by the French singer Edith Piaf in 1946, and has since become a signifier of romance in dozens of films. Appropriately enough, the song is used in WALL-E to accompany a montage of events over the course of WALL-E's initial attempt to court EVE while on Earth. As such, its use in the film initially seems clichéd, especially in light of how cleverly the film as a whole incorporates music within its narrative.

"La Vie en Rose," however, has a direct connection to *Hello Dolly!* through Louis Armstrong's career. In 1964 Armstrong recorded his biggest-selling album, *Hello Dolly!*, an album which dislodged The Beatles from their number one spot on the bestselling albums chart (McAleer 93). Armstrong's album included a Dixie-land jazz version of the song "Hello Dolly!" and also featured cover versions of "Moon River" and "Blueberry Hill." But Armstrong's involvement with *Hello, Dolly!* did not end there. In 1969 he had a cameo appearance in the film version of *Hello, Dolly!* as the bandleader at the restaurant, Louis. Armstrong sings "Hello Dolly!" with Dolly (Streisand), welcoming her "back where she belongs." He only has a minute of screen time before he disappears from the film and Streisand is swept up into a large-scale production number. His inclusion is a clear attempt to capitalize on the popularity of the album and on Armstrong's association with the song outside of its original musical theater context (Nollen 184–186). *WALL-E* thus incorporates the most famous song from *Hello, Dolly!* without ever having to use it directly.

Regarding how the nostalgia of the film functions at the level of technology, not only does WALL-E watch the musical on a VHS, an already obsolete format that undoubtedly holds nostalgia for some of the Pixar film's older viewers, but he has rigged his VHS to play on an iPod, a technology which, to the contemporary viewer, is no more than seven years old. By using an object that is so foreign to any of our current representations of the past and which, instead, is one of the most widely recognizable signifiers of the advancing technology of the 21st century present, *WALL-E*'s makers viscerally mark our present as the film's past. Complicating this, the screen space of the iPod is so small, that WALL-E must employ a rectangular glass magnifier to enlarge the image. Coincidentally, the result of his makeshift home theater is something akin to recreating the experience of watching television. Even this, the simple act of watching a VHS of *Hello Dolly!* on a makeshift TV holds the potential to incite nostalgic inclinations, as now less and less TV is actually watched on TV.

One of the central catalysts for a nostalgic reading of the present is WALL-E's copy of *Hello Dolly!*, which he watches repeatedly throughout the film. The footage from *Hello Dolly!* functions on at least four variously inter-related levels of nostalgia. First, as noted above, the 1969 musical is nostalgic in its own right, depicting a simplistic, perfectly harmonious version of late 19th century American life. Second, the film can be read as one of Hollywood's last major attempts at a big-budget studio musical looking back longingly both to the golden age of the studio system and of film musicals in particular. As noted above, *Hello Dolly!* also invokes nostalgic sentiment on a third level through the technologies employed to watch it. Lastly, while all three of these levels of nostalgia work to portray the present or near past as the ancient past, nostalgia in WALL-E counteracts a possible reading of the film as a post-apocalyptic science fiction horror film by subverting many of the conventions used in science fiction horror through its soundtrack.

Conclusion

As we have shown, reused and recycled cinematic music performs a significant portion of the genre work in *WALL-E*. While the film employs multiple sequences that attempt to converge the two genres — the "define dance" sequence, for example — it is through the soundtrack that the film actually resolves these issues. Using the dualist conventions imbedded in the classic Hollywood musical and activated by the musical sequences from *Hello Dolly!*, *WALL-E* resolves apparent contradictions between science fiction and the musical. In doing so, it points to a shared lineage of nostalgia and utopia that run through and structure both genres.

In Vera Dika's discussion of "returned" images she discusses the distortion of the past in the pervasive practice of using material taken from or referencing older movies as a figure for history. Accordingly, "the image returns not as representational of the natural real, but as simulacra, as a copy of copies whose original has been lost. A play of references is thus engendered, one now highly coded with pastness" (3). This process also engenders the "changed status of the film image, and the return of the classical film genres, both as past coded signifying systems" (3). In the above, we tried to map out this phenomenon as it stood in relation to "returned" sound and more specifically, as manifest in *WALL-E*. Throughout, we discussed ways in which the musical excerpts function differently within the narrative and aesthetic structure of the film as well as the differences between *WALL-E*'s soundtrack and classical Hollywood use of music. If, as Dika claims, "nostalgia films are not new examples of old genres in the usual sense. They are reconstructions of dead or dismantled forms, genres that are now returned after a period of absence or destruction," then *WALL-E* provides ample evidence for the ways in which music can be one of the primary ways of facilitating such a return, and further suggests that the use of previously recorded music in films requires closer attention in order to better ascertain the meanings such music is meant to convey.

NOTES

1. For more details, see Christine Sprengler's discussion on the history and evolution of nostalgia from seventeenth century Europe to the American cinematic present in "Setting the State: The History of Nostalgia" in *Screening Nostalgia: Populuxe Props and Technicolor Aesthetics in Contemporary American Film.*

WORKS CITED

Altman, Rick. *The American Film Musical.* 2d ed. Bloomington: Indiana University Press, 1989.

Anders, Charlie Jane. "Wall-E, Right Wing Hero?" 13 July 2008. Accessed 11 September 2009.<http://io9.com/5024712/wall+e-right-wing-hero>.

Barthes, Roland. *Mythologies.* Trans. Annette Lavers. New York: Macmillan, 1972.

Boym, Svetlana. *The Future of Nostalgia.* New York: Basic Books, 2002.

Brown, Royal S. *Overtones and Undertones: Reading Film Music.* Berkeley: University of California Press, 1994.

Dika, Vera. *Recycled Culture in Contemporary Art and Film.* Cambridge: Cambridge University Press, 2003.

Dyer, Richard. *Only Entertainment.* 2d ed. New York: Routledge, 2002.

Eisenstein, Sergei, V.I. Pudomn, and G.V. Alexandrov. "A Statement," in *Film Sound: Theory and Practice.* Eds. Elisabeth Weis and John Belton. New York: Columbia University Press, 1985. 83–85.

Feuer, Jane. *The Hollywood Musical.* 2d ed. Bloomington: Indiana University Press, 1993.

Gleiberman, Owen. "Movie Review: WALL-E." *Entertainment Weekly* 26 June 2008. Accessed 1 June 2009. <http://www.ew.com/ew/article/0,,20209111,00.html>.

Hutcheon, Linda. "Irony, Nostalgia, and the Postmodern." *Methods for the Study of Literature as Cultural Memory.* Vol. 6, Proc. of the XVth Congress of the International Comparative Literature Association, Leiden, 16–22 Aug. 1997. Ed. Annemarie Estor and Raymond Vervliet. Rodopi, 2000. 189–207.

Jameson, Fredric. *Postmodernism, or the Cultural Logic of Late Capitalism.* Durham: Duke University Press, 1991.

Kislan, Richard. *The Musical: A Look at the American Musical Theater.* 2d ed. New York: Hal Leonard, 1995.

McAleer, Dave. *Hit Singles: Top 20 Charts from 1954 to the Present Day.* 5th ed. Milwaukee: Hal Leonard, 2004.

Nollen, Scott Allen. *Louis Armstrong: The Life, Music, and Screen Career.* Jefferson, NC: McFarland, 2004.

Sobchack, Vivian. "The Virginity of Astronauts: Sex and the Science Fiction Film," in *Cultural Theory and Contemporary Science Fiction Cinema.* Ed. Annette Kuhn. London: Verso, 2000. 103–115.

Sprengler, Christine. *Screening Nostalgia: Populuxe Props and Technicolor Aesthetics in Contemporary American Film.* New York: Berghahn Books, 2009.

"WALL-E Q & A with Writer/Director Andrew Stanton." 23 June 2008. Accessed 1 June 2009. <http://www.collider.com/entertainment/interviews/article.asp/aid/8305/tcid/1/pg/2>.

Williams, Linda. *Hard Core: Power, Pleasure, and the "Frenzy of the Visible."* Berkeley: University of California Press, 1999.

Willman, Chris. "Wall-E Meets Dolly." 28 July 2008. Accessed 12 September 2009. <http://www.ew.com/ew/article/0,,20211943_2,00.html>.

4

Just Imagine: The Musical Effacement of Dystopia in an Early Sound Film

Katherine Spring

Looks Like 1980, Sounds Like 1930

On September 6, 1927, a stage musical comedy, titled *Good News*, opened at Chanin's 46th Street Theatre in the Broadway theatre district of New York City. Featuring the music of celebrated scoring triumvirate George Gard ("Buddy") De Sylva, Lew Brown, and Ray Henderson, the show integrated a number of popular songs into a gag-filled story about a college football star who, benched for failing classes, falls in love with his tutor. *Good News* turned out to be the songwriting trio's most successful show to date, and several songs, including "The Best Things in Life Are Free," "The Varsity Drag," and "Just Imagine," became instant hits, having also been recorded by various artists for the major phonograph record companies of the day.[1] By the time *Good News* closed in January 1929, it had registered 557 performances and had inspired studio executives at MGM to adapt the stage show to the screen as an early sound musical. In the meantime, executives at Fox Film, a studio that was already capitalizing on the commercial success of De Sylva, Brown, and Henderson's songs for early sound films *The Singing Fool* and *Say It with Songs* (both 1929), hired the trio to write and produce two new motion pictures. The first, *Sunny Side Up*, was a generic romantic comedy and vehicle for stars Janet Gaynor and Charles Farrell, but the second manifested a peculiar plot: in 1980, when marriages are determined by government decree, a young aviator is prohibited from marrying the woman he loves until he travels to Mars and proves his scientific competence. For the film's title, De Sylva,

Brown, and Henderson borrowed the name of a hit song from the repertoire of *Good News*; Fox's *Just Imagine* opened in New York in November 1930.

Despite the musical provenance of the film, *Just Imagine* is often cited in critical scholarship as an example of early science fiction cinema or at best a hybrid of the musical and science fiction genres (for example, in Brosnan 40–41, Cornea 7, Desser 114, Richards 28).[2] Certainly, discussion of the film as an example of science fiction cinema is warranted. Its futuristic setting and urban set design, the construction of which allegedly cost Fox $250,000, was undoubtedly influenced by the visual aesthetic of *Metropolis*, Fritz Lang's seminal work of science fiction that opened in North American theaters in March 1927, just three-and-a-half years prior to the release of *Just Imagine*.[3] Moreover, roughly one third of *Just Imagine* takes place on the planet of Mars, a setting that justifies the appearance of an alien species, that integral semantic feature of the science fiction genre.

But when one considers elements beyond its set design and extraterrestrial creatures, the classification of *Just Imagine* as science fiction becomes dubious. As Vivian Sobchack has argued, even while *Metropolis* influenced the visual style of Fox's production, the former presents in unequivocal terms a negative and oppressive portrait of technological progress and aims to persuade its audience that the future bears more distress than the present; by contrast, the 1930 film promotes technology as a positive force (7). J.P. Telotte extends Sobchack's observations and situates *Just Imagine* on a spectrum demarcated at one end by the dystopic vision of *Metropolis* and at the other by the utterly optimistic progressivism of 1933's *The Shape of Things to Come* ("Science" 84–86). In his book, *A Distant Technology: Science Fiction Film and the Machine Age*, Telotte contends that *Just Imagine* represents technology as a means of eradicating social estrangement and anxiety (120). He writes, "Inscribed in all of these wonders [of the future] are promises of comfort, convenience, and accessibility, even a common ability to exercise some control over our world rather than to be controlled by and its technology's implicit agenda for change, speed, and order" (117). The cityscape featured in *Just Imagine* may evoke that of *Metropolis*, but arguably the narrative presents, by standards of science fiction, an unconventionally consoling vision of the future and its technological manifestations. This unconventionality is seconded by the film's soundtrack, which manifests what Philip Hayward has dubbed a degree of "conservatism" atypical of science fiction cinema, a genre often heralded for its innovative sonic designs (7; see also Whittington). As Hayward explains, the songs heard in *Just Imagine* "were not perceived by contemporary critics and audiences as deviating from the songwriters' established formula" (7); Telotte observes similarly that the film "sounds" like 1930 rather than a creative sonic landscape one might conjure up for the setting of 1980 ("Distant" 116).

What accounts for *Just Imagine*'s utopic vision of technology and its "conservative" soundtrack? Drawing on the work of Howard P. Segal, Telotte cites the surge in popularity of technological-utopian literature during the 1920s ("Distant" 120–21), but this chapter considers another influence, one mentioned by Telotte but not explored in the detail I believe it deserves in the context of science fiction studies. *Just Imagine* was produced at the tail end of Hollywood's transition to sound, when institutional and aesthetic factors distinctive of that period rendered the Broadway stage musical comedy the most proximate and salient influence on the visual and sonic style of the film. As a derivative of the Broadway stage and an exemplar of Hollywood's nascent musical genre, *Just Imagine* employs a key element of the musical comedy — the star-song spectacle — in order to mask its narrative's potentially threatening elements of technology with a vision of progress and optimism. While the technological devices on display in *Just Imagine* never "appear menacing or betray a kind of hard-wired social agenda," as Telotte has written, *Just Imagine* requires for the sake of narrative conflict the portrayal of society in 1980 as a risk to individual free will ("Distant" 114). An account of the influence of the musical stage genre, one which situates *Just Imagine* in its institutional and aesthetic contexts of film history, helps to illuminate our understanding of the film's negotiation of dystopic and utopic scenarios and hence its maneuvering between the science fiction and musical genres.

Before examining these contexts, it should be noted that although the musical and science fiction film may seem to share little in common — the musical is typically associated with exuberant song and/or dance sequences and optimistic narrative outcomes in which a romantic union is formed, whereas the science fiction film often evokes nightmarish threats to human safety and, at times, concludes with pessimistic or ambiguous narrative states — they share a central strategy in their emphasis on visual and sonic spectacle and their tendency to position the exhibition of this spectacle against the flow of narrative. Christine Cornea points up this similarity when she remarks, "The numerous moments in science fiction films when the narrative flow is stalled to make way for visual spectacle resembles the way in which song and/or dance numbers are commonly structured into the narrative of a musical film" (7). I would add that the formal opposition of narrative and spectacle also maps onto an opposition of ideological or thematic content. Just as science fiction plots frequently flow from the conflict posited between humanity and aliens/machines, where humanity represents a domain of safety and is threatened by the presence of non-human entities, the musical, as Rick Altman describes it in his seminal book, *The American Film Musical*, associates its song sequences with themes of community, joy, and beauty, all of which are absent from the surrounding narrative world.

In this way, the film musical's song sequences acquire symbolic status. They are microcosmic impressions of utopia that stand in contrast with the diegetic reality depicted by their narrative surroundings. In an oft-cited passage from his essay, "Entertainment and Utopia," Richard Dyer conceives of the film musical as one facet of a broader form of entertainment, which he elucidates as follows:

> Entertainment offers the image of "something better" to escape into, or something we want deeply that our day-to-day lives don't provide. Alternatives, hopes, wishes — these are the stuff of utopia, the sense that things could be better, that something other than what is can be imagined and maybe realized [20].

Songs, as utopian impressions, serve to counter the presence of social fragmentation, malaise, and economic scarcity (26). Considered in these terms, the popular songs of *Just Imagine* function to intimate what everyday life in 1980, despite the era's technological advances, fails to deliver.

Institutional Context: The Coupling of Hollywood and Tin Pan Alley

By the time *Just Imagine* was released in late 1930, the major Hollywood studios — Paramount, Loew's/MGM, Fox, Warner Bros., and RKO — had phased out the production of silent cinema in favor of sound films, a striking proportion of which were musicals.[4] Whether they were adaptations of Broadway shows or original works that adopted the formal conventions of stage musicals, the earliest film musicals fulfilled two significant commercial functions. First, as Donald Crafton writes in *The Talkies: American Cinema's Transition to Sound, 1926–1931*, they exploited the capacity of synchronized soundtracks to make possible the onscreen, vocal performances of singing stars. Filmmakers working with the new technology of sound film "relied on what they knew.... [They] capitalized on cinema's capability to suggest a *virtual* presence, an imagined being-there, in order to bring performer and auditor together in the space of the filmed performance. Broadway, the 'Street of Streets,' was coming soon to the local theatre" (63). Musicals exploited the novelty of sound cinema by emphasizing song-and-dance performances, and, unlike Broadway shows, they could disseminate "virtual" performances to urban and rural audiences. Broadway casts that embarked on regional road shows following their runs in New York could not circulate the country as efficaciously as could film prints that delivered song-and-dance sequences.

Second, at the same time that the onscreen performances of songs infused the nascent sound cinema with commercial appeal, they launched popular songs to mass audiences. In the two decades that preceded the transition to sound, the country's most powerful publishing firms, whose central offices were located in the region of Manhattan dubbed "Tin Pan Alley," advertised and distributed songs by way of sheet music, phonograph records, radio broadcasts, and live Broadway performances. Shortly after the introduction of sound motion pictures on a commercial scale, the music and film industries lauded the new medium for its capacity to serve as an especially effective platform for song distribution. In the 1928–1929 filmmaking season, as motion picture songs topped *Variety*'s weekly lists of best-selling songs, the trade paper observed:

> The picture song, from the music men's viewpoint, is the millennium. It's the quickest, easiest and least expensive means of song hit making ever known.... From the picture producer's standpoint, the song hook-up is invaluable. It gives their celluloid product a new form of plugging and exploitation over the radio, on the records and in the streets, through mass whistling and harmonizing, which no amount of paid advertising could accomplish ["Picture" 56].

For a brief time, sound motion pictures rivaled radio and threatened to supplant Broadway as the country's most important platform for introducing songs to mass consumers, whose response to individual popular songs was measured by the quantity of sheet music and phonograph records sold. During the 1929–1930 filmmaking season, popular songs appeared on the soundtracks of more than half of all synchronized sound feature films, representative of a variety of genres, released by the majors (American Film Institute). In this context of cross-promotion, the film musical, with its emphasis on the presentation of songs by singing stars, was considered an especially lucrative genre.

The perceived commercial value of motion picture songs resulted in significant and lasting changes to the relationship between Hollywood studios and Tin Pan Alley music publishing firms. During the transition to sound, all of the major studios entered into contractual arrangements with publishing firms. The agreements, which ranged from informal mergers to outright acquisitions, granted the studios control over the distribution of motion picture songs and, at the same time, directed the music business toward the new, profitable platform for popular songs. In the remainder of this section I examine the circumstances that precipitated the relationship between Fox Film and the triumvirate of De Sylva, Brown, and Henderson prior to the production of *Just Imagine*.

The chief motivation for the investments by studios like Fox into the business of music publishing was the perceived value of song copyright ownership. During the two decades leading up to the transition to sound, the music industry developed various methods to enforce the laws of the U.S. Copyright Act of 1909, which updated the 1790 Act in order to reflect vital changes in the ways that the music industry produced and distributed songs around the turn of the century. The amended Act granted, among other provisions, two exclusive rights to owners of music copyrights. One was the right for an owner to collect two cents per mechanical reproduction, such as a phonograph record, of his or her copyrighted work. The other provision was the right to perform a work publicly for profit. Individuals seeking to perform a copyrighted work were obligated to obtain a license from the copyright owner. As Tin Pan Alley publishers and songwriters prospered in the early 1900s, the public performance of live music proved to be increasingly profitable.[5]

In order to monitor and regulate the performance and recording of copyrighted works under the laws of the Act, a group of publishers and songwriters gathered in 1917 and formed the American Society of Composers, Authors and Publishers, or ASCAP. In exchange for the right to perform copyrighted music in their spaces, venue proprietors — including owners of motion picture theaters — were obliged to pay annual license fees to ASCAP. Although the organization was ostensibly an equitable collaboration of composers, lyricists, and publishers, the organization's methods of royalty distribution favored the latter, which took in half of mechanical royalties, while the music creators — composers and lyricists — split the remainder (Caldwell 298–99). Within ten years, ASCAP attracted the membership of nearly every one of the country's most important publishers: Irving Berlin, Inc., Sam Fox Publishing Co., Robbins Music Corp., Remick Music Corp., and Shapiro, Bernstein & Co. Many of these companies belonged to another, smaller organization, the Music Publishers Protective Association (MPPA), also formed in 1917, which oversaw the rights to mechanical reproductions — most notably, phonograph records. By the 1920s, publishers had successfully repackaged the popular song into not just a manufactured product but also a marketable commodity.

That ASCAP and the MPPA had secured control over mechanical and performing rights just as the motion picture industry was preparing to convert to synchronized sound film was highly auspicious, because the production and presentation of sound film depended both on mechanically reproduced discs (and, later, celluloid) as well as on public performances of prerecorded music in theaters. Among other responsibilities, the transition to sound shifted the onus of musical accompaniment from theatre managers to studio producers. These producers could no longer rely on theater managers and music directors to maintain libraries of sheet music and to employ musicians; as Kathryn Kalinak has noted, the burden of music performance and copyright shifted to the film studios (66). The large, centralized major studios of the motion picture industry could not evade prosecution brought about by

ASCAP and the MPPA. At the same time, the publishers who comprised these large music conglomerates offered Hollywood producers top-selling songs. For song material for their earliest sound films, therefore, studio executives looked to these publishers.

As motion picture producers sought to exploit the commercial value of popular songs by incorporating them into films, it became increasingly clear to motion picture producers, music publishers, and songwriters that they would benefit from conducting deals directly with one another rather than through a conglomerate of publishers. As I have outlined elsewhere, between the autumn of 1928 through late 1929, each of Hollywood's major studios invested in the business of song publishing, either by purchasing the rights to the song catalogs of the country's most prominent music publishers, by acquiring majority stock in extant publishing firms, or by merging with them (74–76). In August 1929, *Variety* printed an accurate prediction:

> The importance of musical copyrights to pictures and sound recordings has upset the industry so that within a very few months it is believed none of the more important music firms will remain independent in view of the value of a tie-up with either the picture companies or the electrics ["Warner-Harms" 5].

Because the studios had spent the transitional era acquiring not only the copyrights to the country's largest song catalogues but also the means by which to copyright songs composed specially for new motion pictures, a portion of the royalties earned from every piece of sheet music and every phonograph record would proceed to their subsidiary publishing houses.

This brief history brings us to Fox Film, one of the first studios that entered into a contractual agreement with a publishing firm. In October 1928, executives approached De Sylva, Brown, and Henderson, who by that time had created an eponymous, incorporated firm (henceforth referred to as DBH) as a means of publishing their own song material. Fox executives clearly sought to exploit the trio's established reputation as among the best "songsmiths" in Broadway and Hollywood. By the time they met in New York in 1925 to score that year's edition of producer George White's *Scandals*, an annual Broadway musical revue, each of the three had at least ten years of experience writing hit songs that were popularized by celebrity singers on Broadway stages.[6] The edition gave rise to a crowd-pleasing number, "The Girl Is You," and inspired the songwriters' collaboration on subsequent stage productions. This, in turn, generated some of the best-selling and memorable songs of the decade, including: "The Varsity Drag," "You're the Cream in My Coffee," and "The Best Things in Life Are Free." Meanwhile, DBH composed and published several hits for Hollywood films, including "Angela Mia" for Fox's *The Street Angel* (1928) and "Sonny Boy" for Warner Bros.'s *The Singing Fool*

(1928). When Fox signed with DBH in October 1928, the publishing company had grown to employ more than 100 staff members, and the songwriting trio was preoccupied with Broadway shows in New York and Atlantic City ("DeSylva" 55). Three of their musical comedies, *Good News*, *Three Cheers*, and *Hold Everything*, as well as the musical revue, *George White's Scandals*, were running simultaneously, and *Follow Thru* was in production and scheduled for a premiere in January 1929. DBH was in an optimal position to become the exclusive publishers of all of Fox's new motion picture songs ("Film" 73), and one month later, in November 1928, Fox and DBH formed a film music publishing subsidiary, Sound Music Corp., which eventually became the Crawford Music Corp. ("Rapee" 57).

In less than a year, however, a major deal was struck between Warner Bros. and another large publishing firm, Harms, Inc., which owned partial stock in DBH. As a result, DBH songwriters working in Hollywood transferred to the Warner Bros. lot, and suddenly Fox required new songwriting talent as well as a protective publishing strategy so that it would not be forced to publish under the Harms–Warner Bros. conglomerate. In October 1929, the studio announced its creation of a new publishing entity, Red Star, which planned to be in full operation by the beginning of 1930 ("Fox's" 65; "Writers" 73). Under the Red Star label, the studio published its own film songs, arranged music licenses with foreign branches of Fox Films, and offered to farm out its songwriters to other studios ("Fox" 57). At the same time, Fox retained a connection to De Sylva, Brown, and Henderson, and hired them to write, produce, and publish the songs for *Sunny Side Up* and *Just Imagine*. Whether or not Fox profited directly from sales of the songs' sheet music and records is unclear, but the studio nevertheless stood to gain from its association with the trio; the three "masters of marvelous entertainment" were highlighted in advertisements that preceded the release of *Just Imagine* (Kreuger 259).

In summary, *Just Imagine* was produced in an institutional context that championed the popular song as a commercial feature of sound motion pictures. By employing De Sylva, Brown, and Henderson as composers and producers for *Just Imagine*, Fox sought to take advantage of the trio's reputation for producing popular music that was sure to sell in the material formats of sheet music and phonograph records outside the theater. That some of the song numbers written for *Just Imagine* were published and recorded by popular bands two months prior to the film's release further suggests the significant role that songs played in the film's marketing campaign.[7]

Aesthetic Context: Spectacular Songs, From Broadway to Hollywood

While the economic rewards generated by the cross-promotion of film and music help to explain the incorporation of songs across the narrative of *Just Imagine*, it is equally important to consider the impact of the Broadway stage musical on the form and style of the film. In a synoptic history of musicals produced during the transition to sound, Rick Altman writes, "The most important influence of the period was exercised by the Al Jolson tear-jerker *The Singing Fool* (Warners, 1928), along with MGM's 1929 backstage love triangle story *The Broadway Melody*. In imitation, every Hollywood studio immediately and repeatedly turned to production of musical melodramas featuring an unlucky-in-love performer, a faithless spouse, a selfish sister, a gangster subplot, a singer on the skids, or a dying child" ("Musical" 297). Although musical melodramas constituted a vital subgenre of the early sound cinema, I argue in this section that the musical revue and musical comedy of the Broadway stage bore an equally wide-reaching influence. While music publishers crosspromoted sheet music, records, and radio with star vocalists in order to enhance the distribution and sales of popular music, the most successful song hits of the 1920s derived from Broadway performances. There, stars launched show tunes to audiences who, conversely, paid to attend shows in which stars sung. The spectacle of the singing star was a vital tradition of live performance, and its associated song-plugging practices were inherited by motion picture producers during the coming of sound.

Musical revues adopted the structure of early vaudeville and variety shows in that they presented series of unrelated acts or "turns," which included comic routines, song-and-dance numbers, magician shows, animal routines, and dramatic skits. At the same time, revues enhanced the earlier variety show format with spectacular displays of sets, costumes, and massive chorus numbers. Such extravagance entailed high expenses: *Ziegfeld Follies of 1919* cost $170,000, while production of the musical comedy *Irene* in the same year, cost only $41,000 (Mordden 86). Because their high production values led to the presentation of individual songs as isolatable moments of extravagant spectacle, revues served as especially effective platforms for advertising songs. Broadway historian Gerald Bordman describes the staging of Irving Berlin's song "An Orange Grove in California" part of the composer's score for George White's 1924 production of the *Music Box Revue*. As stars John Steel and Grace Moore sang, they were "walking together in an orange grove. Slowly the grove melted away into a kaleidoscope of shimmering orange lights and the audience found itself sprayed with orange perfume" (428). With their performances inextricably linked to such spectacular displays, Steel and Moore helped popularize "An Orange Grove" as well as several other Berlin tunes, including "Lady of the Evening," "What'll I Do?" and "All Alone."

Likewise, in the aforementioned *Scandals* of 1926, the music of which was composed by De Sylva, Brown, and Henderson (with the exception of George Gershwin's "Rhapsody in Blue"), visual spectacle accompanied the launch of the song "The Birth of the Blues." Bordman describes the performance as follows:

> By later standards, the song was overmounted in the show. It would seem to need little except a piano, a good singer, and a spotlight. But the twenties [sic] and White would tolerate no such austerity. There was the inevitable revue staircase flanked for this number by chorus girls dressed as angels. As Richman sang the song, a battle raged between contemporary blues and the classics. The McCarthy Sisters wore gowns suggesting "The Memphis Blues" and "The St. Louis Blues," while the Fairbanks Twins opposed them in costumes symbolizing Schubert and Schumann songs [462].

This dazzling presentation of "The Birth of the Blues" exemplifies the ways in which musical revues married popular songs to two spectacles: lavish sets and star vocalists.

Not all Broadway shows were as episodic as musical revues; musical comedies presented songs within some semblance of narrative structure.[8] Yet even while stars remained in character and in narrative contexts, they still plugged songs by repeating them across individual shows and by linking them to visually striking scenarios. For example, in the first act of *Good News*, the 1927 production mentioned at the outset of this chapter, characters Tom and Connie (John Price Jones and Mary Lawlor) sing the entirety of a ballad, "Lucky in Love" (22–23). Their duet functions not to advance the narrative or to provide narrative information but, rather, to supplement in a visually appealing way a point already disclosed by the scene's dialogue: romance has flourished between two characters. Once established as a love duet, "Lucky in Love" is reiterated at the end of the first act, when Connie discovers that Tom has pledged to marry her cousin if his team wins the next day's football game. When asked by her peers to request a song, Connie replies (while "looking at Tom — bitterly"), "Lucky in Love," which prompts the chorus to sing an abridged version of the song and close the first act. Other songs that repeat across the show include "Good News," "The Best Things in Life Are Free," and the show-stopping dance number "Varsity Drag."

Nearly every presentation of a song in *Good News* is both motivated by tenuous narrative circumstances — a casual line of dialogue, a slight gesture — and constitutes a discrete unit of performance that momentarily arrests the flow of narrative. Conveniently, of course, these "units" were also made available for purchase in the forms of sheet music and phonograph records, supporting what Broadway historian Ethan Mordden has observed: the essential elements of Broadway shows were the stars and scores, not the stories (184). This defining attribute of musical comedy applied equally well to the earliest sound musicals produced in Hollywood.

Just Imagine: Songs as Utopic Respite

As in *Good News*, the advancement of narrative in *Just Imagine* frequently halts in order to accommodate the presentation of an entire song. Moreover, the formal distinction between narrative and number across the film aligns with binary oppositions in both visual style and ideological associations. As illustrated by the table below, song performances are imbued with connotations of emotional individualism and community, while the delineation of narrative from number is mobilized stylistically. Devices of editing and mise-en-scène demarcate the shots that bear the song performances, exemplifying what Richard deCordova calls "syntagmatic specificity" (117).

Form	Visual Style	Ideological Associations
narrative	classical continuity, i.e., style is self-effacing	government regulation, social fragmentation
number	direct address, "syntagmatic specificity"	individual free will, community, nostalgia

Stylistic and Ideological Associations in *Just Imagine*

Before the appearance of a song, *Just Imagine* contrasts two social ideologies and links them with 1930 and 1980, respectively. A title card appears on the screen, and a male voice recites its message: "*Just Imagine* what a difference fifty years can make! Take a look at New York in 1880." A series of shots show an idyllic street scene in which horse-drawn buggies share a cobblestone road with ambling, parasol-toting women and children. The narrator continues, "What a peaceful scene. What calm dignity. What quaint charm. It is so quiet you can even hear the rustle or the bustle. Lovely. No traffic problem in those days. The age of pedestrian was absolutely safe." When a man crosses the street, a buggy comes to full stop, and the driver tips his hat to the pedestrian before each proceeds on his way. The narrator proclaims, "See? What politeness. In those days they did not have electric lights, telephones, radios, wireless, automobiles, or airplanes."

A new title card appears on the screen, and the narrator reads: "*Just Imagine!* The people in 1880 thought they were the last word in speed! Take a look at the same spot today." A cut returns us to a street scene that now boasts the

sight of a double-decker bus, numerous automobiles, and crowds of pedes-
trians. Sounds of traffic — horns honking, engines whirring — embellish the
soundtrack, and a building that in the earlier segment was a three-story structure adorned with awnings now extends beyond the upper reaches of the
frame. "Good ol' Fifth Avenue," quips the narrator. "Changed a bit, hasn't
it?" This time, a man crosses the street and narrowly escapes collision with
the passing traffic. The narrator calls out, "Ah, here's an adventurous soul.
Going to do a little jaywalking, eh? Be careful. Take it easy. Watch yourself.
He made it!" At that moment, a car drives into the frame and strikes the man,
whose body sails upward as the screen fades to black and the voice-over narrator concedes, "No, he didn't."

Having depicted the urban environment of 1880 as bucolic and that of
1930 as perilous, the film offers a third title card: "If the last fifty years made
such a change, *Just Imagine* the New York of 1980 ... when everyone has a
number instead of a name, and the Government tells you whom you should
marry! *Just Imagine* ... 1980!" A cut brings us to 1980, when airplanes fly in
rows between towering skyscrapers as traffic police hover above. Against this
backdrop, two characters, J-21 (John Garrick) and LN-18 (Maureen O'Sullivan), convene mid-air and discuss their predicament: the New York State
Marriage Tribunal has rejected J-21's petition to marry LN-18 and has
approved the application of his rival. In order to reverse the court's decision
and win LN-18's hand in marriage, J-21 must prove his "worth and accomplishments" in society by the time his appeal arrives in court in four months.
Until then, he is forbidden from seeing LN-18. The conversation is disrupted
by a traffic cop, who reminds the pair of the legal prohibition against stop-
ping mid-flight for extended periods.

The opening sequence of *Just Imagine* portrays technological progress as
an ambivalent force. Despite the apparent ease with which citizens traverse
the metropolis in personal aircrafts, and despite the marvelous skyscrapers that
populate the urban space, technology has ushered in a conspicuous degree of
social control that threatens individual free will. As the narrator proclaims,
humans are designated by number rather than by name, and marriages are
assigned by government decree. Progress between 1930 and 1980 comes with
a cost, one which may amuse rather than frighten audiences (as Telotte suggests), but one which nonetheless posits the central narrative conflict between
two entities: the protagonist, J-21, whose personal desire emblematizes an
ideology of individual free will, and a government body whose directives represent an ideology of social control.

In this context, popular songs function to counter *Just Imagine*'s portrayal of the negative aspects of modern life. By nesting songs within narrative contexts that refer to the governmental regulation of individual behavior,

the film amplifies the utopian impressions of those songs, and thereby helps to ensure their success as purchasable commodities beyond the space of the movie theater. An early example of this strategy may be found in the presentation of a ballad titled "(There's Something About) An Old-Fashioned Girl," which first appears approximately ten minutes into the film. Using technological features of the day — button-operated electric doors and videophones — J-21 and his roommate, R-42 (Frank Albertson), receive at their apartment a priggish government employee who is gathering information for a statistical survey. When their conversation reveals J-21's quandary, the surveyor extols the marriage law as a "noble experiment."[9] Following her departure, RT-24 offers consolation to his despondent friend, who replies, "I like a girl like my grandmother used to be. That's why I like LN. She's an old-fashioned girl. I should have lived back in 1930." RT-42 exclaims, "What? With those slow pokes?" and leaves the frame, cuing a cut to a medium shot of Garrick, who subsequently performs "An Old-Fashioned Girl." In direct address to the camera, Garrick strums a lute-like instrument and sings the first lines of the ballad. As he completes the first verse, wherein he professes a high regard for the women of 1930, a sparse, nondiegetic musical arrangement enters on the soundtrack. This background music continues as the film cuts to a medium close-up of the star, who proceeds to sing the refrain, the lyrics of which convey an unmistakable tone of nostalgia for the subject of the song's title; the performer even expresses his envy at a hypothetical male suitor of an "Old-Fashioned Girl" of 1930. Throughout the performance, three devices of visual style — a relatively tight shot scale, static framing, and a long take — focus our attention on the singing star and the showcase of the discrete unit of star-song spectacle.

An encore presentation of "An Old-Fashioned Girl" supplies a different but equally appealing depiction of the past. Immediately following J-21's first performance, RT-42 declares, "You said it, boy. Can't you just picture them?" which seemingly prompts J-21 to repeat the number's refrain. This time around, Garrick no longer sings to the camera. Instead, his voice underscores a series of lap dissolves that alternate shots of RT-42 and J-21 with three shots of "flappers": the first dances with a martini shaker, the second succumbs to a kiss from a young man, and the third rocks a baby cradle with her foot while holding a cigarette in one hand and a book, titled *Ex-Wife*, in the other. In RT-42's fantasies, an "old-fashioned girl" is a 1920s flapper, an icon whose overt display of sexual and personal freedom contrasts starkly both with the woman whom J-21 has in mind and with the staid surveyor who moments ago praised her government's rigid marriage policies.

Just as the performances of "An Old-Fashioned Girl" are motivated by J-21's voiced frustration with the policy of arranged marriages, they are also bracketed by a showcase of technology. RT-42 uses a videophone to usher in the surveyor whose reference to the government's policy prompts the song, and, following the performance, RT-42 walks to a screen on the wall and uses a videophone to call his girlfriend. In other words, the narrative scenarios that allude to technological progress and social control also circumscribe the performance of a song whose lyrics and visual mode of representation offer a period of utopic respite.

A similar example is found in the use of the publicized theme song of *Just Imagine*, a ballad titled "(I Am the Words) You Are the Melody." The song is introduced as a diegetic performance in a scene that takes place after J-21 and RT-42 steal into the flat inhabited by LN-18 and her roommate. Again, J-21 and LN-18 deliberate over the decision of the Marriage Tribunal, and LN-18 assures J-21 that his accomplishments mean more to her than do his rival's. "All he's done is published that old paper his father left him," she tells him. J-21 responds, "But the Tribunal doesn't see it that way," to which LN-18 asserts, "The Tribunal doesn't know anything about love." J-21 smiles and muses, "Love is beautiful when the loved ones are together," to which LN-18 responds, "But it's terrible when they're apart." A cut to a medium-close up of the couple accompanies J-21's launch into the first verse of the theme song, the lyrics of which, in their comparison of love to a song, reiterate the unabashed banality of the lovers' dialogue.

Although Garrick and O'Sullivan do not sing in direct address to the camera (they gaze alternately offscreen and at each other), the camera's static position, long take, and tight shot scale again supply the "syntagmatic specificity" that results in the stylistic demarcation of the song from its context of classical decoupage editing. Moreover, as with "An Old-Fashioned Girl," the change in visual style that characterizes the representation of the song accords with a change in the trajectory of the narrative: the protagonists iterate through dialogue the conflict between J-21 and the tribunal, but their potential progress toward resolution is circumvented momentarily for the sake of the star-song spectacle.

The final appearance of "(I Am the Words) You Are the Melody" in *Just Imagine* emphasizes the song's status as spectacle. In order to prove his competence to the Marriage Tribunal, J-21 travels to Mars along with RT-42 and Single-0 (played by Swedish comedian El Brendel). Shortly after their arrival, the Earthlings encounter a band of Martians who seem anything but menacing: dressed scantily in glossy outfits, these aliens bear a remarkable resemblance to humans — indeed, to a Broadway chorus line. (Edwin Bradley accurately diagnoses the Mars segment of *Just Imagine* as one that "degenerates into contrived silliness" [146].) The Martian queen, named Loo Loo (Joyzelle Joyner), leads J-21 to a telescope, whereupon the young explorer peers through the eyepiece and sees the face of LN-18 superimposed onto an image of Earth. Framed in close-up via the iris of the telescope, and accompanied by soft orchestral music, LN-18 utters the lyrics to "(I Am the Words) You Are the Melody." As she gazes directly at the camera, and a tear trickles from her eye, LN-18 performs simultaneously for J-21 and for the film's audience, thereby enacting Rick Altman's conception of the relationship between narrative and number in the music genre:

> Far from simply providing an alternative to silence — as does background music in other Hollywood films — the musical's music (as well as its dance) enters into a process of signification whereby it comes to stand for personal and communal joy; expressing a romantic triumph over the limitations of nature, of time, of society, and of economics, music becomes the signifier *par excellence* of the value of the couple and of courtship [109].

In addition, this final iteration of the theme song serves up spectacle by way of both O'Sullivan's close-up and the celebration of a scientific apparatus, the powerful telescope, as a means of fostering intimacy, since it connects J-21 and LN-18 across the vastness of outer space. When removed from Earth, perhaps, technology acts as a positive force towards social cohesion.

Up to this point, the primary threat levied against J-21 is his government's Orwellian policies. The film's final musical number, a chorus sequence performed on Mars, addresses a different threat but one which is equally commonplace to the genre of science fiction: a hostile alien species. Loo Loo, it turns out, has an evil twin, named Boo Boo, whose own tribe captures J-21, RT-42, and Single-0. In the midst of discussion of their plight, the three Earthlings witness a spectacular scene in which the female members of Boo Boo's tribe (who, like Loo Loo's clan, are conveniently redolent of a Broadway chorus line) dance before the base of a massive, four-armed effigy, which they eventually ascend in orgiastic pleasure. Throughout the eccentric performance, the soundtrack manifests orchestral music marked by a pulsing bassline and chromatic melodic runs in minor tonalities — in other words, musical features at odds with the saccharine popular ballads sung previously by J-21 and LN-18. To some extent, then, this musical sequence connects Loo Loo's tribe and non-popular music with connotations of danger, sexuality, and alien savagery. At the same time, however, the pleasures associated with the choreographed performance militates against the potential hazards posed by Loo Loo's tribe, and transforms the sequence into an attraction for the enjoyment of the Earthlings as well as the film's audience. Immediately following the song's conclusion, J-21, RT-42, and Single 0 resume their conversation and discuss their plan for escape.

Thus, although the sequence is preceded and followed by bleak narrative circumstances, the number itself lacks a narrative function other than to underline the eccentricities of the Martian tribe. That the sequence fails to advance the narrative in any salient way suggests its existence for the sole entertainment of the audience. (The entertainment is amplified by the integration of verbal jokes into the dialogue. For example, pointing to the idol, Brendel asks, "Who is that fellah?" RT-42 replies, "He's an idol," prompting Brendel to quip, "He is idle? With all those girls?"—the point being, too, that the Earthlings view the Martians as attractive women and not alien species). As it is positioned as a self-contained performance with no narrative function, in which the Earthlings serving as our surrogate audience, the musical sequence showcasing Boo Boo's tribe indulges a film audience that was already accustomed to the intrusion of song-and-dance numbers into otherwise coherent narrative structures.

Conclusion

Scholarly works that cite *Just Imagine* often conceive of the film as an unsuccessful hybrid of two genres. For instance, one scholar labels the film a "misguided science-fiction musical" and notes that the "mythos of the Hollywood musical is utterly incompatible with the tradition of dystopic fiction and the film alternates between a vision of a dehumanizing future and a standard 'boy gets girl' musical" (Kerman 114). In a similar vein, critical reviews published upon the release of *Just Imagine* treated the film as a musical comedy rather than as an instance of science fiction. A review printed in *Photoplay* underlined the comic aspects of the film and considered the "fantastic" (i.e., science fiction) elements as mere "background" to the plot. The reviewer chided audiences "who can't get a kick out of this sort of thing!" and branded *Just Imagine* "delightful buffoonery, backgrounded by an ironical, fantastic conception of life in 1980. You shouldn't and can't take a second of it seriously," wrote the author, continuing, "which makes it top entertainment. Imagination explodes everywhere — especially in your funny-bone....There are beautiful songs, romance enough, and a wealth of beauty" (Kreuger 254). A reviewer writing for *Variety* stressed *Just Imagine*'s unimaginative treatment of its fantastic elements and worried that the film would flop in the absence of a strong marketing campaign.[10] Indeed, *Just Imagine* earned only a small profit at the box office.

Judging by both contemporaneous reviews and more recent assessments of the film, it may be tempting to explain the film's poor box office performance as the result of its attempt to unite two "incompatible" genres. I offer two rejoinders to this claim. First, as I hope the preceding pages have shown, the value of *Just Imagine* need not be measured in terms of its adherence to generic elements. Rather, tonal inconsistencies across the film may be accounted for by its immediate historical context, in which a major studio endeavored to capitalize on the cultural and economic power of popular music as it was promoted by the Broadway stage of the late 1920s. Value in *Just Imagine* resides in its deployment of the popular song as a significant aesthetic and commercial force.

Second, a more compelling explanation for *Just Imagine*'s disappointing box office receipts derives from concurrent reports in the trade press, which suggested that audiences were tiring of motion picture songs and were avoiding musicals altogether (Spring 82). That *Just Imagine* failed to earn substantial revenue for Fox points to shifting trends of mass taste among filmgoers in the United States but does not necessarily indicate the film's deficiencies as a genre picture. Indeed, as a product of Hollywood's earliest sound cinema, itself a period of experimentation with the norms of classical narration vis-à-vis the spectacle of the popular song performance, *Just Imagine* exemplifies a wondrous amalgamation of two genres in their embryonic, and arguably most malleable, phases.

NOTES

1. The song "Just Imagine" was recorded by Jean Goldkette and His Orchestra (Victor, July 1928), Abe Lyman's California Ambassador Hotel Orchestra (Brunswick, June 1928), and Ben Selvin and His Orchestra (Columbia, July 1928). Lyman and his band also recorded "Varsity Drag," "Good News" and a "Good News Medley" (Brunswick, March 1928).

2. Two noted exceptions are Bradley 144–47, and Barrios 256–58.

3. The figure $250,000 appears in Bradley (147), while a full-page advertisement printed in the fan magazine *Photoplay* proclaims set expenses totaling $168,000 and requiring for its construction the labor of 205 engineers and craftsmen over the course of five months (Kreuger 241).

4. During its embryonic years as a genre, the Hollywood musical possessed a highly fluid definition. As Donald Crafton has written, "Around 1929–1930, it was the rare movie that was *not* a musical in some sense of the term," because a great number of them incorporated song performances (315–16). On the other hand, reviews and descriptions of the earliest sound films in contemporaneous trade sources suggest at least a loose characterization. Bradley identifies and analyzes 171 of these musicals in *The First Hollywood Musicals*, while my own survey of entries in the American Feature Film Catalog corroborates Bradley's findings and suggests that roughly 200 musicals, both adapted and original, were produced during the period.

5. By 1912, for example, *Variety*'s Abel Green and Joe Laurie, Jr., reported that cabaret presentations cost approximately $1000 to stage in 1912 but could gross as much as $25,000 per week (78, qtd. in DeWhitt 1).

6. De Sylva had composed "Look for the Silver Lining" (1920, with Jerome Kern) and "California, Here I Come" (1924, with Joseph Meyer), both of which were sung by Al Jolson. Brown worked for venerable Tin Pan Alley composer Albert von Tilzer, with whom he wrote "I Used to Love You (But It's All Over Now)" in 1920. Henderson, a classically trained musician who chose to become a popular music composer, worked as a song plug-

ger for Leo Feist, Inc., and other Tin Pan Alley firms before writing "That Old Gang of Mine" (1923, with Mort Dixon and Billy Rose), "I'm Sitting on Top of the World" (1925, with Sam Lewis and Joe Young), and the million-copy sheet music seller, "Alabamy Bound" (1924, with lyrics by De Sylva and Bud Green).

7. Phonograph recordings of selected songs written for *Just Imagine* were issued in September 1930 by the "Big Three" record labels: Columbia, Victor, and Brunswick. Featured recording artists were Abe Lyman's California Ambassador Hotel Orchestra, Harry Reser and his Orchestra, Ben Selvin and His Orchestra, and McKinney's Cotton Pickers.

8. Numerous Broadway historians credit the narrativization of musical comedies to the Princess Theatre shows penned by composer Jerome Kern, lyricist P.G. Wodehouse, and librettist Guy Bolton between 1915 and 1920. The relatively small size of the venue — 299 seats — encouraged the trio to develop "intimate" musicals in which songs arose plausibly from narrative situations and that, in Bolton's words, "[depended] as much upon plot and the development of their characters for success as upon their music" (qtd. in Bordman 376–77). Although during the late 1890s and early 1900s, composers Jacques Offenbach, George M. Cohan, and Gilbert and Sullivan had made efforts in the same direction, the Princess Theatre shows of the 1920s contrasted starkly with the episodic structure of contemporaneous musical revues.

9. The potential sincerity of the surveyor's statement is belied by her subsequent comparison of the marriage law to the Volstead Act, a piece of pro-prohibition legislation introduced in the United States in 1919 and which, by the time *Just Imagine* was released in 1930, had lost much of the public's support.

10. One exception to the negative critical reaction garnered by *Just Imagine* issued from Mourdant Hall, reviewer for the *New York Times*, who praised the way in which "fantasy, fun and melody are shrewdly linked," and noted the film's combination of "songs and dances, a highly imaginative conception of New York fifty years hence and a Jules Vernesque journey to Mars" (23).

Works Cited

Altman, Rick. *The American Film Musical*. 2d ed. Bloomington: Indiana University Press, 1989.

_____. "The Musical." *The Oxford History of World Cinema*. Ed. Geoffrey Nowell-Smith. New York and Oxford: Oxford University Press, 1999. 294–303.

American Film Institute Catalog. Proquest (Chadwyk-Healey). Wilfrid Laurier U Lib., Waterloo, Canada. 15 Mar. 2009 <http://afi.chadwyck.com/home>.

Barrios, Richard. *A Song in the Dark: The Birth of the Musical Film*. New York and Oxford: Oxford University Press, 1995.

Bordman, Gerald. *American Musical Theatre: A Chronicle*. 3d ed. Oxford and New York: Oxford University Press, 2001.

Bradley, Edwin M. *The First Hollywood Musicals: A Critical Filmography*. Jefferson, NC: McFarland, 2004.

Brosnan, John. *Future Tense: The Cinema of Science Fiction*. New York: St. Martin's Press, 1978.

Caldwell, Louis G. "The Copyright Problems of Broadcasters." *Journal of Radio Law* 2.2 (April 1932).

Cornea, Christine. *Science Fiction Cinema: Between Fantasy and Reality*. Edinburgh: Edinburgh University Press, 2007.

Crafton, Donald. *The Talkies: America's Transition to Sound, 1926–1931*. Vol. 4 of *History of the American Cinema*. Ed. Charles Harpole. New York: Charles Scribner's Sons, 1997.

deCordova, Richard. "Genre and Performance: An Overview." *Star Texts: Image and Performance in Film and Television*. Ed. Jeremy G. Butler. Detroit: Wayne State University Press, 1991. 115–24.

Desser, David. "Race, Space and Class: The Politics of the SF Film from *Metropolis* to *Blade Runner.*" *Retrofitting Blade Runner: Issues in Ridley Scott's* Blade Runner *and Philip K. Dick's* Do Androids Dream of Electric Sheep? 2d ed. Ed. Judith Kerman. Madison: Popular Press, 1997. 110–123.

"DeSylva, Brown & Henderson's First Year Finds Remarkable Record." *Variety* 15 February 1928: 55.

DeWhitt, Bennie L. "The American Society of Composers, Author, and Publishers, 1914–1938." Diss. Emory University, 1977.

Dyer, Richard. "Entertainment and Utopia." *Only Entertainment.* 2d ed. New York: Routledge, 2002. Originally published in *Movie* 24 (Spring 1977): 2–13.

"Film Theme Song Near Monopoly of Publishing Trade." *Variety* 17 Oct. 1928: 73.

"Fox Red Star Co. with Complete Dept. Lineup." *Variety* 18 Dec. 1929: 57.

"Fox's Red Star Music Co. Start of Film Concern's Own Organization." *Variety,* Oct. 16, 1929: 65.

Green, Abel, and Joe Laurie, Jr. *Show Biz, from Vaude to Video.* New York: Henry Holt, 1951.

Hall, Mourdant. "The Screen." *New York Times* 22 Nov. 1930: 23.

Hayward, Philip. "Introduction: Sci-Fidelity: Music, Sound and Genre History." *Off the Planet: Music, Sound and Science Fiction Cinema.* Ed. Philip Hayward. Eastleigh, UK: John Libbey, 2004. 1–29.

Kalinak, Kathryn. *Settling the Score: Music and the Classical Hollywood Film Music.* Madison: University of Wisconsin Press, 1992.

Kreuger, Miles, ed. *The Movie Musical: From Vitaphone to 42nd Street: As Reported in a Great Fan Magazine.* New York: Dover, 1975.

Mordden, Ethan. *Make Believe: The Broadway Musical in the 1920s.* Oxford and New York: Oxford University Press, 1998.

"Picture Song Working for Pub. and Screen." *Variety* 31 Oct. 1928: 56.

"Rapee Takes Charge of Firm's Sound Music." *Variety* 14 Nov. 1928: 57.

Richards, Gregory B. *Science Fiction Movies.* New York: Gallery Books, 1984.

Schwab, Laurence, and B.G. De Sylva. *Good News: A Musical Comedy in Two Acts.* New York: Samuel French, 1932.

Segal, Howard P. "The Technological Utopians." *Imagining Tomorrow: History, Technology, and the American Future.* Ed. Joseph J. Corn. Cambridge: MIT Press, 1986. 119–36.

Silverman, Sid. "Just Imagine." *Variety* 26 Nov. 1930: 18.

Sobchack, Vivian. "Cities on the Edge of Time: The Urban Science Fiction Film." *East-West Film Journal* 3.1 (December 1988): 4–19.

Spring, Katherine. "Pop Go the Warner Bros., et al.: Marketing Film Songs during the Coming of Sound." *Cinema Journal* 48.1 (Fall 2008): 68–89.

Telotte, J.P. *A Distant Technology: Science Fiction Film and the Machine Age.* Hanover, NH: Wesleyan University Press; University Press of New England, 1999.

_____. *Science Fiction Film.* Cambridge, UK: Cambridge University Press, 2001.

United States Copyright Act of 1909. 4 Mar. 1909. 35 Stat. 1075.

"Warners-Harms Big Deal." *Variety* 21 Aug. 1929: 5.

Whittington, William Brian. *Sound Design and Science Fiction.* Austin: University of Texas Press, 2007.

"Writers Going with Fox's Red Star Co." *Variety* 23 Oct. 1929: 73.

PART III

BECOMING THE STAR-CHILD: MUSIC AND THE CONSTRUCTION OF SUBJECTIVITY

5

Ambient Reverberations: Diegetic Music, Science Fiction, and Otherness

Seth Mulliken

Science fiction cinema bears the responsibility of its origins in utopian literature. For however far science fiction may drift from its literary origins, the notion of constructing a vision of a future time is consistently underlain by the presence of utopia. The weight of this responsibility is a historical one; science fiction cinema must construct a full trajectory of history, a past, present and future, and code a linear pattern of movement that reinforces a utopian vision. This utopia is ideological one; the future it presents speaks directly to our own ideological subjectivity today.

I am interested in "futurization," the process by which a future time is connoted by the content and formal elements of science fiction cinema. Through this process, a future space and time is created that bears some level of familiarity to our own present, while coding the future as having surpassed certain elements of that present day life. The analysis of *Back to the Future*, a film that does not take place in a time future to our own present, will show that the trajectory of history present in futurization is not limited to those films that take place in a future time. Though *Back to the Future* places our viewership as "present" to the film's "past" the politics of representation using futurization remain as strong as in the "future" films.

In science fiction cinema, the most common practice of futurization is through the visual content. The alteration of mundane objects, including clothing, vehicles, buildings, weapons, or food are the connotative signs of the futuristic time-space. Adorned, complex clothing becomes a singular unadorned jumpsuit, as manifested by the various incarnations of *Star Trek*, implying a lesser focus on fashion vanity in the future: less need to use clothing to structure individual identity. In *Star Trek*, the individual self, as constructed by fashion, is replaced by a colored jumpsuit, where the color defines the subject's place within the power structure of the spaceship. In *Blade Runner* (1982), however, the clothing continues our modern Western idea of attire as a performance of individual identity; the only futuristic alterations are purely cosmetic. The colors that are fashionable, the shape of the color or cuff, the manner of jewelry ... these changes are the only formal alterations to the presence of clothing in the future.

It is not only that these futurized visual elements suggest future, but also that they propose a progression of history, a movement of culture that arrived at the point that is displayed. *Star Trek* suggests that our vanity, and need for individual identity, will dissipate in the next centuries. *Blade Runner* suggests just the opposite, that declaration of identity through clothing will continue in the same process by which we understand it.

Given the predominance, saturation and necessity of futuristic visualized objects in sci-fi cinema, my interest here is to look at the futuristic auditory realm. In science fiction cinema, while it is crucial that the visual space connotes "future," the auditory space rarely is presented in this manner, with the exception of films like *Alien* (1979) and *Solaris* (2002) where the silence of the spaceship is a kind of silence our present-day environments cannot create. It is a sound-space only truly possible in the future. In most science fiction, however, the sound space remains fundamentally unaltered from our present understanding of it. Future objects may have strange sounds, but their function within the sound environment is the same.

My analysis is limited to one single auditory aspect of the future science fiction film, the presentation of futurized diegetic music. The futurizing process is a combination of the abstract and the direct. The abstraction of an object into a future shape is necessarily a work of imagination; in order to be plausible as future, it must have an element of mystery, of Otherness to it. In order to be recognizable in its ideological coding, it must be familiar, be coded in a language we recognize. Futurized diegetic music operates at a particularly incisive intersection. Music, as an abstracted form of language, is not coded like spoken language. Equally, it cannot be said to operate by the same methods of signification that visual objects do. As sound, it is subject to the unique properties of the sonic, as distinct from the visual. Music is best described as being stained and infected by the presence of the present, by the presence of the ideological. This is its "familiar" within the futurization of the science fiction film. The elements of futurization in the music constitute a form of Otherness: a dialectic with the familiar elements.

Through the analysis of those instances of futurized diegetic music, I wish to show how the intersection of the historical identity, the "familiar," and abstracted, Othered futurization is a unique form of representation by its existence as musical sound. Sound creates a constitutive subjectivity, one that has tended to be ignored in the analysis of representation. The question of how sound, in and of itself, defines a subject is one that necessarily requires a close reading of the unique properties of sound. Reading sound beyond its content, beyond the content of language, for instance, is an approach to the reading of sound as a carrier ideology. Music, as a coded language that is communicated through form, not only content, lies at the intersection of sound's unique properties of representation.

Anahid Kassabian, in *Hearing Film*, attempts to define a process by which Hollywood film music proposes identity. She says that considering music as a carrier of ideological meaning has been long outside of acceptance. However, she says that

> film music constitutes society while being constituted by it. The well-established code communicates groupings of ideas that are associated with each other in dominant ideologies, and by communicating these groupings on a nonconscious level, the code can buttress and reproduce the very ideologies that produced it [Kassabian 29].

Musical ideological markings include both the formal qualities and structure of the music, as well as our historical understanding of those qualities; she calls them the "extramusical" elements.

Diegetic music has tended to operate within a small range of functions in the cinematic space. Most often, diegetic music is created to establish a sense of historical time, and to place the viewer and the characters within a familiar historical location. Martin Scorsese's scores, which tend toward source music in *GoodFellas*, *Mean Streets*, or *Bringing Out the Dead*, are used most often to define the larger historical movements within which the characters operate; the songs are the external, familiar universe that verifies the plausibility of the character's lives. In Scorsese's films, while he is often choosing music that is aesthetically compelling to the scene, he does not vary from chronological appropriateness. He has not had a song playing in the film, off a car radio, in a nightclub, that has yet to be written within the film's diegetic space. This has tended to be true of most examples of diegetic music within narrative cinema: a contract of appropriateness defines how the music is used in the scene. We can have a bending of the contract, such as in *Back to the Future III*. ZZ Top, the rock band who wrote a song for the film's soundtrack, appears in the film playing that song. The story year is 1885, so while ZZ Top is a modern rock band playing a modern rock song, they play using musical instruments appropriate to 1885. While this contact can be bent, it is rarely ever broken.

The presence of futurized diegetic music is fairly uncommon occurrence in science fiction cinema. There are a great many examples of modern (that is, our present-day) music used in a future time. In the television series *Star Trek: The Next Generation* characters listen to jazz from the 1950s and '60s, or perform baroque classical music. This music would be centuries old within *Star Trek*'s narrative, and the show never suggests what music might have been written in the ensuing centuries. In J.J. Abrams' newest *Star Trek* film (2009), this is taken to almost comic levels, where a young James Kirk has stolen a 20th century car, and turns on the radio to play a song by The Beastie Boys, "Sabotage." Despite that fact that this song was written 300 years before the film's narrative, it is still used to connote the same exact cultural meaning as it does today, in the 20th century, that of youthful anger and rebellion. This use of music is quite ubiquitous in many sci-fi films.

The Sound of the Cantina

Star Wars (1977) contains what is likely the most iconic scene involving futurized diegetic music in science fiction.[1] Luke Skywalker, after leaving his decimated home, travels with Obi-Wan Kenobi to Mos Eisley, a town referred to as a "wretched hive of scum and villainy." Luke enters a bar, the Mos Eisley Cantina. Inside, we see, for the first time in the film, a large collection of strange and unique aliens and a band playing. The band, called the "The Modal Nodes," plays two pieces of music, "Mad About Me" (often referred to as "Cantina Band #1") and a second, slower piece, "Cantina Band #2."[2] Director George Lucas' original concept for the music of the cantina band was to "imagine several creatures in a future century finding some 1930s Benny Goodman swing band music in a time capsule or under a rock someplace ... how they might attempt to interpret it?"[3] Lucas' statement is especially revealing, already noting the constitutive power of the merging of the familiar and the futurized.

"Mad About Me" is a fairly simple jazz melody, upbeat, with an AB structure. John Williams, who composed the music, calls the piece a "five-part rondo." The structure of the music itself, the form of the song, does not, in and of itself, connote futurized or Otherness. It uses drums, percussion, bass, and melodic instruments in a manner completely recognizable to modern Western popular music. The one element of the song that does perform is in the choice of musical timbres. The notion of timbre stained by ideology is a familiar one in popular music, and quite often, is the only musical element the divides one genre from another. Genre division in popular music is an ultimately a political one, a necessity of capitalism to define popular according to an audience. But, as Kassabian states, the ideological divisions of genre in popular music also serve to reconstitute the listening subject, and to define the subject in an auditory sense. In the cantina, this attention to timbre serves to construct our own auditory subject-hood as listeners.

In "Mad About Me" Williams uses instruments whose timbres feel as though they are just on the edge of recognizability and familiarity. There is an ARP synthesizer playing the song's bass line, a few very thin-sounding wind instruments, and most strikingly, a steel drum that doubles the melody. The presence of the steel drum here is especially revealing, as the sound of the instrument is coded, more than the other instruments to very specific musical tradition, found in Afro-Caribbean musical culture. The presence of this timbre is coded as a sound of Otherness with a western understanding of popular music. In the cantina, it is timbre, exclusively, that is used to futurize and code the music as Other. Here, the two processes merge into one. In a wider sense, the futurization of the musical sounds in the cantina suggests that these sounds will retain their Other status far in the future; that there are inherently Western and inherently Other sounds.

In *Star Trek 5: The Final Frontier*, a scene early in the film operates as a parody of the cantina band scene, and challenges the easy relationship of Other present in the cantina. A robed, masked character rides a horse up to a bar on the planet Nimbus 3. As the character enters, we see that the bar's entrance is a swinging wooden door, common in many western films, but here the door slides, rather than swings. The camera pans around the bar, finding characters playing a game much like billiards, but with water on the table. On the bar, a creature resembling a woman in a cat Halloween costume dances, only to let out a comic cat yelp when her tail is struck. All of those carefully designed elements from the Mos Eisley Cantina, objects with a precise combination of the familiar and the alien, are here rendered satirically. The swinging western doors don't actually swing; the billiards game just looks wet.

The one element of curiosity in the Nimbus 3 bar is the diegetic music. Unlike the Mos Eisley Cantina, where the music contains familiar ideas to place us as listeners in relation to it, as subjects constructing by listening, the music here is a series of long synthesizer drones, containing no structure we can recognize. Western ideas of popular music have no hold in this place, and appear to have never touched it. We can notice that down to the very level of the note, music seems to function differently. In Mos Eisley, the very notion of "upbeat" and "lively," the simplest adjective definitions of music, serve the same function as we understand them. The music is coded according to our western understanding; at Nimbus 3, we cannot read even a simple code into the music. We have no code system to understand the use of music as a sonic wallpaper in this space.

The New Sound You've Been Looking For

While not a futuristic film per se, *Back to the Future* (1985) serves to reveal the process by which diegetic music in the sci-fi film comes to signify Otherness, and proposes a progression of musical history. Because the musical Otherness in this film places us on the side of the future music, rather than the original, we can witness the process from another standpoint. *Back to the Future* locates itself mostly in the year 1955. Marty McFly, a young man from 1985, through a series of chance occurrences, acquires a time machine that transports him to 1955. He meets his parents as high school students and interrupts their courtship that will serve to create him. His mission becomes a dual one; he must return to his home time, but first must re-establish his parents' future relationship, guaranteeing his future existence.

In the first scene of two scenes of interest here, Marty dons a radiation suit, masquerading as "Darth Vader from the planet Vulcan," and appears to his [future] father late at night, in the private space of his bedroom. His attempt is to create a nightmarish vision, one that will frighten his father into action. His nightmare is not limited to a visual one, however; he places a pair of headphones on his father, and plays from a Walkman a guitar solo by Eddie Van Halen. This is an unaccompanied guitar solo played high on the guitar's neck, and filled with Van Halen's unique use of noises derived from his fingers and the feedback possible from the electric guitar. Rhythmically complex and un-infected by any sense of central melody, this music produces fright and horror in Marty's father.

To our modern ears, the scene is a joke, a humorous way to further signify Marty's dad as cowardly. But if we place our auditory subjectivity into the father's space, we find that it is a further use of musical timbre as a "horror of Otherness." The music contains a familiar sound source, the electric guitar, but played in a foreign and alien manner. It is in the timbre that the horror is found, the mutilation of familiar sounds.

A second scene in *Back to the Future* occurs near the film's climax. Marty has brought his parents together, but to assure the permanence of their bond, they must kiss at the school dance, the "Enchantment Under the Sea Dance." Through a series of accidents, Marty must fill in for the injured guitarist in the band playing the event. He strums his way through "Earth Angel," during which his parents kiss, bringing about the conclusion of this film's central emotional conflict. With his task completed, Marty suggests to the band

that they play something else, and he proceeds to play "Johnny B. Goode."
Once the song reaches the guitar solo, Marty's temporary hold over crowd
begins to break down. His guitar solo starts off well, suggestive of the "rock"
music present to 1955, but Marty reaches beyond the comfortable timbres,
and plays sounds that are referential of rock music to come.

Again, we find that it is in the timbre that horror and Otherness are
found, but even more so in this second scene from *Back to the Future*, a historical progression is proposed. Marty's playing is initially the "new sound"
of rock that will soon appear; as his guitar solo progresses, however, he crosses
a line of auditory alterity where what contained a level of familiarity crosses
a line to the realm of aural Other. We are witnesses to the creation of the
auditory Other, a creation based on progression of musical history; we can
see the inter-relationship of the auditory with history, how Otherness in sound
is tied to an ideological construction of history, and of the auditory subject
as a historical creation.

We can extrapolate further that the threat of the Other as presented in
the dance scene from *Back to the Future* is the threat of noise, as defined by
Jacques Attali. Attali, in his *Noise: The Political Economy of Music*, he discusses
the role sound plays in the political order:

> Any organization of sounds is then a tool for the creation of consolidation of a
> community, of a totality. It is what links a power center to its subjects, and
> thus, more generally, it is an attribute of power in all of its forms. Therefore,
> any theory of power today must include a theory of the localization of noise and
> its endowment with form [Attali 6].

In *Back to the Future*, Marty has violated the consolidation of power through
the ignorance of the distinction between noise and sound (in this case, musical sound) in 1955. He threatens the center of power. Curious is the line of
dialogue present in some versions of the film. After Marty relinquishes the
instrument upon which he played the threatening noises, the other members
of the band ask him, "What was that?" Marty answers, "It's rock and roll."
If rock music is a signifier of auditory subversion, as Marty's response seems
to indicate, then it should always be working in opposition to the consolidation of power through the definition of noise. If rock music presents any
threat at all, it is to this definition, that which describes acceptable from unac-
ceptable noise.

It is no mistake, however, that in this scene from *Back to the Future* a
visualized Other is present, a racialized Other. The other members of the
band at the dance are black, and the climate of racial segregation in 1955 is
established earlier in the film by one of the film's white antagonists, who refers
to one member of the band with a racial epithet. Working against the idea

that race is entirely and only a visual phenomenon, the film suggests the possibility of the racialized auditory subject. By linking this auditory subject to a history of musical progression, and through the political distinction of noise from musical sound, the film suggests those noises traditionally attributed to the African American origins of rock in blues and jazz (and, in the film's narrative, this is personified through the musical identity of Chuck Berry) can be re-subjectivized into a white (as personified by Marty himself) origin. This scene is dealing in an economy of racialized auditory subjective identities; the racialized auditory identities are traded within the economy of power, establishing dominance and submission in relation to musical history. In terms of an analysis of the racial, auditory Other, the film both creates an auditory black identity, through Chuck Berry's presence and the style of the band's music, but then attempts to define a white auditory identity (Marty's "future music") as the truly subversive one, the auditory identity that can create community, and define historical progression.

The Sound First

The final example here is from the cartoon television series *Futurama*. The show tells the story of Philip Fry, a young man who is accidentally frozen on New Year's Eve, year 2000, and is unfrozen a thousand years later, in the year 3000. He has various trials and tribulations as he adjusts to the unfamiliar world of the future. In the episode entitled "Parasites Lost" Fry becomes infected by parasitic worms, who energize and improve his body. Using his newfound competence and intelligence, he attempts to learn a musical instrument called the holophonor. "Only a few people in the universe can play it, and they aren't very good," he is told. Fry uses the holophonor to woo Leela, the woman he has been lusting after.

The holophonor is a curious creation, one especially fascinating in contrast to the mutant guitar of *Back to the Future*. Physically, the holophonor resembles a clarinet, or a south Asian instrument called the Pungi, popularly used in classic Warner Brother's cartoons when played before a large basket to "charm" a snake. The conceptual origins of the holophonor are found in Isaac Asimov's novel *Foundation and Empire*, described under the name Visi-Sonor.[4]

When initially played, the holophonor sounds like a synthesized oboe. As the playing continues, other instruments are added to the mix, soon sounding as a full orchestra. Precisely how the holophonor functions to create this orchestra is never clear; nor is it clear to what diegetic space these musical sounds belong. The instrument appears a number of times in the show's run, and while it can create any manner of sounds, theoretically, it does not seem to be able to create vocals. In the final episode, Fry writes a holophonor opera; he can "play" the entire orchestra himself, but requires singers for the actual vocals. Equally, while it may be theoretically possible to replicate any music, it invariably is used to create orchestral classic music in a Romantic style.

Most interesting about the holophonor is its visual component; the instrument emits a series of images, seemingly controlled by the music. As Fry plays for Leela, a montage of scenes not unlike "The Dance of the Sugar Plum Fairies" from *Fantasia* (and containing an implicit reference to Kurt Vonnegut's novel *Galapagos*) are preformed, all featuring the characters of Fry and Leela dancing. The visual space is presented as a kind of sublimated space, where the degree of the character's participation in the hologram is never clear. The holophonor is marked by a blurring of the characters subjective reality and our own. As soon he begins to play, the hologram ceases to be a framed space within the frame of the cartoon's diegesis, and extends to fill the entire frame; where Fry and Leela begin by staring at a bubble in which the hologram appears, almost immediately it becomes the entire screen.

As a device marked by futurization, the holophonor suggests, as none of the other examples do, a fundamental shift in the very nature of the musical instrument. Here, in the show's year 3000, musical instruments, and music itself, no longer occupy only the sonic realm, but bleed into and merge with the space of the visual. Unlike *Star Wars*, where music operates in much the same commodified manner as it does now, *Futurama* suggests a shift in what the boundaries of music are.

Even more intriguing about the holophonor are the suggestions of shift in sound's relationship to subjectivity and Otherness. Sound, as an ontological creation, remains situated beneath the visual as a verification of truth. Sound is, at best, a support for the visual, and not as truth onto itself. The sonic realm is marked by a slippage of signification, where a sound can signify, but does not absolutely signify. We can hear a voice, and at best we can offer an educated guess about the identity, but the voice is not considered the truth of identity per se. Our primary sensory modality is the visual. It is through this understanding of the sonic realm that the understanding of subjectivity of an inherently visual one comes.

Julian Henriques, in his article "Sonic Dominance and the Reggae Sound System," investigates those locations where the sound realm is the primary sensory modality. Sporting events, he says, and especially the event of the street reggae sound-system performance, are places where the visual ceases to be the dominant mode of interaction with space. Even more importantly, it is in these spaces that a new definition of power is created, by virtue of sound's relationship to it. The sound realm is marked by a blurring of boundaries, where the distinction between sound "objects" cannot be considered with the same strict boundaries as the distinction between visual objects. Further, in the sonic realm, the boundaries of the subject itself blurs, complicated a more "visualist" reading of the subject.

In *Futurama*, this blurring of subjects is notated in a number of ways. First, that our subjective boundaries, as watchers and listeners of Fry's playing, traditionally marked by our knowledge of the boundaries of diegetic spaces, dream spaces, and sublimated spaces, is confused. We are not sure what precisely the characters are seeing and how that differs from our gaze. Because the narrative within the holographic space is one of "magic" (that is, we move from one moment to another in highly abstract ways), we are never situated by a visual understanding of space, that is, an architectural blueprint of rooms, hallways, and connecting passages.

Second, in music, we see that the holophonor is a single device, with a series of keys. The question of how exactly it produces the orchestra is not obvious. But in our confusion, we blur the line between diegetic and nondiegetic music, a line that is underlain by a visual understanding of the subject. We understand our subjective position in relation to the characters' because we can see that music does not belong in the specific cinematic space we are viewing; we can clearly distinguish our reality from theirs.

In the universe of the holophonor, this visualist understanding of the subject vanishes, replaced by a subjectivity whose relationship to the Other is defined by the unique properties of sound. Because we are never sure exactly how the instrument functions, we do not know if Fry is improvising; we never are sure to what degree the notes he plays have control over the visual. A scene at the end of episode, after Fry has lost the worms that granted him his intelligence, shows him attempting to the play the holophonor. He conjures up a discordant musical passage, and a poorly rendered image of the Frankenstein monster. His reply, that he was distracted and started thinking about neck bolts, would seem to indicate the auditory images produced by the holophonor are connected to a kind of Freudian subconscious "bubbling up" of images into the conscious mind.

We can say that in the universe of the holophonor, the sounds controls the construction of the image and the image remains subject to the sound's agency. Fry's playing merges with our listening, so that we can be both inside and outside his holographic space; equally, Leela's position as listener merges with Fry as the player, as we are never sure what level of agency she has over the holographic representation of herself. In this way, *Futurama* depicts the most compelling idea of futurization, one where the very foundations of subjecthood and Otherness are challenged by the presence of diegetic music.

However, this challenge to subjectivity remains firmly in the sonic realm, and does not seem to infect the visual narrative.

In the presence of technology as the link to the possibility of the perfected human life, the "future" as a science fiction construct is wholly tied to the present. Utopia is a project, one that when reached will continue to carry the ideological signifiers of our present, to reassure us of the correctness of our ideological choices. We can, through the analysis of futurized diegetic music in science fiction, see the possibility for a new definition of cinematic Otherness, one that depends on the unique qualities of the sonic.

In *Futurama*, the holophonor exposes most clearly a "sonic resistance" that bubbles beneath the surface of the other examples, like static noise in an otherwise clear radio broadcast. The holophonor tells a narrative about sound becoming dominant, about sound occupying the space of the visual, a narrative where visual boundaries are eschewed in favor of auditory ones. The ontological reality of the visual space, of temporality and spatiality neatly arranged for logical visual understanding is replaced by a construction of the visual according to the rules of auditory reality. In *Futurama*, visual subjectivities blur, and we are never quite sure to what degree the consciousnesses of Fry and Leela inhabit their surrogate bodies. The space flows from one location to another, merging spatiality by means of the sonic. The wave breaks on the ocean, then crashes on the shore; visually, this is a surrealistic flourish, but in the auditory realm, it a presents a reality in keeping with our experience of sound, a method of sensory construction compatible with a sonic perspective. The holophonor allows the sonic to take dominance, and in doing so, releases the sonic from its imprisonment by a visualist perspective.

The attempt to use diegetic music as an ideological signifier is never a complete process; sound resists being completely defined by visual logic. Cinema sound requires a different type of analysis, a different definition of subjectivity, one that takes into account an auditory construction of the subject. Only then can it be understood how sound transmits ideological information, through its idiosyncratic properties. It is through a sonic resistance that oppressive definitions of Otherness in cinema can be further critiqued.

NOTES

1. While the title crawl on *Star Wars* considers its time frame "a long time ago," most critiques of the film, including the makers' own, consider it to be a time future to our own, rather than past. Therefore, I will consider it in the same way.

2. The song and band name, as well as their canonization in the *Star Wars* official universe, were confirmed for me by an unnamed LucasArts employee.

3. Quoted, amongst other places, in the *Star Wars: A New Hope Special Edition* soundtrack liner notes.

4. "He croaked, 'A Visi-Sonor — and of a make to distill joy out of a dead man's heart.' His long fingers caressed softly and slowly, pressing lightly on contacts with a rippling

motion, resting momentarily on one key then another — and in the air before them there was a soft glowing rosiness, just inside the range of vision" (Asimov 112).

WORKS CITED

Asimov, Isaac. *Foundation and Empire.* New York: Spectra. 2008.

Attali, Jacques. *Noise: The Political Economy of Music.* Minneapolis: University of Minnesota Press. 1985.

Henriques, Julian. "Sonic Dominance and the Reggae Sound System." *The Auditory Culture Reader.* Eds. Michael Bull and Les Black. New York: Berg, 2003. Pp. 451–480.

Kassabian, Anahid. *Hearing Film.* New York: Routledge, 2001.

Lucas, George. Liner Notes. *Star Wars: A New Hope: The Original Motion Picture Soundtrack (Special Edition).* RCA, 1997.

6

Sci-Fi Film and Sounds of the Future

Matthias Konzett

The Excess of Sound

In her discussion of Roland Barthes' notion of the "third meaning," Kristin Thompson points out that "the materiality of the image goes beyond the narrative structures of unity in a film" (514). In invoking the notion of excess, Thompson refers to non-diegetic elements that stand outside the film's logical narrative structure. Spectacle, musical dance scenes, extravagant costumes or breathtaking shot sequences often function to arrest the narrative progression of a film and return film to its earliest manifestation of the burlesque and vaudeville as so tellingly described in Tom Gunning's essay "Cinema of Attractions."[1] It is interesting to note that sound as excess is mostly acknowledged in musicals but rarely in other film genres where non-diegetic soundtracks are seen as mostly supportive of the narrative and the image.

Recreated almost entirely in postproduction process, film sound can be compared to a complex orchestral score where every note is deliberately and methodically composed. Dialogues are redubbed and enhanced, ambient sound such as room tone is added as well as sound effects, Foley sounds, and music. Indeed, the intensive labor and extreme detail that goes into the production of a film soundtrack, mixing it, and marrying the soundtrack to the image track is staggering in its complexity and effort. This time consuming process literally requires thousands and thousands of hours, especially prior to the early 1990s when sound editing became digitalized. And yet, despite major advances in sound technology and sound production, film sound continues to be treated mainly as a supporting function in cinema, one that is said to enhance the visual image as well as manipulate the moods of its audience.

The dominance of the visual image in cinema is understandable. The act of perception amounts to nothing less than a cognitive act, establishing our visual and symbolic order in the world. And yet, we cannot afford to relegate sound to a subordinate role in film since we not only see a film, but hear it as well. Film is not simply a visual medium but an aural one as well, if not to say multi-sensory. It is to this end that Mary Ann Doane in 1980 called for a new "politics of the voice" in film, bringing attention to classical Hollywood's rigorous regulation of sound so as to maintain the illusion of a unified subject and "[stave] off the fear of fragmentation"(383). Managed and edited classical sound, according to Doane, creates a "oneness" that "is the mark of a mastery and a control" (Doane 383). Sound in Classical Hollywood cinema, notes Doane, is used specifically to create and support a three-dimensional phantasmatic body that moves through the space of the diegesis (the world of the story), the space of the screen made visible through synchronized sound, and the quasi-realist auditory ambience in theater that "envelops the spectator" in sound (377). This illusion of the phantasmatic body, argues Doane, functions much like Jacques Lacan's mirror stage supporting the illusion of an imaginary subject and agency (380–382). However, Robert Bresson similarly draws attention to the constructed nature of sound and views it as complex interplay of contrapuntal impressions of sound and image: "Image and sound must not support each other, but must work each in turn through *a sort of relay*" (149). Sound thereby becomes non-synchronic while still critically communicating with the image. As with Doane's politics of voice, sound breaks free from the mere "service of a representational illusion" (385).

This essay explores the construction of soundscapes in sci-fi film, illustrating how sound literally creates a vision of the future that allows viewers to realize a conceptual and embodied world that does not yet exist as a concrete visual image. Sci-fi films are highly suitable vehicles for experimentation with sound, since the genre as such aims to project and imagine new and alternate worlds. The sci-fi soundscape, pointing to an imminent future, as I will argue, rejects the classical supportive function of sound and its subordination to the dominant code of the visual. Given that non-synchronic sound in sci-fi film breaks with the classical formula, I will further ask how it reconstitutes, if at all, the illusion of presence and of three-dimensional worlds inflected by futuristic speculation. In this essay, then, I will discuss several examples of futuristic sound, namely Boris Sagal's *The Omega Man* (1971) along with Stanley Kubrick's *2001: A Space Odyssey* (1968); Ridley Scott's *Blade Runner* (1982); Steven Soderbergh's *Solaris* (2002); and Alfonso Cuaron's *Chil-*

dren of Men (2006) and examine the independence of sound from image and its heuristic nature in sci-fi films.

In the first four examples, as we will see, sound increasingly asserts its independence and priority over the visual image in order to create its utopia via sound. The philosopher Ernst Bloch refers to the utopian imagination as a "not-yet" already reaching into the present: "Concrete utopia stands on the horizon of every reality" (223). Concerning our examples, this claim can certainly be made as these films project worlds of the future that are already with us but have not yet found full expression. These futuristic worlds depict the struggle of myth and enlightenment (*The Omega Man*; *2001*), the seductive mythology of technology (*Blade Runner*), and the disembodied phantom appearance of subject and object in space as simulacrum (*Solaris*). As such, these projected utopian/dystopian worlds are already known to us in theories on culture articulated by such thinkers as Theodor Adorno and Max Horkheimer, Roland Barthes, and Jean Baudrillard. However, rarely have these utopian visions been analyzed as soundscapes that in creative interplay with the visual image introduce us to these worlds in audio-tactile fashion, intensifying the presence and absence of cinema's phantasmatic body. In a final example, Alfonso Cuaron's *Children of Men* (2006), I will ask the question if sound supports the possibility of social agency in spite of its discontinuous and relayed relation to the image. Sound, when divorced from the image, raises doubts about the viability of the subject as a fragmented sensorium. However, is it possible, we shall ask, that sound restores a renewed materiality and plasticity to the image, albeit in a broken and provisional fashion, as a rhythm of reality? Could this then be the sound of the future, of social agencies caught in continuous revisionary loops, which provide the rhythm and drama for our changing social, cultural and communicative worlds?

2001 and *The Omega Man*: A and B Genre Conventions

Until Stanley Kubrick's *2001* sci-fi films were mostly made in the mold of B genre conventions. B genre films are usually produced on low budgets, quickly shot, and receive little public promotion, hence falling under the radar of critical public scrutiny. The sideshow and burlesque status of B films allows the genre to indulge in more graphic and crude terms in specters of social fear to the point of political incorrectness. Since A films in American film history were subject to the Hays code of censorship, their topics dealing with social and cultural conflict had to be handled delicately. While this code was no longer in force during Kubrick's *2001*, it still resonates in the high seriousness of its arthouse cinematic treatment. Thus, while Kubrick helped to secure sci-fi film a more respectable standing, his A genre arthouse film was also contained by the very attempt of gaining wider currency and acceptance. In contrast to a B genre film like Boris Sagal's *The Omega Man*, Kubrick's *2001* had to deal with universal questions in the abstract and hence allowed for little historical specificity in its depiction of imminent social and cultural problems.

Kubrick's use of Richard Strauss's tone poem *Thus Spoke Zarathustra* in the opening sequence of *2001: A Space Odyssey* (1968) offers a case in point. Not only does this unusual soundtrack brilliantly illustrate the independence of sound from image but it also underscores an esoteric arthouse and experimental effort in construing film sound. In stark distinction to the dissonant overture of electronic music preceding the film's opening scene, the main musical theme by Richard Strauss accompanies two crucial scenes, namely the dawn of the world with the sun rising behind the planet Earth and, later, the discovery of the instrumental use of animal bones by a primate as a tool or weapon capable of destruction. Initially, a three-note musical figure stated by trumpets rises over an ominous pedal point held by the organ and the double-basses, while the orchestra is gradually augmented. The pedal point, a monotonous drone, is presented simultaneously with the image of the dawn of the world, a future imagined backwards into an irretrievable and phantasmatic past.[2]

The fanfares of the brass section sounding out the triumph of the will, the domination of man over nature, are ambivalent in its association with progress and savagery. The rising cadence produces the auditory hope for progress and better worlds achieved via the brassy and steely sound of technology. However, this expectation is disappointed as the triumphant theme ends on the savage rhythms of large kettledrums, animal skins vibrating with a heavy clumsy beat. The savage beating of the kettledrum is repeated in the film's image of the skull-crushing use of animal bones, a use that is eventually appropriated to subdue the tribal enemy.

Both music and image underscore the theme of enlightenment culture as irrevocably implicated in barbarism. Thus, before the intertribal murder among primates is shown, the non-diegetic soundtrack has already anticipated this type of violence for the viewer. However, it is mostly the visual image of the discovery of the hammer-like function of animal bones, hence serving as a tool of destruction, which directly foreshadows the later scene of tribal murder in which another living primate's skull will be crushed. The sound image during this scene conversely harks back to the earlier triumphant scene of the dawn of the world. Via the relay of sound and image, both triumph and barbarism of civilization are invoked as inextricably intertwined, opening up an ambivalent space of triumph and murder that governs the world of technology.

Eventually, in the film's famous graphic and match-on action jump cut, the upwardly thrown animal bone merges with the instruments of modern technology, namely the free-floating spaceship and later the airborne pen used by the astronaut. Richard Strauss's music is subtly replaced by the comforting Viennese waltz of Johann Strauss, suggesting a softer and more balanced use of technology in which the violent proclivity of civilization is seemingly sublimated. While one could make the claim that image and sound are perfectly synchronized, it is more interesting to note the apparent ironic tension that opens up between them. Sound no longer supports the image but comments on it ironically. The waltz music of Strauss does not provide a continuity match as given in the images. The substitution of Richard Strauss by Johann Strauss is merely a verbal pun on their shared surname. Otherwise, the two worlds of music have little in common. It is rather the image of the animal bone converted via graphic match into the technological achievement of the spaceship and the pen, a tool of writing, which makes us rethink the connection between the two differing soundtracks.

Again, the ironic relation of sound and image comes to the fore. The Strauss waltz is thus perceived as underscoring the deceptive ease of soft technology, while also recalling its anti-thesis in the savage sounds of Richard Strauss. In addition, the use of classical music also supports Kubrick's attempt to raise the sci-fi film from its B status to an A level film. Kubrick's skillful use of sound and sound-image relay captures in concrete audio-tactile terms the clash of myth and enlightenment, which, according to Adorno and Horkheimer, characterizes Western civilization: "Myth turns into enlightenment, and nature into mere objectivity. Men pay for the increase of their power with alienation from that over which they exercise power" (9). As the repressed content of technology, myth eventually returns as delayed or sanitized barbarism. In Kubrick's *2001* this reversal is shown tellingly in the growing independence of the spaceship's computer system, the HAL 9000. HAL's voice, once the achievement of interactive voice command technology mimicking human voice, assumes total independence from its master and dominates man as a machine that was originally created for the obverse purpose of subduing nature. As Horkheimer and Adorno comment on the double bind of science and technology: "The instrument achieves independence. ... On the way from mythology to logistics, thought has lost the element of self-reflection, and today machinery disables men even as it nurtures them" (37). HAL's disembodied voice underscores this loss of reflective agency and in its deceptive and nurturing mildness of sound once again mocks the achievement of technology as did the waltz by Johann Strauss.

Eventually, HAL will be associated with the absence of sound, as he is able to read lips and hence spy on the crew, allowing HAL to avert their covert attempts to disable his computer system. In its use of sound, then, the film creates auditory worlds that rival the supremacy of the image and that can no longer be forced into harmonious synchronization. The anarchic nature of sound reveals a constant struggle in which the more primitive sensory perception, sound, can no longer be subdued by the image, standing in for the organized perception of instrumental reason. The ultimate achievement of technology, namely its self-emancipation from man's domination, is depicted as soundless much like the objectifying human gaze. It comes therefore as no surprise that HAL eventually assumes this image of soundlessness, as he usurps man by becoming the absolute reason, the pure gaze of a Western logo-centric perspective.

Boris Sagal's *The Omega Man* (1971) still follows the B genre conventions of sci-fi film that dominate much of American cinema until Kubrick's *2001*. As such, its soundtrack is not forced to put on airs of sophistication through the use of classical music. Rather, in accordance with its implied theme of the Civil Rights struggle and 1960s hippie socialism as eruptive forces in society, it deploys a more mainstream jazz and electronic music score composed by Ron Grainer, known for his scoring of BBC's TV sci-fi *Dr. Who* series. As the producer Walter Seltzer notes about the soundtrack for *Omega Man*: "The temptation was to make it kind of weird. We wanted a certain element of exotic sound but we didn't want it to sound like a futuristic party, and he got the idea very quickly. It's melodic and not atonal, which is always a temptation. That was all by design; that's the way we wanted it."[3] And yet, contrary to this statement, Lukas Kendall points out that the score proved to be extremely ambitious in spite of the production constraints placed upon it:

> The score essays a light pop vibe in keeping with the music of the period while remaining highly dramatic and effective: Grainer's strategy was to keep the acoustic forces of the orchestra tonal and accessible, while assigning the score's more unusual sounds to two early Yamaha synthesizer organs — the EX-42 and YC-30 — and a unique instrument called a waterchime. Eschewing trumpets and tuba, Grainer's brass forces feature four French horns and as many as eight trombones, even in the quieter passages, to give the score a mellow, masculine feeling. To this end, cues involving the "Omega Man" theme (the main title) feature horns, while those with Neville's theme and the Family theme feature trombones — no cue has both. Likewise the string section focuses on the lower shades of viola, cello and bass, with violins added only to some of the largest passages (such as "Zachary Makes His Move"). The beefed-up percussion section features timpani, cymbal, marimba, xylophone, tabla and African drums as well as the aforementioned waterchime. For the pop-styled cues, a rock drum kit joins piano, guitar and electric bass to act as a rhythm section ["Liner Notes"].

The sound score fulfills in its unique orchestration and use of instruments a double function. On the one hand, it abides by the rules of realism and would appear almost like a supportive and conventional soundtrack. However, its "pop vibe" and heavy emphasis on percussion instruments creates an ambient sound that reflects the new voices in American society at the time, namely the hippie youth revolt of the 1960s (pop vibe) and the voice of the Civil Rights Movement (African American/Afro Caribbean percussion instruments).

In *The Omega Man*, the undead Zombies of Los Angeles prominently appear as hippies in medieval garbs and are known as "The Family." Their anarchic and futile bohemianism is underscored in a retrospective Woodstock sequence viewed by their hero Colonel Robert Neville in an empty theater as well as certain flippant musical themes that often run counter to the seriousness of a scene. The Family also evokes association with the Charles Manson Family and its criminal and socio-pathological pursuits. In addition, close-up shots of Zachary, a key black member of The Family, and his grotesquely bleached African American physiognomy and the character of Lisa, reminiscent of blaxploitation's Foxy Brown, highlight racial conflict as equally central to society. The theme of barbarism versus enlightenment, as seen in Kubrick, no longer possesses the high pathos of civilizational endeavor that undermines itself increasingly through its excessive use of technology. Instead, it is bluntly depicted as the conflict of race and social class in society through the use of crude images and stereotypes.

U.S. Army Colonel Robert Neville, M.D., played by Charlton Heston, appears as the last white survivor in a post-biological warfare scenario in which mankind has been drastically reduced and its remaining members are threatened by a rampant plague. Through mutation, The Family has been able to survive the plague virus but has now become itself a predator upon society. Fears of miscegenation, race riots, hippie bohemianism play into the demonized image of The Family. Robert Neville is disparagingly referred to by The Family and its club of mutated albino survivors as an out-of-touch and obsolete "man of the wheel and machine." Colonel Neville, in this dark tale of sci-fi horror, appears to fight a losing battle on behalf of white Anglo-American norms in trying to produce a vaccine that reverses the plague virus and restores society to its original health. While donating his blood for the vaccine, he comments to Lisa, his African American lover, in the flippant language of the hipster: "It's genuine 160-proof old Anglo-Saxon, baby." And shortly thereafter with white Eurocentric arrogance: "I'm the only game in town."

The film, in the sloppy manner of B films, manages to promote at once interracial love (Neville and Lisa), and at the same time brings back notions of white Anglo-American racial supremacy in the couched language of the hipster. To use David Desser's term, the "politics of cityscapes" breaks into a crude binary of dehumanized science that has caused the original disaster and a pre-scientific return to medieval lifestyles as demonstrated in The Family's use of monks' capes, caterpillar launchers for fire bombs and their inquisition-like methods of interrogation. The social stratification of the above and below pattern, discerned by David Desser in the cityscape of Fritz Lang's *Metropolis* as a motif for class struggle, is here simply replicated into a horror show type of night and daytime opposition, stressing white and black binaries.[4] Nevertheless, apart from its sensational elements, the film accurately reflects the race and class upheavals of the 1970s in the U.S. as a potential threat to the status quo of society, rather than treating these questions in the abstract. However, this historically more specific depiction is gained at the cost of demonizing the oppressed minorities of African Americans and other bohemian elements that appear sympathetic with America's marginalized groups. While the image of the zombie, an undead person, for example, may correctly refer to the status of social death that has been imposed upon slaves in America, the film mostly exploits race fear as its main motivation rather than analysis of race relations.[5]

Unlike A films, B films often embrace politically incorrect views and hence succeed in exposing a social conflict more directly. Concrete Civil Rights strife of the present rather than archaic struggle of man vs. technology lend *The Omega Man* a strange historical topicality. At the same time, B films, due to their low budgets, often tend to be more slaves to convention. In *The Omega Man*, the soundtrack appears at first less so in an against-the-grain or relay mode, as do the unusual classical Strauss scores in Kubrick-matched with the unlikely genre of science fiction. However, the jazz-soul soundtrack in *Omega Man* anticipates a type of ambient soundtrack that was eventually to become highly popular in sci-fi films. The sound of the future is thus depicted as that of a minority culture and its hip and subversive beats. In fact, while the film upholds the status quo of white normative culture, the music score undermines this complacent view and points out that the new emerging culture is to be found elsewhere. The closing scene, in which Neville hands the blood serum needed to cure Lisa to other non-infected survivors, can be seen as a passing of the torch from an old to a new order. However, Richie's and Lisa's proximity to The Family also evoke fears whether social emancipation can ever take place, thus striking a more conservative and reactionary tone. The B film genre in the end does not provide constructive solutions to social problems but serves merely as mood indicator of imminent cultural conflict.

Blade Runner: Postmodern Spectacle

Ridley Scott's *Blade Runner* (1982) revisits the scenario of *2001*, man's struggle with technology, adding, however, a postmodern twist to this conflict. In its fusion of high and low art, the film appears to have merged the vision of *Omega Man* with *2001*. Unlike the opening of *2001* where the musical score showed internal conflict and contradiction, *Blade Runner's* opening scene seems to have smoothed over the discontinuities of the earlier film, giving its soundtrack more of an ambient resonance as seen in *Omega Man*. The savagery of technology is mostly depicted through the images of a post-apocalyptic Los Angeles and flames flaring up in the close-up shot of a human eye. The electronic music by Vangelis conversely accomplishes a more thorough integration of technological and synthesized orchestral sound, belying the conflict altogether. The opening theme still relies on slow and deliberate Wagnerian cadences as with Richard Strauss's music and is additionally enhanced by sound-bites of technological machinery such as the diegetic engine sounds of a spacecraft and non-diegetic artificial technological sound such as bleeps, high bells, xylophone sounds, percussion effects, etc. In addition, we also hear diegetic sounds of thunder, lightning, and bursts of flames from refineries, thus creating a thick soundscape of realistic and artificial sound. As the establishing shot slowly tracks in a pyramid-shaped building, electronic sound bleeps and high bells are synchronized with small light flashes apparently emanating from the architectural structure. Hence the illusion is created that perhaps the architecture itself could be the source of the soundscape, as if technology were now able to create its own sound. This autonomous sound of technology, a blend of non-diegetic soundtrack and diegetic sound, also heard when the camera pans over the advertising billboard in the sky, functions curiously as the new mythology in this utopian setting. Myth, according to Roland Barthes, naturalizes arbitrary signification: "myth operates the inversion of *anti-physis* into *pseudo-physis*" (142). It appears as if technology, an artificial product of human origin, has now taken on quasi-natural status. This myth of the autonomy of technology and its "naturalness" underscores the film's central theme in which man-made replicants appear more human than humans and rival the human race in humanity and ethics.

Deckard, the blade runner hired to retire potentially threatening replicants, is initially depicted as a degraded noir hero, lacking total insight into the ethical dimension of his assassinations or "retirement of skin jobs." The question asked by Rachael, whether he has ever retired a human by mistake, points to Deckard's inability to define himself as a human being as opposed to the non-sentient replicated human species of the Tyrell company. As with the music of Vangelis, artifice and the natural are blurred and raise doubts whether Deckard may not himself be a replicant. Slavoj Žižek, in fact, reads the entire film in reverse, arguing that the film depicts not so much "the sub-jectivization of the replicants" but rather asserts that "our 'human' memories [are] also implanted in the sense that we all borrow the elements of our indi-vidual myths from the treasury of the big Other" (212). Discourse, in this sense, precedes the voice of the human subject. "Are we not," asks Žižek, "prior to our speaking, spoken by the discourse of the Other?" (212). In short, the illusion of human subjectivity is only achieved, as we begin to integrate our memories into our symbolic universe, hence lending it the mythical support of truth and reality. Human subjects, in this more radical reading, are fictions and resemble replicants rather than differ from them.

It appears that the synthesized soundtrack by Vangelis, electronically mimicking the Romantic music of Wagner and Bruckner, likewise points to the constructed nature of all sound, and hence all reality. The presumed ante-riority of orchestral music as quasi-natural sound over electronic music as artificial sound is ultimately questioned, just as the difference between repli-cant and human being becomes increasingly indistinguishable in the film's postmodern shakeup of the epistemological certainties. The melancholy main theme no longer expresses the initial serene confidence of Richard Strauss's dawn of the Earth theme in *2001* but instead mourns the absence of a loss that can no longer be identified. Human memories become only reliable in so far that they may temporarily fool the interrogator in his effort to unmask replicants but ultimately appear fictive. When Deckard eventually tells Rachael that her memories are implants, she leaves his apartment visibly upset. Deckard then turns his attention to his family pictures scattered throughout the apart-ment to reassure himself of his own human status. Looking at various fam-ily pictures with little emotion, he also leafs through Polaroids of an android that are part of his investigative police work. These photos seen in the same pile of pictures become indistinguishable from the family pictures and stress that there is no difference between them. A jazz piano soundtrack of repeated quizzical chords further adds to the blurring perception of all these images. This scene precedes the scene when the replicant Pris meets the genetic designer Sebastian and his artificial puppets. Both interior scenes thus mir-ror one another in their emphasis on artifice.

A parallel cut eventually returns us from Sebastian's home to Deckard's apartment. We hear soft piano notes electronically enhanced with echoes. Deckard's family pictures are displayed above an old piano to underscore that they are relics of a bygone era and thus have no merit or substance and are hollow like the enhanced echo sound. The director's version (1992) stresses this point even more so when inserting a new intercut of a fable animal, a unicorn, while the camera is panning over Deckard's family pictures and thick electronic sound sets in. Deckard picks up a single family picture and then turns to the image enhancement system processing the photos of a suspected android, thus highlighting the construction of all images. In a later scene, after Rachael saves Deckard's life, we return one more time to Deckard's apartment. The music played in this scene places Rachael on the piano, associating her with "naturalness" and her desire for it. The soundtrack likewise points to the implanted nature of all visual memory, motivating the musical dreams of the drunk and sleeping Deckard. In this scene, the soundtrack moves from a sexy noirish saxophone tune, as Rachael is nostalgically leafing through his family pictures, to a snippet of a classical piano chords played by Rachael and quickly returns to the seductive jazz sounds followed by electric piano chords. It appears that the natural diegetic piano sound is framed by the non-diegetic noir jazz and electronic sound. The "natural" piano music is thus conveyed as a diminishing category giving way to a jazz-electronic fusion sound. Desire and artifice have become one in the soundtrack. This scene is followed by a quick intercut to the oversize advertising billboard in the sky and then cuts to a close-up of Pris doing her facial makeup, framing and mirroring the prior scene once again in its emphasis on artifice. Unlike the masculine world of *2001*, *Blade Runner*'s softer electronic soundtrack and its prominent women characters (Zhora, Pris, Rachael) offers a challenge to the gender hierarchy upon which the inhumane male visions of technological utopias are built. Thus, while the film may question the distinction between the natural and artifice as its central theme, it also begins to undermine conventional gender binaries in its strong women characters that repeatedly challenge Deckard's noir hero status.

Solaris: In the Realm of the Simulacrum

Steven Soderbergh's film *Solaris* (2002) takes artificiality to the next level in which an unexplored solar ocean appropriates human memory, decodes its DNA information, and replicates human beings. In contrast to *Blade Runner*, it is no longer a man-made machine that eventually exceeds man but an extraterrestrial force that now replicates and simulates man. This escalation of dehumanization pushes the vision of this utopian scenario into the realm of the simulacrum, whereby all tangible relationships with reality cease to exist. In successive order of intensity, one could say, using the terminology of Jean Baudrillard, that the sound image "perverts basic reality" in *2001*, "masks the absence of basic reality" in *Blade Runner*, and "bears no relation to any reality whatever" in *Solaris* (11). A key scene, illustrating that the sound image has become "its own pure simulacrum" occurs when the film's hero, Kris

Kelvin, sent to investigate the strange events aboard the spaceship Solaris, meets Rheya, his former wife, seemingly resurrected from the dead after her suicide many years ago (Baudrillard 11). The scene can be read in many ways, such as the return of repressed guilt on the part of Kelvin, a psychologist who chose to overlook the warning signs of his wife's unstable mental state. Additionally, it stresses the theme of gender that returns from its repressed status in a male dominated world of technology. Rheya, as Kelvin finds out, cannot simply be gotten rid off, both in their prior life and aboard the spaceship where she miraculously returns and easily recovers from critically sustained injuries. Overall, the film stresses a profound sense of self-alienation via its musical score, which in many key scenes relies on ambient sound, and thereby questions human subjectivity and agency altogether.

The composer Cliff Martinez, former drummer of The Red Hot Chili Peppers, follows in *Solaris* in the tradition of Brian Eno who is credited with the invention of ambient sound with its deliberate sub-audible sound worlds. In the film's sound world, the sound of technology and minimalist musical chords a la Philip Glass mix into a scenic sound that is removed from conveying the emotion of human characters. Just as the Solaris constellation rejects human invasion, sound refuses to become subordinate to the interest of character and instead manifests itself as a background hum or white noise in many scenes, suggesting steely isolation and even more so the illusionary phantom existence of the human subject. Contrary to the earlier films, the soundtrack no longer conveys a clearly identifiable emotion. For example, when Kelvin falls asleep and Rheya appears for the first time, we hear mostly vibraphone and synthesized music stylized in percussionist and rhythmically repetitive fashion.

While such music may realistically evoke technology with its sanitized and functional worlds, it does not depict for the listener an emotion. Rather increasing and decreasing intensities of volume of sound and a sense of rhythmic monotony create an ambient soundscape beyond the repertoire of human emotional response. In the scene, sound further creates a fluid bridge between past events, Kelvin's and Rheya's first encounter, and their uncanny re-encounter on the spaceship. As Kelvin awakes and finds Rheya in his room, sub-audible sound, white noise, is heard in the background. The soundtrack falls completely silent and the exchanges are mostly quiet and erratically assume at one point the form of screaming on Rheya's part. When Rheya is eventually tricked into being ejected from the spaceship, orchestral chords proceed in quiet descending manner, yet without any pathos. And once again this scene turns quickly to white noise background sounds rather than allowing for any audible emotion to emerge. Sound is thereby associated with social death administered silently and via soft technology. The ejection of Rheya further links social death specifically to gender and its oppression in techno-utopias.

Sound functions mostly in *Solaris* to isolate and detach the viewer from emotional identification with the main character, turning the viewer instead into a critical observer. Hence, the relation of audience to screen drama becomes analytic and sterile, reduplicating the sterile scientific gaze that pervades the drama. The use of ambient sound creates ambiguity, since diegetic and non-diegetic sound become interchangeable and indistinguishable. For example, when the electronic bass sound overlaps with the diegetic humming noise on the spaceship, it is unclear whether sound ultimately emerges from the diegesis or beyond it. In the film's play with auditory ambiguity against the backdrop of sterile homogeneity, the scientific gaze is unsettled in its certainty as shown in the dissociation of the scientists from their mission. Gibarian's skeptical insights, taken almost verbatim from Lem's novel, are shortened in the film version in order to render his sober reflections in a more simple and powerful manner: "We take off into the cosmos ready for anything: Solitude, hardship, exhaustion ... death. We're proud of ourselves. But when you think about it, our enthusiasm's a sham. We don't want other worlds. We want mirrors."[6] Gibarian's thoughts are related via video monitor with Kelvin turning his back to it, thus stressing a separation of voice and image. Moreover, the film image frames the human voice as a technological construct emanating from a monitor in the remote background of the scene. Yet on the level of sound, this voice can be heard via amplified voiceover clearly as a sound emanating at the front of the screen image. Sound thus asserts itself as a critical voice over the image, which, according to Gibarian, reflects unreliably the narcissistic need for mirrors rather than reality.

No Exit: *Children of Men*

Solaris ultimately shows that man is forever entrapped by his own narcissism and memories that prevent any communication with phenomena outside the context of a human perspective. While *Solaris* depicts this contextual anthropomorphic limitation mostly as a failure of man's will to domination, Alfonso Cuaron's *Children of Men* (2006) views this existential limit as a productive force, creating a utopia/dystopia of realism. Rather than projecting remote worlds, autonomous machines and robots, or inexplicable extra-terrestrial forces, this film returns man to man by focusing on an inexplicable inability among humans to procreate. Cuaron's dystopian world of infertility, set in the not too distant future of a realistic London in the year 2027, has many post-apocalyptic features such as civil anarchy, degraded technology, and biological dysfunction of the human species. It harks back to social realist sci-fi film such *The Omega Man* (1971), *Soylent Green* (1973) and *ZPG*

(Zero Population Growth, 1972) in its dystopian vision of imminent social and ecological disaster. Romantic and post–Romantic orchestral sound as well as ambient sound no longer appears appropriate for this suspicious, realistic and critical vision of technology. Instead, the film shows a disposition for ecological worlds in its yearning for the resurrection of the "natural." A sci-fi retelling of the birth of Jesus as savior, the film depicts a dystopian world where humankind is facing extinction. Gender once again comes to the fore as the corrective force to male technology. The miraculously pregnant mother, a young black woman from Africa, further invokes race as a redemptive force against the backdrop of xenophobia and anti-immigrationist measures that lend the film a highly realistic setting filmed in documentary and newsreel style.

In a key scene, former activist Theo Faron (Clive Owen) meets with Jasper (Michael Caine), an older political activist friend, who has a hideout in the remote woods. Jasper's appearance is that of a disheveled pot smoking hippie who indulges in food, drink, and the telling of raunchy jokes. Contrary to the antiseptic appearances of space crews in the above films, he is a person of human and bodily functions. *Children of Men* can in fact be understood as a Bakhtinian carnivalization of the sci-fi genre via emphasis on physiological materiality, low bodily function, and grotesque realism which return the quasi-superhuman and high-serious domains of sci-fi and its technological worlds to the tangible Earth. In the film, sound supports this vision by remaining for the most part diegetic, emerging as everyday sounds of street noise, chaos, sirens, conversations, overheard music, and so forth. In the encounter between Theo and Jasper, we hear music associated with the past "natural world," such as an aria sung by a soprano, a rendering of Ruby Tuesday by the Bee Gees, and a few bites of heavy metal music played by Jasper for comical and disruptive effects. The music remains stubbornly diegetic, stressing the realism of the setting. Even in key scenes such as the delivery of the baby and the escape, the soundtrack, consisting of small citations from classical orchestral compositions of Penderecki and Mahler, quickly gives way to diegetic sound and fades into the background.

The non-diegetic soundtrack as the quasi-grand narrative of the film thus disintegrates into the diegetic sound of reality. By means of this reversal, sound is relieved from its conventional functions of emotionally manipulative musical accompaniment and the illusionary framing of a phantasmatic body and world. Instead, it transforms into an active sound generated foremost in the diegesis, refusing to remain anonymous and ambient in nature. Sound merges with human drama, stressing the film's political and interventionist view. The film, however, cannot cover up the fact that its politicized and realistic sound image is likewise a construct and the film is therefore forced to return to an almost classical mode of sound synchronization. Hence some doubts remain as to the revolutionary nature of sound in *Children of Men* as sound is once again subordinated to the primacy of the visual image. However, the use of de-saturated images throughout the film can be said to stem against a naive realist mode with the effect of assimilating sound into a type of ambient image. In his DVD commentary on the film, Slavoj Žižek further points to the film's stylistic use of anamorphosis whereby the main characters serve as mere focal points for the many significant background scenes, depicting a rivaling drama of the collapse of social and civil society. In similar fashion, an ambient sound image constructed via color manipulation of the screen image and added diegetic sounds stresses a new type of cinematic image that has assimilated to the notion of ambient sound. Once again, it becomes difficult to determine where the film's mood or melodramatic tone of experience actually originates and we see image and sound working in relayed forms of interface rather than classical synchronization.

As our examples have shown, the creative function of sound appears when it breaks with the power of the image and either comments critically on the image via Bresson's notion of sound relay or challenges the image altogether. Thus, the political and critical function of sound cannot be attributed to any single specific film in our examples. Rather, as the final example shows, sound may re-inject renewed materiality and plasticity to the image, albeit in a broken and provisional fashion, as a rhythm of reality demanded to be heard in savage drum beats, ambient technological sound or realistic sound. In analogy to Bloch's notion of imminent utopias, the future is thus already with us, sub-audible in the changing contexts and demands of social communication.

Notes

1. See Tom Gunning, "The Cinema of Attraction: Early Film, Its Spectator, and the Avant-Garde," *Film and Theory: An Anthology*, eds. Robert Stam and Toby Miller (London: Blackwell, 2000), 229–235.

2. This pedal point re-appears again in Steven Soderbergh's *Solaris* (2002), now played by an electronic instrument, capturing the ambivalent hum or white noise of futuristic technology. As a sound, it is at once comforting and threatening and re-occurs in several key scenes of the film.

3. Walter Seltzer, quoted in "Liner notes," *Film Score Monthly 2000*, FSMCD Vol. 3, No. 2.

4. See David Desser, "Race, Space and Class: The Politics of Cityscapes in Science Fiction Films," *Alien II: The Spaces of Science-Fiction Cinema*, ed. Annette Kuhn (London: Verso, 1999), 80–96.

5. See Orlando Patterson, *Slavery and Social Death* (Cambridge, MA: Harvard University Press, 1982).

6. See Stanislaw Lem, *Solaris*, trans. Joanna Kilmartin and Steve Cox (New York: Harcourt, 1987), 72.

Works Cited

Barthes, Roland. *Mythologies.* Trans. Annette Lavers. New York: Granada, 1983.
Baudrillard, Jean. *Simulations.* Trans. Paul Foss, Paul Patton and Philip Beitchman. Cambridge, MA: Semiotexte, 1983.
Bloch, Ernst. *The Principle of Hope.* Vol. 1. Trans. Neville Plaice, Stephen Plaice and Paul Knight. Cambridge, MA: MIT Press, 1986.
Bresson, Robert. "Notes on Sound." *Film Sound: Theory and Practice,* eds. Elisabeth Weis and John Belton New York: Columbia University Press, 1985.
Doane, Mary Ann. "The Voice in the Cinema: The Articulation of Body and Space." *Film Theory and Criticism,* eds. Leo Braudy and Marshall Cohen. Oxford: Oxford University Press, 2004.
Horkheimer, Max, and Theodor W. Adorno. *Dialectic of Enlightenment.* Trans. John Cumming. New York: Continuum, 1990.
Kendall, Lukas. "Liner notes." *Film Score Monthly 2000.* FSMCD Vol. 3, No. 2.
Thompson, Kristin. "The Concept of Cinematic Excess." *Film Theory and Criticism,* eds. Leo Braudy and Marshall Cohen. Oxford: Oxford University Press, 2004.
Žižek, Slavoj. "'The Thing That Thinks': The Kantian Background of the *Noir* Subject." *Shades of Noir,* ed. Joan Copjec. London: Verso, 1993.

PART IV

MOON/SPOON/CROON: SCIENCE FICTION AND POPULAR MUSIC

7

"It's Hip to Be Square": Rock and Roll and the Future

Cynthia J. Miller and A. Bowdoin Van Riper

It's not that rock has no future, but that we usually imagine a future that does not rock.

When we think of "The Future," we don't think of rock and roll.... The vibrant, often unruly genre, better-known for its sins than its saintliness — as well as for lyrics like "Gonna live while I'm alive, I'll sleep when I'm dead" — seems firmly rooted in the present, literally, light years away from our received knowledge of futures and frontiers. Brimming over with sexuality, drive and aspiration, rock and roll is a defining element of who we are *now*, not who we aspire to be. "The Future" — a storehouse for our brightest hopes and darkest fears, always so distant in our imaginings — should be something vastly different.

Our dominant cinematic images of the future are brought into being through broad brush strokes and sweeping scores, the outcomes of our best, and worst, selves. At one pole, we find images of a world of order and efficiency — clean, crisp, bright, and gleaming — where desires are dampened, and transgressions are controlled. Balance, intellect, and certainty are over-arching themes in the images of this brave new world grounded in science and technology, found in films such as *2001: A Space Odyssey*, *Logan's Run*, and *Minority Report*. At the other end of the futuristic spectrum, we find a second, darker set of cinematic images: humanity gone horribly wrong. Dull, worn, broken, and limping, these dystopian futures, found in such films as *Blade Runner*, *Mad Max*, and *Children of Men* are nearly stripped bare of hope, and gasping to survive.

Both of these dominant images are, in very different ways, lifeless ... soulless ... void of the messy, spontaneous, depth and passion of the human spirit. And it is that spirit — chaotic, rebellious, and inconvenient as it may be — that rock and roll brings to cinematic portrayals of the future. Futuristic science fiction films, like *Flash Gordon* (1980), *Heavy Metal* (1981), and *Strange Days* (1997), have occasionally employed rock scores to create a specific mood, in very contained, bounded ways. Of greater interest, though, are those science fiction films which have woven rock and roll through the narrative fabric, and used it to define characters and drive plots, with written-to-order songs like "The Zombie Stomp," "Beware the Blob," and "Monster in the Surf," as well as more mainstream rock and roll fare. It is those films and uses that are the focus of this article. Here, we will explore the ways in which the function of rock and roll in science fiction films has changed, from its introduction in the 1960s to its futuristic heyday in the late 1980s to mid–1990s. Socially, culturally, and politically, rock and roll has always been an agent *for* change, but as its path becomes interwoven with science fiction in film, rock becomes an agent *of* change. Unlike the sweeping orchestral or electronic soundtracks discussed elsewhere in this volume, rock and roll isn't the sound of the future ... it's the sound of how we get there.

You've Got to Live a Little: Sun, Surf, and the Status Quo

The 1960s were a time of "endless summer" in teen culture, characterized in film, on one hand, by sun, surf, and freedom from cares, and on the other, by sexuality, rebellion, and transgression. Beach party and surf films, like *Gidget* (1959), and the American Independent Pictures (AIP) surfsploitation sequence: *Beach Party* (1963), *Muscle Beach Party* (1964), *Bikini Beach* (1964), *How to Stuff a Wild Bikini* (1965), and *The Ghost in the Invisible Bikini* (1996), were populated by clean, carefree, hip-shaking teens like Frankie Avalon, Annette Funicello, James Darren, and Sandra Dee — several of whom were already mainstream singing idols of the late 1950s — and the morally more complex bikers and fast women cast as their opposite numbers. The soundtracks of their lives brimmed over with the driving rhythms and reverb of surf music — the '60s new sound that drew on the styles and energies of rockabilly and rhythm and blues, to represent the ocean landscape (Lueras 1984). The "king of the surf guitars," Dick Dale, and his band, the Del-Tones, along with bands like the Bel-Aires ("Mr. Moto"), the Chantays ("Pipeline"), and the Surfaris ("Wipe Out") were revolutionizing popular music on the West Coast, and across the country. Music historian John Blair observed that "it was white, danceable, and non-threatening. Kids all over America picked up on it, despite the lack of beaches and surfboards" (Blair 7). Their sound spread through motion pictures like wildfire. Songs like "Muscle Bustle," "If it's Gonna Happen," and "Surfin' and a-Swingin'" became the standards of beach party movies, as well as (often re-recorded) movie-related singles and LPs, produced by labels like Buena Vista, Wand, and MGM.

Typically painted in the broad brush strokes of an older generation's morality, the clean-living teens conformed to overarching social norms, as they danced, sang, surfed, made-out, and fell in love. The "troublemakers" smoked, drank, actively defied authority, and often skipped love and went straight to sex — a rebellious holdover from the 1950s who alternately resented, disrupted, and subconsciously desired, the lives of their carefree counterparts.

For many, this opposition mirrored, and addressed, what was happening in the world around them, and the recognition that teens were a social and cultural force to be reckoned with loomed large. In the 1960s, the post–World War II baby boom generation was beginning to come of age, forming a social and economic demographic that was willing to turn up the volume to be heard. Teens of the previous decade had been characterized in the public consciousness as transgressive — a threat to the moral order — with J. Edgar Hoover describing juvenile delinquency as a threat to the American way of life that was equivalent to communism, and directly implicating the film industry as "trash mills which spew out celluloid poison destroying the impressionable minds of youth," asserting that "in the face of the nation's terrifying juvenile crime wave, we are threatened with a flood of movies and television productions which flaunt indecency and applaud lawlessness" (Doherty 40, 96–97). The seemingly-unfettered teen culture of the 1960s drew on the icons and artifacts of 1950s rebellion against prosperous-but-textureless American conservativism, such as James Dean, Marlon Brando, Lee Marvin, Chuck Berry, the writings of Beat authors Allan Ginsberg and Jack Kerouac, as they engaged with new cultural forms early in the decade — the politics of the Counterculture, with its anti-establishment, anti-corporate stance; the heady, highly sexualized music of Elvis and the British Invasion; high-energy innovative surf music of groups like the Ventures, Jan and Dean, and the Beach Boys; ideologies of experimentation and freedom, given form in the projects of Andy Warhol and the artists, actors, and filmmakers of the Factory — creating a range of teen identities with a complexity that mainstream cinematic portrayals of the times only hinted at.

By the late 1950s, the teen demographic — along with its disposable income — was the locus for innovation, advertising, and exploitation in the consumption of fashion and other lifestyle consumer goods, but perhaps nowhere more so than in entertainment forms such as film and music. Motion picture studios were quick to capitalize, through various strategies, on the teen market. Particularly successful were those strategies that linked the two forms — music and film. In 1955, Metro-Goldwyn-Mayer's teen drama *The Blackboard Jungle* propelled the Decca single "Rock Around the Clock" to significant sales success. Capitalizing on the song's popularity, Columbia Pictures' Sam Katzman produced the country's first rock and roll exploitation film, *Rock Around the Clock*, in 1956 (Fred Sears, director), pushing motion picture production strategy even more strongly toward the teenpic (Doherty 57). The following year saw the release of the first cycle of popular films produced for and about teenagers in the American International Pictures trio, *I Was a Teenage Werewolf*, *Blood of Dracula*, and *I Was a Teenage Frankenstein* (Tropiano 33). These formula films spoke directly to teen-adult relationships, with teens becoming literal monsters, rather than the figurative monsters of juvenile delinquency. "The teenager was the most valued force coming to the theaters," noted AIP producer Samuel Z. Arkoff, and thus began motion picture studios' pursuit of the teen box office dollar (Voger 76).

As the teenpic market continued to grow and expand, the early 1960s brought yet another new cycle of teen films to American theaters — the beach party film — adding an additional dimension to the ever-increasing body of rock and roll exploitation films. Surf movies, like the AIP surfsploitation releases mentioned earlier, reached out to touch teen fantasies of romance, sand and sun, and gave them a soundtrack to groove on. Studios like Columbia (*Ride the Wild Surf*, 1964), Paramount (*Girls on the Beach*, 1965), and 20th Century–Fox (*Wild on the Beach*, 1965) all rode the wave of popularity that rock and roll brought to teen films. These films capitalized on the explosion of rock and roll's popularity in the wider teen culture — the Beatles, the Beau Brummels, Frank Sinatra, Jr., Freddy Cannon, and others — to create the perfect teen utopias, where bikini-clad girls and their surfer boys twisted the nights (and days) away. It was only when the popularity of these films of endless summer began to wane, however, that film studios, eager to retain their teenage moviegoers, began experimenting with genre-blending, and brought forth the rock and roll–science fiction hybrid. This was a combination that had been explored several years earlier, in *I Was a Teenage Werewolf*, with the inclusion of Kenny Miller's single "Eeny Meeny Miney Moe." This sub-genre began rock and roll's now four decade-long coming-of-age, hand-in-hand with science, the fantastic, and the future.

"Everybody Do the Zombie Stomp"

And what a journey that was.... As the wider culture whirred and boomed with space launches, and forays into futuristic technology, early rock and roll science fiction films stayed much closer to home and the present. They ushered teen audiences through familiar territory, now beset by giants, monsters, prehistoric cave dwellers, mad scientists, menacing slime, and of course, alien life forms, exploring the nature of science, adulthood, rebellion, and the status quo along the way. It typically began innocently enough: a teen, on her way to the country club dance, drives along a darkened road, full of anticipation ... a bikini-clad girl tosses sand at her boyfriend, and laughingly runs off to hide among the rocks on the beach ... a cat inquisitively laps at a spill on the floor of a young boy's "lab" ... and with that, the door is opened into the world of the fantastic. Here, rock and roll became an iconic element of hedonistic, rebellious teen culture, which must negotiate a relationship with the world of science, in order to vanquish their common foe. Science, in these "monster-rock" films, is cast as the antithesis of the rock ethos. Detached, objective, and empirical, regulated by reason and rubric, science, and those associated with it, embody the dull, lifeless, responsible existence against which teenagers rebel. However, in order for either pole to succeed and survive, collaboration becomes necessary. While bongos, Stratocasters, and outboard reverbs provide sonic markers of the teenagers' territory, teen protagonists would need to venture out of earshot, bringing with them only the energy and ingenuity that remained. And in so doing, cinematic teen characters take on additional range and dimension, creating a continuum of identities that replace the simple good/bad binary opposition of 1950s teen films. Conservative, squeaky clean teen characters still exist in these '60s monster-rock films, along with 1950s-style rebels and delinquents, but greater space exists for essentially "good" teens who are also frivolous, or risqué— following in the footsteps of Steve McQueen's drag-racing, girl-chasing, too-cool-for-his-own-good character, Steve Andrews, in *The Blob* (1958). These basically good protagonists, often serve as conduits to draw their equally risqué peers into the battle against both the threat of monsters and of rebellion. Science, in its turn, begins to incorporate (and often, is rescued by) teenage vitality and imagination, in its strivings to save humanity.

At times, that fledgling relationship has faced setbacks.... The collaborative foothold between science and teens, gained in films like *The Blob* and later, *The Horror of Party Beach* (1965), is stripped away in *Beach Girls and the Monster* (1965). Promising "beach party lovers, making hey-hey in the moonlight, while the monster watches," the film is promoted in the upbeat, over-the-top style of 1940s and '50s exploiteers. Its trailer boasts "the glamorous Watusi Dancing Girls from Whiskey A-Go-Go" and a rousing surf soundtrack ("Dance Baby Dance," "More Than Wanting You," and the playful "There's a Monster in the Surf") that includes music credited to Frank Sinatra, Jr., but the film's content offers the genre's most wholesale indictment of science, adults, and adult-teen relationships. *Beach Girls and the Monster* creates a monster as real as it is fantastic in oceanographer Dr. Otto Lindsey (played by director Jon Hall). After his son Richard (Arnold Lessing) adopts a "live before you die" philosophy that leads him to spend his days in the sun and surf, Lindsey dons a monster suit and begins killing the "tramps" and "loafers" who congregate on the beach, determined to protect his son's promising career with him in the laboratory. The sea monster's on-screen appearances are accompanied by eerie guitar strains from a Fender Jaguar that create a sharp contrast to the bold staccato of the surf guitar numbers that characterize the teens' carefree sexuality and play. The movie fails to create a successful negotiation between teens and science, but that failure is largely because the youths are victimized by *human* nature, rather than a freak of nature.

When the threat of the fantastic in these films is "real," though, "monster-rock's" multi-dimensional teens sometimes singlehandedly save the day, with little adult intervention. In *Eegah* (1962), Arch Hall, Jr., as Tom, armed with a guitar, a rifle, and a dune buggy sporting whitewall tires, saves his girl-friend, Roxy (played by Marilyn Manning), and her explorer father (director Arch Hall, Sr.) from the title character (Richard Kiel), a prehistoric caveman who has fallen in love with Roxy, and then triumphantly rocks out with his band, The Archers. Scattered throughout the action are swinging tunes of freedom and rebellion, like the hot dance number "Tag Team Tequila"; "Whizzing Interlude," where surf guitar and electric piano provide the soundtrack for a dune buggy romp; and the crypt-kicking "Brownsville Road," about a vacant house that hosts ghostly rockers.

Similarly, in *Village of the Giants* (1965), based loosely on H.G. Wells' *The Food of the Gods* (1904), there is little adult intervention to be found. When the car belonging to a gang of rebellious youths (led by Beau Bridges) gets stuck in a mudslide, they wander into the quiet California town of Hainesville, and tumble to the fact that a local girl's younger brother, known to all the teens as "Genius" (played by eleven-year-old Ron Howard), has accidentally created "Goo," which causes giant growth. A performance by the Beau Brummels, singing their hits "Woman" and "When It Comes to Your Love," frames the youths' arrival with hip-shaking rhythms, camera close-ups on breasts and bottoms, and cutaways to giant ducks on the dance floor, comically mimicking the gyrating teens — initially homogenizing all teens within the mindless, sexualized, hedonistic context set by rock and roll.

As the plot progresses, however, various stances toward authority and the moral order take shape among both the "clean" teens and their delinquent counterparts, as the unruly gang ingests the Goo, and force the townspeople to serve them. The now-giant youths (dressed as Greek gods) defiant and mocking of authority, are firmly situated in the rock ethos through an extended, surreal, sensual dance sequence, while the local teens shed their ties with frivolity and rebellion to combat the menace. Ultimately, science, in the form of another laboratory accident, saves the day, and allows young "Genius" to rescue the teens.

Offering a more sophisticated exploration of the "teens in need of science/science in need of teens" narrative, *The Horror of Party Beach* (1964) continues the standard use of surf music soundtrack to define both the setting and characters, while taking the relationship between teens and science a step or two farther down the path toward its continued evolution. The film allows for a greater range of teen character types and positive adult interaction, yet still holds "science" strictly the under the watchful eye of the mature. Laying claim, in the opening credits, to status as "The First Horror Monster Musical," the voice-over of the film's trailer sets the stage:

> While the beach set twists to the big beat sound of the Del-Aires, swinging out with six rocking hits; while the cycle gangs burn up the road and strong-arm their way into the party with fists flying; while teenagers prepare for a secluded slumber party; terror strikes from the bottom of the sea — an invasion of ghoulish atomic beasts who live off human blood [*The Horror of Party Beach*, 1964].

Whether risqué rockers, delinquent bikers, or naïve slumberers, teens in *The Horror of Party Beach* are cast as "kids," frivolous, undisciplined, and unprepared for the horror that awaits. The Del-Aires blend of surf rock and Doo-Wop netted three singles from the film — "Elaine," "Drag," and "Wigglin' Wobblin'" (as "Just Wigglin' n' Wobblin'") — in addition to "Joy Ride," "You Are Not a Summer Love," and "Zombie Stomp," which appear exclusively on-screen. Driving bongos over the opening credits are joined by surf guitar picking, then a jazz sax riff, as images of a whitewall tire, a car radio, and finally, the speeding MG to which they belong, set the tone for this coming-of-age monster tale. As a bickering teen couple, hard-drinking, good-time girl Tina (played by Marilyn Clarke) and the more mature Hank (John Scott) struggle to stake out their respective ground in adulthood.

> TINA: Say, what happened to the campus big shot who'd do anything for kicks?
> HANK: Campus big shot's grown up. Times have changed, Tina, we're not kids anymore. I've got plans, and you can do all the partying you want, but you'd better stay out of my way.
> TINA: Stop preaching. I know about your plans — your experiments in that laboratory. Well, let me tell you something — I have a few experiments of my own I'm just itching to try and they don't have one thing to do with test tubes and Bunsen burners.

When a momentarily remorseful Tina asks what's happened to their relationship, Hank lectures her that "life isn't all fun and games." A furious Tina snaps back: "...If that's the way you want it, you go your way, and I'll go mine.

We'll see who gets the most out of life. Oh, brother, you ain't seen livin' 'till you've seen Tina swing!" She then throws herself into the crowd of rebels, already dancing in the sand.

After her aborted striptease to the Del-Aires' on-camera performance of "Wigglin' Wobblin,'" Tina, in short order, is dead: a morality message delivered by a humanoid monster that has emerged from the sea. And there are more. The monsters, the result of vegetation merging with human remains, and animating, after radioactive waste is dumped in the water, prey on teens in increasing numbers in the small East Coast town. Hank finds a kindred spirit and budding romance in Elaine (Alice Lyon), the equally mature, science-oriented daughter of his employer, research scientist Dr. Gavin (Allan Laurel). As the killings and panic escalate, and a solution is accidentally discovered, the scientific trio becomes central to destroying the monsters. Leaving aside the issue that the monsters, like the larger-than-life delinquents in *Village of the Giants*, were a product of science gone awry, science, in the joint, if unequal, custody of Gavin and the two teens, has saved the day. With that, an additional dimension has also been added to the roles of teens in monster-rock films. Hank and Elaine, whose maturity had already begun to set them apart from their beach party peers, now straddle the worlds of hedonistic, carefree swinging and objective scientific research. With one foot in each, the two function to join, if only tentatively, the energy and imagination of rock and roll with the discipline and control of science.

Scientists of the "monster-rock" era, however, typically only serve to regulate our relationship with the fantastic. Even as science, in the wider society, is taking its first significant steps into the unknown, cinematic scientists are lauded for their abilities to mitigate catastrophe and keep the present intact, rather than to propel American society into the future. In their role as protectors of life, limb, and America's frail sense of stability, they maintain the mainstream status quo in the face of threats from monsters, technological change gone wrong, and alien invaders, alike. Only as science's relationship with rock and roll deepens and becomes more complex do they move forward into the future together. And while, in the 1960s, passage into the scientific realm implicitly requires shedding the identity of unfettered rocker, soon, that would no longer be the case.

The Future Belongs to Those Who Rock

Shifts in American attitudes toward science during the late 1960s and 1970s robbed it of its once-unquestioned cultural authority. Movie scientists changed as well. They no longer stood, and spoke, for a monolithic entity called "Science": bland, uninspired, and interchangeable. As early as 1970, in films like *The Andromeda Strain*, scientists began to emerge as distinct characters with whom audiences could identify — role models who spurred imaginations and made pulses race, rather than humorless authority figures dedicated solely to preserving the status quo. The 1980s brought an additional spark of quirky independence and individuality to men of science on the silver screen. Heroic scientists in films as diverse as *Raiders of the Lost Ark* (1981), *E.T.* (1982), and *Creator* (1985), were outright rebels, defined by their individualism, ingenuity, and disdain for convention. The emergence of the rebel-scientist as a hero revived a subgenre of science fiction film that had languished in the sixties and seventies: stories of brash, exuberant dreamers pitted against dull, plodding naysayers. It also spawned a tight cluster of "teen genius" films in the mid–1980s (Tropiano 177–181; Bernstein, 137–150; Shary 180–195). Rock — the music both of rebellion and of youthful enthusiasm — re-entered science fiction through those films, which began with *Zapped!* (1982) and extended through *War Games* (1983), *Revenge of the Nerds* (1984), *My Science Project*, *Weird Science*, and *Real Genius* (all 1985), and *The Manhattan Project* (1986). Like their cinematic ancestors — the wholesome Disney heroes of *The Misadventures of Merlin Jones* (1964) and *The Computer Wore Tennis Shoes* (1969) — the heroes of the teen genius cycle were trickster figures who wielded scientific and technological know-how in place of magical powers. Unlike those ancestors, they bedeviled not just corrupt authority figures (gangsters, crooked politicians, unscrupulous businessmen) but *all* authority figures — just for the sheer fun of doing so.

It is an article of faith in science fiction that scientific and technological knowledge gives those who wield it the power to remake the present and shape the future. The teen genius films used rock soundtracks to paint their heroes as typical, fun-loving teens who just happened to have world-changing powers — teens for whom solid-state physics, advanced biochemistry, and cutting-edge computer science went hand-in-hand with the elemental pleasures of getting high, getting laid, and getting even. The cumulative effect was to suggest that giving up fun and youthful exuberance was no longer a requirement for becoming a great scientist or inventor.

Hard-Rocking Scientists:
Genius with a Driving Bass

The Adventures of Buckaroo Banzai Across the 8th Dimension (1984) was among the few films of the time that explored the adult side of the equation. Buckaroo Banzai, played by 37-year-old Peter Weller, holds the movie's ultimate scientific credentials: brain surgeon *and* rocket scientist. He's also a musician whose band ("those hard-rocking scientists, The Hong Kong Cavaliers") is shown taking the stage in a small club to the cheers of adoring fans. The club's manager, Artie, is quick to remind them that futuristic science is all well and good, but it's the music that matters:

> ARTIE: I don't care if you drove through a mountain in Texas. This is New Jersey, and when you play my ... when you play my joint, you're just another act. I want some music outta you characters.
>
> RENO [one of the Cavaliers' sax players]: You want it, Artie? You got it.

The Cavaliers' lineup (electric guitars and bass, alto and tenor saxes, piano, drums) suggests a musical style that moves between rock and jazz. Banzai is clearly at home in both idioms, taking a brisk distortion-filled solo on his guitar before slinging it behind him and, without missing a beat, producing a cornet and soloing on *that*. Later, he accompanies himself on piano for rendition of the Skyliners' "If I Don't Have You," demonstrating his mastery of the rock ballad as well as his unwavering love for Penny Priddy, who sits in the audience, overcome by emotion. He is far removed from the bright young men of 1960s monster-rock movies, for whom success in science meant giving up "childish things" like rock and roll. Buckaroo Banzai has it all: "the President on line 1," a faster-than-light propulsion system in his workshop, *and* a hot band behind him.

The principal function of rock in mid–1980s science fiction films was to mark the innovative heroes as fun-loving rebels rather than dull tools of the establishment. Martha Coolidge's *Real Genius* (1985) went further, however, associating rock with the *act* of innovation itself and the process of bringing a newer, hipper future into being. Set at fictional Pacific Tech (a thinly disguised version of the California Institute of Technology), *Real Genius* pits a group of brilliant student scientists and engineers against an unscrupulous professor who wants to use their work to support an illegal CIA weapons program. When 15-year-old freshman Mitch Taylor steps from the staid atmosphere of a garden-party reception into the wild anarchy of the students' dorm, the sonic shift from string quartet to thundering rock heralds the transition. Thereafter, whenever a group of Pacific Tech students join forces to make the (seemingly) impossible happen — but only then — a rock song throbs behind them on the soundtrack. "Summertime Girls," by Los Angeles metal band Y & T, backs scenes of a winter carnival staged (on artificial snow) in a dorm hallway. "One Night Love Affair," by Bryan Adams, accompanies a beach party (complete with sand and water) set up in a lecture hall. Chaz Jankel's "Number One," with its driving beat and aspirational lyrics, plays over an all-out, all-hands effort to perfect an experimental laser. Rock, in *Real Genius*, is the sound of brilliant minds bumping up against each other in wild, unruly improvisation: defying conventional wisdom to create a future where science and technology make the impossible routine.

"The Power of Love"

Back to the Future (1985) is not strictly a teen-genius film, but it embraces their central premise: that the future belongs to those who rock. Its central relationship, between teenaged rocker Marty McFly and middle-aged scientist Emmett "Doc" Brown, mirrors the one between Hank and Dr. Gavin in *The Horror of Party Beach* and the one that Dr. Otto Lindsay aspires to create with his son Richard in *Beach Girls and the Monster*. Marty is not just Doc's assistant, but his trusted junior partner, and Doc is not just an adult friend but a mentor to Marty. The bond between them rests on shared personality traits: a disdain for convention, a talent for on-the-fly improvisation, and an unshakable calm in the face of the unexpected and the fantastic. Those traits, the film suggests, are equally essential to the rocker and the scientist. Far from giving up rock to embrace science (as Hank or Richard were expected to do), Marty is free to be both an aspiring rocker and an apprentice rebel scientist.

Doc — played by Christopher Lloyd in conscious *homage* to the eccentric scientists of 1930s and 1940s horror movies and 1960s comedies — lives in a rambling house on the edge of town and creates wonders in his basement and garage. He is a master of improvisation, building a time machine out of a limited-edition DeLorean sports car and scamming Libyan terrorists out of plutonium in order to run it. His younger self, whom Marty meets in 1955, improvises the means to send Marty back to his own time with a large reel of electrical cable, a public clock, and Marty's knowledge of an impending lightning strike. His house, with a gigantic speaker-amplifier system in the basement and an absurdly complex machine in the kitchen for automating his morning routine, suggests that he improvises for the sheer joy it brings him. Creating the technological future from bits and pieces of the technological present is, for Doc, not a means to professional advancement (since he has no visible professional ties) or economic security (since he is independently wealthy) but a form of play.

Marty — played by Michael J. Fox as a teenaged everyman who dreams of a cooler car, a less-embarrassing family, and time alone with his girlfriend — also creates wonders, but they are musical rather than technological. Marty lives for rock and roll in the same way that Doc lives for science. It is the background to everything Marty does, from Van Halen blasting out of his clock radio in the morning to Huey Lewis and the News singing about "The Power of Love" as he skateboards to school. His garage band, The Pinheads, is dismissed by clueless school administrators as "just too loud" to play at the school dance, but their audition hints at solid skills overlaid with enthusiasm and a willingness to push the musical envelope. Marty's before-school encounter with the giant speaker-amp in Doc's basement is also telling. Picking up a tiny Erlewein Chiquita guitar, he plugs in and powers up with the crisp assurance of a pro. When the first chord he plays generates a wall of sound that blows him across the room, he lays in the wreckage of a bookshelf slightly stunned, but mostly intrigued, by its power and possibilities. Marty's blend of serious action and playful intent is clearest when he takes the stage at his parent's 1955 high school dance, filling in for the band's injured guitarist. Picking up the leader's Gibson as if it was his own, Marty tells the band that "it's a blues riff in B, watch me for the changes and try to keep up" before launching into a full-throttle cover of "Johnny B. Goode" ... a year before Chuck Berry would write it.

The parallel between Doc, the scientist, and Marty, the rocker, goes beyond their personalities, however. Just as Doc creates the future in his workshop and laboratory, Marty — like Doc, a natural innovator willing to let go of what *is* to bring to what *will be*— creates the future on the stage of his parents' high school gym. Taking the place of the dance band's injured guitarist and ensuring that the dance goes on, Marty ensures that his parents will fall in love with each other: a "natural" process that Marty accidentally disrupted when he first arrived in 1955. The act of playing a song — and not just *any* song, but one of the seminal songs in the rock and roll tradition (Marsh, 2–3) — thus erases the accidentally created future in which Marty's parents never connect and Marty is never born and replaces it with one in which they do and he is. In *Back to the Future*, Marty's rock and roll is — just as much as Doc's nuclear-powered DeLorean — the tool with which the future is (re)created. It is, perhaps, not coincidental that "Johnny B. Goode" is a song about a boy who shapes his own future through his guitar playing.

Back to the Future suggests, however, that in playing the song Marty has also participated in two larger acts of creation. The first, implied, is revealed in Marty's return from 1955 to a 1985 different than the one he left. In the original 1985, his parents are downtrodden failures; in the revised 1985 (the one Marty creates by rocking the school dance and strengthening his once-ineffectual father), they are vibrant and successful (Jeffords 65–78). The audience is left to conclude that the spirit of rock and roll — the drive and daring that Marty has shown throughout the film — touched them in 1955 and shaped the next three decades of their lives. The second, explicit, is revealed during the dance scene. The pivotal moment comes at a 1955 high school dance where an all-black dance band (electric guitar, upright bass, piano, drums, and tenor sax) has been playing jazz ("Night Train") and sedate mid-fifties pop ("Earth Angel"). The injured bandleader (whose name has been subtly established as "Marvin Berry") excitedly dials his "cousin Chuck" from a backstage phone and holds up the receiver to give him a taste of what may be "the new sound you've been looking for." Marty thus acts as midwife at the birth of rock and roll, whose future he previews by successively mimicking Chuck Berry, Pete Townshend, Angus Young, and Eddie Van Halen in the long guitar solo that ends the song.

Magic Carpets and Time Machines

Bill and Ted's Excellent Adventure (1989) takes the idea of rock as a creative force to its logical extreme. Skipping through the past in a borrowed 27th century time machine, amiable slackers (and aspiring rockers) Bill and Ted discover that the spirit of rock and roll runs through the heart of Western culture. They impress Socrates with their profundity by quoting the lyrics of "Dust in the Wind," woo two Elizabethan princesses by composing lyrics in lieu of poetry, and introduce a delighted Beethoven to the wonders of electronic keyboards and Bon Jovi. They also visit the utopian future society that produced their time machine: a world where pollution is a distant memory, the music is (in their words) "most excellent," and the benevolent rulers — the Three Most Important People in the World — are played by John "Fee" Waybill of The Tubes, Martha Davis of The Motels, and Clarence Clemmons of the E Street Band. The missing key to the story — revealed at the end of *Excellent Adventure* and developed in the 1991 sequel *Bill and Ted's Bogus Journey*— is that Bill and Ted are the spiritual forefathers of the utopian society whose agent, Rufus, lent them the time machine. The music of their band Wyld Stallyns will, they learn, become the foundation of that civilization in the most literal sense. It will usher in a golden age: ending war and poverty, aligning the planets, and bringing about universal harmony and communication between all forms of sentient life.

Bill and Ted, Marty, and the teen-genius heroes of the mid-eighties — unlike their fun-loving predecessors in mid-sixties monster-rock movies — take it for granted that they can rock out even as they build the future. *Buckaroo Banzai* suggests that adults can also blend the fun of rock and the seriousness of future-defining science. The clearest sign that rock had come of age as an emblem of the future came, however, in 1992. That year, rock finally penetrated the most iconic of all Baby Boom visions of the future: the *Star Trek* universe.

Star Trek: First Contact (1992) sends the crew of the starship *Enterprise* back three centuries in time, to the mid-twenty-first-century moment when humankind's first tested a faster-than-light spaceship and encountered representatives of an alien civilization. Zefram Cochrane — hero of that moment and designer of the "warp drive" that sets humans on the road to the stars — proves to be every inch a rocker. Living in the aftermath of World War III, surrounded by people whose principal goal is day-to-day survival, he alone seems determined not just to survive but to live, and to *enjoy* the act of living. He drinks, he dances, he enjoys the company of beautiful women, and he dreams of retiring to a tropical island. He holds a PhD and is destined to make the most important discovery of the twenty-first century, but his favorite song on the bar's jukebox — Roy Orbison's "Ooby Dooby" — is a rockabilly ode to the sheer, elemental joy of moving your body to the beat (which he does, with enthusiasm):

> Well you wiggle to the left, you wiggle to the right
> You do the ooby-dooby with all of your might
> Ooby-dooby, ooby-dooby, ooby-dooby, ooby-dooby
> Ooby-dooby, ooby-dooby, ooby-dooby, dooby-do-wah-do-wah-do-wah

Cochrane is also among the few who, amid the shattered cities and ruined dreams left behind by the war, is willing to imagine a future that is more than just an endless reiteration of the present. His spaceship is an instrument of that vision, and her name — *Phoenix* — reflects it.

When *Phoenix* prepares to take off, Cochrane's last act is to slip a disc into the stereo system that is (naturally) built into her cockpit. As the ship rises into a bright blue sky on a pillar of fire, taking humankind's first step on a three-century journey that will lead to the *Enterprise* and the United Federation of Planets, has three distinct audio elements. The first is the roar of the rocket engines. The second is Cochrane's exuberant battle cry: "Let's rock and roll!" The third is the song booming through the cabin: Steppenwolf's "Magic Carpet Ride." In the initial, interior shots of the cabin, the lyrics are lost (to all but Steppenwolf fans) in the roar of the engines, while the pounding drums and staccato guitars of the opening verse blend seamlessly with the din. The camera then cuts away to an exterior shot of the *Phoenix* rising from its underground silo, watched by amazed Montana locals from the bar and the ground outside. They cannot hear the music — they see only a loud, noisy spectacle — but on the soundtrack the engine noise slides under the music for the first time, allowing the audience hear lines from the final refrain:

> You don't know what we can see
> Why don't you tell your dreams to me
> Fantasy will set you free

Cochrane, it is now clear, wanted not just "music" but this specific song, with its driving beat and its delicate lyrics about dreams and quests and freedom. Neil Armstrong prepared his famous "one small step for a man" speech well before he used it; Zefram Cochrane, ever the rocker, made his historic statement with a song.

Rocking into the Future

Dreams ... quests ... freedom ... these are the stuff of which rock and roll and visions of the future are made. While seeming to inhabit two different social, intellectual, and aesthetic universes, these two imaginative phenomena have, for generations, given expression to our greatest hopes, fears, joys, and sorrows. No wonder, then, that the past four decades of science fiction cinema would bear witness to them coming of age together.

The monster-rock movies of the sixties, brimming over with youthful exuberance, rebellion, and hedonism, used rock and roll to express terrestrial explorations — as the battle cry of a generation stepping out into the unknown, and making its voice heard. The future was "tomorrow" and of little concern amidst the pleasures of today. Science, the province of those older, wiser, and duller, held little appeal to the younger, bolder, and more vibrant. It was, however, society's bulwark against things that went "bump" in the night — monsters, aliens, and other inhuman menaces — a counterpoint that rebel youth needed to preserve their well-being. But young rockers had something science desperately needed — the energy and ingenuity to venture beyond the status quo and into the future.

And so, the sharp dividing line between scientist and rocker eroded over time. By the mid-eighties, scientists and inventors who rocked entered science fiction films in force. Rock became the cinematic hallmark of rebel scientists who followed their own vision of the future, owing allegiance to no master or mainstream ideology. Whether serving as background music that played as brilliant minds went to work, or a symbol of innovation itself, rock and roll provided the driving rhythm that would energize the journey to the future. If the future was to be made by those bold enough and brave enough to make that journey, then it stood to reason that they — and it — would rock.

WORKS CITED

Bernstein, Jonathan. *Pretty in Pink: The Golden Age of Teen Movies.* New York: St. Martin's Press, 1997.

Doherty, Thomas. *Teenagers and Teen Pics: The Juvenilization of American Movies in the 1950s.* Philadelphia: Temple University Press, 2002.

Jeffords, Susan. *Hard Bodies: Hollywood Masculinity in the Reagan Era.* New Brunswick, NJ: Rutgers University Press, 1994.

Lueras, Leonard. *Surfing, the Ultimate Pleasure.* New York: Workman, 1984.

Marsh, David. *The Heart of Rock and Soul: The 1001 Greatest Singles Ever Made.* New York: Da Capo Press, 1999.

Shary, Timothy. *Generation Multiplex: The Image of Youth in Contemporary American Cinema.* Austin: University of Texas Press, 2002.

Tropiano, Stephen. *Rebels & Chicks: A History of the Hollywood Teen Movie.* New York: Back Stage Books, 2006.

Voger, Mark. "Call me Sam (Arkoff, that is)." *Filmfax 73* (April/May 1991): 76.

8

The Intergalactic Lounge:
Barbarella and Hearing the Future

Mathew J. Bartkowiak

The 1968 cult film *Barbarella: Queen of the Galaxy* wastes no time establishing the nymphomania-cal realities of the future. Our protagonist, a galactic, barely dressed diplomat of the "Republic of Earth" (portrayed by Jane Fonda), is shown in the film's opening scenes encased in an aluminum foil–esque space suit. She begins an interstellar strip-tease as a hipster orchestra plays in the background. We are cued into the mysterious vastness of space as the camera focuses on a pulsating spaceship and are quickly warmed with the shag-covered interior of our strip-tease dancer's spaceship. The presence of the tremolo of the strings and isolated percussive tings give way to a tambourine, hipster horns, and flowing woodwinds. The lounge for the space-age bachelor is created not only through the image of our space woman baring all, but is sonically constructed, helping us to discern the weird and unknown, from the warm and sexual. Barbarella pulls us in from the cold of space, and is able (in zero-gravity, no less!) to skillfully peel away each layer of clothing.

The entirety of *Barbarella* is made up of this dichotomy of the momentary unknown and the very human tour-de-force known as the sexual romp. Any fear or discomfort the viewer feels in the next hour and a half or so will be momentary, as peppy horns and lyrical celebrations of our "Barbarella Psychedelia" help the viewer get past the unknown of distant worlds that are signified by more ominous uses of "primitive electronics and odd studio tricks" (Dusty Groove). In essence, the soundtrack is an essential part of the narrative and is a decoder for the visual. It may, according to several critical reviews, do more than the script does in telling the story of this odd but ultimately familiar tale of the future "Other." It is thanks in large part to what some may call its "lounge" or "exotica" soundtrack, that Barbarella posits the future while remaining firmly planted in the post-war bachelor pad. Though set in distant worlds in space, the tale is an intrinsically human one. The music featured in the film acts as a central character, transporting the listener to the exotic, with an eye always on the timeless and familiar topic of sex.

The soundtrack to the film was a product of songwriter/producer/artist Bob Crewe and composer/producer Charles Fox.[1] Bob Crewe, by the time *Barbarella* was in production, had a long, storied life within popular music. Crewe, who had scored several hits in the '50s, penning songs like "Silhouettes," found his greatest fame when he joined up with writing-partner Bob Gaudio. The team was responsible for the Frankie Valli and the Four Seasons hits: "Sherry," "Big Girls Don't Cry," "Walk Like a Man," and numerous others. "The Bob Crewe Generation," an assemblage of studio musicians, was one of Crewe's many musical projects that came after this period, amongst other writing, producing, recording, and scouting projects. The Bob Crewe Generation's "Music to Watch Girls By" in 1967, "a prototypical easy listening/pop crossover instrumental with a '60s party, go-go beat and Herb Alpert–like brass," as Richie Unterberger describes, became a hit ("Bob Crewe"). Crewe hoped to capitalize on the success that the Generation experienced, when he signed up to craft the soundtrack for *Barbarella*. Crewe, in addition to the Generation, brought in a New York State outfit, The Glitterhouse, one of his pet production projects, to provide some vocals.

Charles Fox, collaborator for the film's soundtrack, had success with scoring the film *The Incident*, as well as penning TV scores including the *Wild World of Sports* theme. Fox would take off after *Barbarella* in film, popular music, and television. Fox's theme for *Happy Days*, his work on soundtracks like *Nine to Five*, and his composition "Killing Me Softly with His Song" highlight some of his more well-known works as a composer.

The team was entrusted to create a sonic world for this campy, psychedelic interpretation of a French comic originally authored by Jean-Claude Forest. The answer for such a task came in the form of launching Crewe's contemporary bachelor pad into space. The approach taken in "Music to Watch Girls By" was jettisoned not only into an interstellar journey, but also into the inner journey of the psychedelic experience. The unknown corners of the galaxy and of the inner mind provided enough of a sense of dissonance and playful potential that the music became a new, to borrow a phrase, bachelor "Music to Watch Space Girls By."[2] The soundtrack proved to be a space-age interpretation of "exotica" music: bringing an experience of "the Other" from the hi-fi systems of the post-war leisure nation, to a new generation of listeners. This musical form would provide the cornerstone as well as a bridge to the worlds of the future that were sonically constructed within the film.

In his *Mondo Exotica: Sounds, Visions, Obsessions of the Cocktail Generation*, Francesco Adinolfi describes "exotica" music or what is commonly referred to — to some critics and fans' chagrin — as "lounge" or "cocktail" music, as one that was born out of a fascination with "the Other." Originally seen in the rise of the post-war "Tiki" culture fad within popular culture, the "dream of escape and sexual liberation" was connected to this "adults only" hunt for the "incredibly strange" (2 & xii). Such music and other associated products of popular culture in the jet-set age produced representations of life far-removed from the banality of the 1950s culture-scape. This could mean a trip to the South Pacific on an album, or in the case of *Barbarella* in the late 1960s, it could mean a journey into the last great unchartered territory: space.

The subset of lounge known as space-age bachelor pad music was born to "invoke visions of machines, outer space, and the unknown" (Goldsmith 1072). It was the ultimate "Other" put into musical form. The music was created to both celebrate and anxiously deal with the "postwar obsession with the future and all that was associated with it: the atom, space, and science and technology more generally," (Taylor 73). Through the consumption of technology, one could perhaps more easily face any such fears of the unknown.

Adinolfi contends that the rise of this practice of lounge music in popular culture and its subsets, like space-age bachelor pad music, was directly tied to the notion of recreation. The so-called "swinging bachelor" was the undisputed king of the land. He was the colonizer consumer of the unknown, both terrestrially and beyond. Plenty of disposable income meant a healthy appetite for stereo equipment, a subscription to *Playboy*, plenty of ingredients for cocktails, and a comparatively low-key attitude towards sexuality (8–9). The bachelor could grab a cocktail, place the needle in the groove, and be transported to distant lands and worlds: a place to free himself from the suit and tie realities of the everyday. This was an environment in which he was ultimately in control and could have all he desired through consumption.

The Rise of the Bachelor

Thanks to such celebration of the status in the pages of *Playboy*, in music, and in everyday life, "the bachelor," as Howard P. Chudacoff explains in his *The Age of the Bachelor: Creating an American Subculture*, is a much different entity than it once was. Our modern conceptualizations of this social identity, although often looked down upon in the past, was shaped into a potentially romantic ideal during the end of the 19th century and the beginning of the 20th. As men took more control of their careers, education, and moved to the city, a re-examination of the bachelor came into focus that ascribed the bachelor as the very definition of unadulterated masculinity (6–7). With the rise of *Playboy* in the mid part of the century, "a newer, more assertive image of bachelorhood came to dominate American styles" (260–261). This was an assertive argument for pride in the bachelor lifestyle that had not been seen by previous generations.

No longer seen as a result of selfishness or a mental illness, as it may have been considered in earlier centuries, the image of the bachelor was unashamedly adopted. It put the experience of the immediate, and the pleasurable at the center of life. It was a life that could be obtained with consumption; it was the unabashed search for pleasure where "seductive and available young women constituted the reward for sophisticated consumerism" (262). Like their art, their music, and their living space, women were a source of cultural capital to be consumed. Chudacoff asserts that *Playboy* "elevated the bachelor life to desirability, perhaps even respectability, it had never before experienced. It also reinforced a common bachelor attitude that divided women into three categories: nuisances to be avoided, namely wives and women in search of marriage; objects of sentiment, mostly mothers and sisters; and sexual playthings — all the rest" (263).

Women as subject of this music, that celebrated and that was created for the consumption of the "bachelor," were focused on as the latter, as "sexual playthings." The bachelor's hi-fi was a place to play a musical product that was meant be a form of recreation, including being music "To Watch Girls By." The music took the search for the primitive and the sexually-unabated from distant islands to the cosmos (146). In terms of this genre-heavy discussion of "lounge" space-age bachelor pad music," "exotica," and so on, music, aside from any such definitive ascriptions of sub-genre, was meant to be an experience of transcendence and escape from other geographical locations, and other mores, sexuality included. All of this was to be tested on one's hi-fi: a bastion of technological innovation in the post-war period that Timothy Taylor in his book *Strange Sounds: Music, Technology and Culture* refers to as "commodity scientism" (79). The hi-fis "do not simply occupy the space in the living room; music can fill a room like nothing else — men and their hi-fis could colonize the entire living room and beyond" (Taylor 80). Through music, the strange and the unknown could be conquered through the consumption of new technological forms. Women, primordially fixated on sex, along with all of these other great unknowns, could be colonized too. Thanks to this march towards progress that could be brought into the living room, the bachelor simply had to only embrace the notion of expendable income, and surety in unsure times was his.

The Bachelor Swings Into the 1960s

It is within this space of the unknown that *Barbarella* fits so succinctly. Even while pulling in supposedly a new generation of influence in the psychedelic and the counterculture, the message remains the same as the one communicated in the post-war bachelor pad. Somehow the square-ness of the '50s was being partnered with the swinging sexual mores of the bachelor pad, and carried into the sexual revolution of the 1960s. The music, like the film, although kitsch, was also communicating an inherent zeitgeist of a social movement of the time into a vision of the future. The pre–AIDS world of the sexual revolution was finding a comfortable home on shag-carpeted spaceships of the future. Like other space-age bachelor pad music, the soundtrack was meant to "bring together the bachelor, his stereo system, and his martini" (Goldsmith 1072).

In the case of *Barbarella*, though, one can see that these intended targets are linked in earnest with more contemporary visions of hedonism via the march of the counterculture. Psychedelic blob patterns and musical texts that look to explore the uncharted spaces within the mind are married into these earlier musical visions of the unknown. By the time the film was made, the psychedelic movement was much less a concentrated social experiment and more a general fad within popular culture. The use of LSD and later the idea or culture of psychedelia promised a potential for escape. As Martin A. Lee and Bruce Shlain in *Acid Dreams: The Complete Social History of LSD: The C.I.A., the Sixties, and Beyond* describe it, "LSD was a means of exciting consciousness and provoking visions, a kind of hurried magic enabling youthful seekers to recapture the resonance of life that society had denied. Drugs were a passport to an unchartered landscape of risk and sensation" (131). LSD became a chemical means to experiencing the authentic, the exotic, "the Other."

Much as exotica wanted to transport the post-war bachelor, psychedelia was promising a journey into some kind of authentic unknown as well. It is useful to point out here that such allusions could be referring to the actual drug experience, as well as the more general stylistic fad of psychedelia. One didn't need to take the drug, to partake in popular culture products that were meant to mirror the experience stylistically, whether visually or sonically. "Psychedelic" texts represented a vast spectrum of products from concert posters to lunchboxes. Though separated in time, exotica and psychedelia were a perfect match, as they both were part of the industry of escape from the everyday, from the ruled, and from the known. Like the path to freedom through consumption of "the lounge," the psychedelic "experience" was also a concentrated and consumed mode of escape that could be used as recreation. If looked at in the right light, both could also be considered challenges to dominant social and cultural life, though both re-emphasize the systems they attempt to escape through the consumptive habits built around them.

The space-age bachelor pad music used in the film was one that incorporated a plethora of influences to create a sound of the future including fuzz-driven guitars and other tropes à la psychedelia. The psychedelic, the aforementioned peppy horn sections, along with twangs, beeps, and electronic noise, came together to form the postmodern sound of space and distant lands. As Andinolfi describes such "space-age bachelor music":

> The music had to be surprising, and yet at the same time entertaining, passing from honey-sweet sounds to striking rhythmic compositions, rife with unusual noises and bizarre instruments like the theremin, together with marimbas, xylophones, timpani, bongos, electric organs, big band–style wind sections, guitars, and animal cries [122].

Barbarella uses these collections of cues to take the listener beyond their stereo and into the film-going experience. Odd animal cries created by electronic dissonance, psychedelic guitar effects, and Aldinofli's cited musical practices become the greatest indicators of the distant and primal. The controlled psychedelic and its incorporation into easy listening motifs counters this and bring us back to Earth. The music of the film eases the film-goer into comfortable spaces that act as a binary to the mysterious, uncharted lands our protagonist discovers. As one reviewer put it, the soundtrack incorporates a "mad mix of styles that blends '60s adult easy with spacier themes"— using the aforementioned primitive electronics and odd studio tricks "to capture the cartoony space landscape of Jane Fonda's world in the move." The same reviewer continues on, describing the soundtrack as a "sonic film" (Dusty Groove). With sparse dialogue and sometimes confounding imagery, the music is able to tell much of the tale.

When one looks at *Barbarella* with such considerations in mind, it is interesting to see how the very real, and one could argue sexist traditions of the bachelor, help the viewer of the film to experience "the Other" or the unknown through the futuristic sounds of space-age pop and visions of the psychedelic. Conversely, a part is played by the more traditional role of "easy" or "lounge" music to reaffirm the very real and terrestrial view of sex and gender of the times in which the music was produced. No matter how far into the future, or how far outside of Earth's orbit we get, the conventions of female sexuality are apparent in the visual and aural form.

This developing theme of importance placed on the music to further the narrative, and to create audience understanding, potentially offers a challenge to the canonized perspectives that focus on the absoluteness of the visual in studying, consuming, and interpreting cinema. Craig Sinclair in his "Audition: Making Sense of/in the Cinema" deals with this challenge specifically, taking issue with the focus taken by scholars such as Laura Mulvey: "Audition serves to undermine the very hegemony that Mulvey posits in the visuals and in doing so appeals to 'other' elements of the audience from those who choose to merely gaze at the screen" (21). Indeed, the lasting presence of film scores and soundtracks in popular culture, including the numerous pressings of soundtracks like *Barbarella*, showcase a definitive appeal and possible alternative sense of narrative and meaning to a film. Sinclair continues that "sound challenges the assumed power, the assumed superiority and supremacy of the image, and thus challenges the perception of the experience." He adds, "This may not necessarily promote agency" but it does "position the experience as the producer of meaning, while the viewer was a mere passive recipient" (24).

In *Film Music*, Peter Larsen discusses that there is a fundamental need to use the music to establish a sense of context and direction. Larsen contends that in its simplest use, a film-maker utilizes music within a film to "support and structure the narrative" (Larsen 206) in predictable ways. The music can "set boundaries, it measures out and rounds off the individual narrative event...." He continues, "With the aid of its own structure, the music structures the events on the screen, separates them from each other or links them, points out connections and transitions, closes sections off and opens new ones" (208). However, music, along with the other sensory stimuli involved in film, allow not only the producers of the film to communicate a message and narrative, but it also provides the raw materials for audiences to do the same: "When music, images and dialogue are coordinated and appear as a perceptual whole, we automatically expect there to be an underlying intention. We search for a meaning, and we find it — no matter whether the coordination was actually intentional or not" (205).

An extreme example of audiences creating such a coordination between the visual and music is exemplified in the great dorm room/urban myth experiment of watching *The Wizard of Oz*, while listening to Pink Floyd's *Dark Side of the Moon*. Though the band contends that no relation exists, listeners have sometimes vehemently linked the album to the film, saying that the musical-visual links are too numerous to ignore.[3] The power of Larsen's contention is especially on display in that, in this instance, the audience is doing all of the creation. The producers of the texts have been left behind. Music and the visual are being used to create a certain sense of narrative or meaning.

The music, like the film itself, is a hodge-podge of mixed messages about sex, space, the unknown, and the familiar. Ultimately, it is the viewer who is left to make sense of the trippy narrative. Whatever message is taken though is linked inherently to the sonic cues that alert us to this binary. There is a give and take with the film and its soundtrack that maintains an ability to keep the film in two musical worlds: the lounge and the psychedelic. These divergent messages create a variance of audience interpretations. Above all, though, sex was something to be sonically celebrated. What this focus on sex meant for the film's audiences, and how the music aided in creating the narrative, seemed to be up for grabs in this time of social, political, and cultural upheaval.

Variety did not see any libratory possibilities of the film when it stated upon the film's release that the film can be reduced to the following: "Jane Fonda stars in the title role, and comes across as an ice-cold, antiseptic, wide-eyed girl who just can't say no. Fonda's abilities are stretched to the breaking point along with her clothes." Louette Harding, mirroring such concerns, claimed in a recent article that for Vadim (Fonda's director and husband at the time) Fonda "turned herself into the film sex doll *Barbarella*, and became one privately too. He told her fidelity was bourgeois and pressured her to join the swinging 60s by participating in threesomes on three occasions with prostitutes" (26). Fonda, in these perspectives, was a representation of the timeless consumption of women as a sort of cultural capital, regardless of the social, political, filmic, or musical prognosis of the time.

The film has and continues to also still solicit comments from critics that see within the film, a sense of potential challenge through countercultural embracement of sexual taboo. Susan McLeland in "Barbarella Goes Radical" sees "Fonda as *Barbarella* was both symbol and product of a 'revolution' that capitalized on free love and sexual pleasure as shocking and therefore resistant." She continues in a discussion of images of Fonda as *Barbarella* that Fonda is "challenging the viewer to possess Fonda and constructing Fonda's body as the repository of a healthy, liberated, utopian sexuality that promises a host of once-forbidden pleasures." Yet the "effect is not indifference to the objectifying gaze but open provocation of it" (234). Such discussions continue in other critical work on the film. Pauline Kael from *The New Yorker* remarked how Barbarella "is playfully and deliciously aware of the naughtiness of what she is doing" (qtd. in Fonda 178). Such readings allow us to bear witness to the fact that the film, with its dependence on music to support the narrative, creates seemingly archaic as well as combative messages about sexuality and women's roles in such changing times. The act of consuming the sights and sounds of a film can yield and support these divergent views. As Peter Larsen contends, watching a film is an activity, an interpretive act.

> We are constantly interpreting the information presented to us. We classify it, we assess it in relation to other information, we scan against our own background knowledge, and we contemplate how it is to be understood and posi-

John Phillip Law and Jane Fonda in a promotional still from *Barbarella* (1968).

tioned in relation to the narrative and its narrators. This is also what we do
with musical information [200].

When combining these forms, the plethora of raw materials in a film such as
Barbarella, can enliven debates from those who see Barbarella as a feminist
icon, and those who see her as an intergalactic tramp.

The track "Ski Ride" for instance uses a mixture of the forms. Our protagonist, after being rescued from flesh-eating dolls, thanks her rescuer, the

"catchman," and agrees to make love to him as a thank you (he also promises to see what is wrong with her ship's stabilizers). The use of electronic shrills and screams in the doll den is replaced with the safety of horns and upbeat electric guitar as they board the sailboat. Aboard the spaceship, a walloping tuba line and other horns join together for the romp around the lake that feels like Herb Alpert meeting the Strawberry Alarm Clock in an orchestration of climax. A new woman, Barbarella steps off the ship in bliss. She is now experienced in physical love-making versus the supposedly more efficient and logical pill-induced equivalent in Earth's future society. Any oddness or feeling of discomfort created by the visual and the soundtrack depicting strange worlds up to this point, is alleviated with a soothing string arrangement that is joined by a vocal sweetly delivering the songs thesis of "I Love All of the Love in You." Flesh-eating dolls, and pills that take the place of sex be damned, the traditional cues of the afterglow are sweetly delivered to the film-goer.

Soon after, Barbarella is saved again. This time she falls into the arms of Pygar, the arch-angel of "The Labyrinth." The oddness of the place, the destitute nature of its inhabitants, which include Marcel Marceau as a whimsical professor, includes a complimentary soundtrack of the future unknown. There is a continuous chiming of bells, and occasional stabs from a heavily overdriven guitar. The music alerts us along with the visual that this isn't a safe or normal place. It is at this point that the music pushes the viewer into "the Other" with electronic whirls and screams indicating that the evil "Tyrant's Guard" is nearby. Pygar saves her from the guards and this cold, unfeeling world. Of course now that she is safe, she must have another sexual encounter, this time in a giant nest.

Barbarella is then shown enjoying the spoils of such nest-making, where another swirl and crescendo of horns and winds create a sense of dawning. We hear Pygar explain, "I've regained the will to fly." The professor, as he sees the arch-angel fly, remarks, "Interesting therapy." Again, a confusing and surreal vision of the future is quickly brought back to contemporary contexts of sex and space-age bachelor music.

Psychedelia is a partial indicator of "the Other," but is overwhelmingly held at bay by the comfort of the post-war lounge, and is used to communicate, in part, along with more traditional fare, the sexual act. It thusly is employed as a creator of dissonance, as well as peppering in its influence on the music of redemption, through sex and the body. Somewhere between the ill-feelings created in a world of machines, and the comfortable world of a peppy horn section, psychedelic music is used as a sort of bridge in the narrative, sometimes erring towards either binary, depending on the context.

In "Spaceship Out of Control" the space between complete dissonance and familiar musical forms is actively engaged via use of "psychedelic" musical stylings, along with semiotic indicators of the same. Barbarella embarks on a journey through "temporal space" in the scene. Barbarella lays down on her see-through bed, chest first, for a long pill-induced nap. This occurs amidst the lullaby of beeps and bops, and dreamlike, whispering brass lines. The viewer is invited to lay beneath the girl in intergalactic lingerie. Our protagonist is awoken, with only a few minutes to wipe the sleep out of her eyes, when an alarm of electronic organs and shrill, psychedelic guitar chords pierces the calm rumpus room. Add to this the visuals of "space" that Barbarella sees in front of her: liquid-projected patterns of colors, bubbles, and electric collage. Simply put, space seems to be the sonic and visual equivalent of a Moby Grape concert at the Fillmore or Avalon Ballroom in late 1960s San Francisco.

The music, representing not only a strange new generational "Other" musically, but also culturally, fits perfectly into the realm of the unknown. Taylor, when discussing space-age pop, describes that "different" was enough to distinguish an interchangeable range of music in indicating "the Other."

> The ways that all of these different sounds from different (sub) styles and/or (sub) genres were used points to how interchangeable all of these categories were. *Exotic* could mean Hawaiian, "Latin," Indian, Middle Eastern — it was a single musical sign system to which electronic instruments such as the theremin were added to signify "space." Others were others, and you have to travel to get to them, or they to you, either by jet or spaceship [92].

Who needs a spaceship though or even a jet-set frequent-flyer membership card, when a small tab of LSD can take a person on their own trip into the unknown? Luckily, no matter the journey, we are constantly brought "back to Earth" by the sex-capades of our protagonist.

The only real exception to the practice of sex as relief and recognition for the viewer musically and visually, comes in Barbarella's run-in with the leader of the resistance. It is at this point that the sound of a militaristic march combines with psychedelic musical cues to showcase the now, in Barbarella's mind, soulless and ridiculously efficient practice of sex through pill form: the exultation transference pill. Begrudgingly, Barbarella agrees to take the pill, as a thank you to Dildano for saving her life. Relegating the level of intimacy to simply touching a single hand to each other, the scene is the antithesis to all the viewer has known so far. Devoid of sensuality, the worst fears of the future come true for the bachelor. The usage of the zealous horn section, and the newly technologically engaged psychedelic sound, including overdrive, distortion, etc. are employed together to showcase the ridiculous in the unknown: sex through efficiency, and without physical intimacy.

Just when one thinks our protagonist maybe onto something a bit more redemptive, Durand Durand, the evil antagonist of the film, traps Barbarella in his "Excessive Machine." The examination of the machine by the camera is joined by a fuzz-driven guitar, string tremolo, and various plinks and plonks. Here "the Other" is created. Thankfully, the viewer/listener quickly learns Durand Durand uses the machine to kill via pleasure. A slew of strings and horns indicate the playfulness. Suddenly, as he describes her forthcoming death via the machine, the musical score bounces between horns, guitars, and furious cadences as the machine does its best to kill our hero. The horns retake the center stage though as Barbarella shamelessly challenges the machine, taking on all of its excessiveness. Again comfort is sounded, and finally in a psychedelic crescendo mixed with whirls, wheezes, and of course horns, any sense of oddity or unfamiliarity created through the music and the visual of the machine is trumped as climax is blaringly indicated on Barbarella's face. The viewer/listener is comfortable that any threat has been neutralized and what we are hearing is the sound of the peak of sexual experience. Thanks to the score that bridges a generational hipster divide, the promiscuity and hipness of the 1950s lounge/bachelor pad is met with the psychedelic vision of hipness and its perspectives on the role of the sexual being.

Dissonance, created through primitive electronica, tech-driven sounds of the psychedelic, and other accompanying whirls and beeps create a sense of the unknown, of the primal, and/or even of the feared. It is in the familiar sounds of the lounge, that all of this is taken away. Oftentimes momentary, these important sonic cues provide a space of relief and familiarity in an unfamiliar world. Combining the two can bring visions of the inner self, of excess and climax. No matter the psychedelic or the lounge, sex is intrinsically related to the sound. It is within this theme that the two styles share a basic meta-narrative; no matter "the Other" to be explored, the experience whether in distant cultures on Earth or in the massive "Otherness" of space, is always related to a sense of primal sexuality. Sex trumps time, space, and technology. Perhaps the generational divide between the swinging bachelor of the 1950s and the psychedelic, sexual celebration in '60s popular culture weren't too far apart.

Sex as repression or sex as empowerment can not only be seen but also heard in *Barbarella*. In this version of space-age pop, the sounds of the lounge and the sounds of the psychedelic combine into a polysemic and polysonic orchestration that delivers mixed messages at best. Are we seeing and hearing an empowered sexual being or are we seeing and hearing the continued exoticization of other places and the primitive sexual mores that must exist in such places? The music of the film and the history of "lounge" or "exotica" would seemingly point to the latter. In essence, from Tiki to the planet Lythion (the setting for the predominance of the film), a changing same exists. Regardless of its countercultural context, the lineage of the music continues a practice of sonic and voyeuristic representation and imagination: it is music to *watch* girls by.

Still, the ability of audiences to use the combined elements of music and the visual to create meaning is a prolific one. Time and context shape texts like Barbarella into raw materials that can be embraced or rejected as challenges to dominant societal norms. Due to its connection to the time, the social milieu, the visual cues, and the musical cues, *Barbarella* occupies numerous ideological potentialities. Though the musical legacy present in the film and the conventions of musically interpreting the future, represent a terrestrial consumption of women, the cues given by the film, including its amalgamated sound, seemingly provide enough raw materials to construct a potential challenge to this consumption. Under the guise of the sexual revolution, or empowerment, these cues, with their countercultural signification, are enough to challenge the idea that this is another conventional playboy exercise.

The score and soundtrack, like the film, leaves some gray area in terms of giving the receiver a definitive message. It is within these mixed messages, including sonic cues that create a film which some can see as empowering and some as regressive. As stated, the divide can be significant and the debate elongated when focusing on the messages of the film and its role as a supposedly "countercultural text." Such sentiments need to be seriously considered and weighed against each other when trying to make sense of the text, and the usability that audiences demonstrate with the text. However history continues to deal with the film, including possible remakes on the horizon, a central place should be reserved for the narrative created by the film's soundtrack. How we hear the film and how we make sense of sonic narrative in cultural and historical terms, can do a great deal in terms of placing how far we have come or, in the case of *Barbarella*, how much we have potentially remained in the bachelor pad of the '50s.

NOTES

1. Composer Michel Magne is also said to have worked on the film, going uncredited.
2. This actually is the title of a Leonard Nimoy cover of the song.
3. See Barron and Inglis.

WORKS CITED

Adinolfi, Francesco. *Mondo Exotica: Sounds, Visions, Obsessions of the Cocktail Generation.* Ed. and trans. Karen Pinkus, with Jason Vivrette. Durham: Duke University Press, 2008.
"Barbarella." *Variety.* 1 January 1968. (Retrieved from Variety.com.)
Barron, Lee, and Ian Inglis. "'We're Not in Kansas Any More:' Music, Myth and Narrative Structure of *The Dark Side of the Moon.*" *Speak to Me: The Legacy of Pink Floyd's Dark Side of the Moon.* Ed. Russell Reising. Burlington, VT: Ashgate, 2005.
Chudacoff, Howard P. *The Age of the Bachelor: Creating an American Subculture.* Princeton, NJ: Princeton University Press, 1999.

Dusty Groove America. *Dustygroove.com.* 19 September 2007.

Fonda, Jane. *My Life So Far.* New York: Random House, 2005.

Goldsmith, Melissa Ursula Dawn. "Lounge Caravan: A Selective Discography." *Notes* V.61, 4, June 2005: 1060–1083.

Harding, Louette. "Jane Fonda's Emotional Workout." *Mail on Sunday* (London) 26 February 2006: YOU MAG Pg. 26.

Larsen, Peter. *Film Music.* Trans. John Irons. London: Reaktion, 2005.

Lee, Martin A., and Bruce Shlain. *Acid Dreams: The Complete Social History of LSD: The CIA, The Sixties, and Beyond.* New York: Grove Press, 1992.

McLeland, Susan. "Barbarella Goes Radical: Hanoi Jane and the American Popular Press." *Headline Hollywood: A Century of Film Scandal.* Ed. Adrienne L. McLean and David A. Cook. New Brunswick, NJ: Rutgers University Press, 1995.

Sinclair, Craig. "Audition: Making Sense of/in the Cinema." *The Velvet Light Trap* 51 (2003): 17–28.

Taylor, Timothy. *Strange Sounds: Music, Technology, & Culture.* New York: Routledge, 2001.

Unterberger, Richie. "Bob Crewe Biography." *Allmusic.* Retrieved 3 March 2008.

9

Proposing an Alter-Destiny:
Science Fiction in the Art
and Music of Sun Ra

Jerome J. Langguth

My purpose here is to explore the ways in which science fiction imagery and tropes function within jazz composer and bandleader Sun Ra's aesthetic philosophy. I argue that Sun Ra's appropriation of science fiction iconography was expressive of what I will term Ra's "comic-sublime cosmopolitanism." Sun Ra's art is an art of the sublime in its persistent interest in the cosmic, the unrepresentable, and the impossible. At the same time Ra's art and music, as well as his persona, are resolutely comic. Ra routinely combined the experimental with the accessible, the humorous, the traditional, and even the deliberately cheesy. As I will argue, this is an important part of Ra's aesthetic philosophy and one that is often overlooked or downplayed. Finally, though Ra's work is foundational for the genre sometimes termed "Afrofuturism," his art is nevertheless cosmopolitan in its intent. His vision of the "alter-destiny"—an impossible future that brings with it an alternative history—for planet Earth is universal, or perhaps one should say, following Ra's own usage, "omniversal," and includes, ultimately, the entire planet and all civilizations. As I hope to show, all three of these aspects of Ra's philosophy found ideal vehicles in the soundscapes and visual language of classic science fiction.

Sun Ra and Science Fiction

Beginning in the mid–1950s, Herman Sonny Blount, who would later officially change his name to Le Son'y Ra, incorporated futuristic images, elaborate space-themed costumes, and sounds suggesting visions of a future space utopia into his performances and recordings. Ra's aesthetic, spiritual, and political vision combined his intense interest in ancient Egypt as an image of beauty and black achievement with a futuristic iconography and mythology that owed much to the science fiction serials and comics of the 1940s, and to the B science fiction films of the 1950s and 1960s. Throughout his forty year recording career, Ra's record sleeves were adorned with fantastical images of ancient Egypt and intergalactic travel, his compositions bore titles equally suggestive of ancient worlds and a utopian future in which current societal and racial strife and division has been overcome, and what he saw as the spiritually depraved condition of present humanity transcended. Perhaps most memorably, his many "Arkestras," dressed always in brightly colored sequined robes and hats, traveled and performed extensively under Sun Ra's direction for over forty years. The Arkestra itself, which still performs with alto saxophonist and composer Marshall Allen as leader, was continually changing names and personnel. Here are just a few of the Arkestras mentioned by John Szwed in his magisterial biography *Space Is the Place*: "The Cosmic Space Jazz Group, the Myth Science Arkestra, the Solar Arkestra, the Solar Myth Arkestra, The Intergalactic Arkestra, The Intergalactic Research Arkestra, the Power of Astro-Infinity Arkestra, the Solar Hieroglyphics Arkestra, ... the Omniverse Ultra 21st Century Arkestra, and so on" (95). Ra also wrote poetry and polemical philosophical tracts, many of which have now been published in volumes such as *The Immeasurable Equation* (2004) and *The Wisdom of Sun Ra* (2006).

As Graham Lock observes in *Blutopia*, his study of the works of Ra, Duke Ellington and Anthony Braxton, science fiction is one of the twin poles of Ra's personal mythology, the other being ancient Egypt (13). Ra's art centrally features a metaphorical outer space informed by his intense and lifelong interest in science fiction films and comics. Ra's brand of science fiction combined the cosmic with the comic, and was at times equally suggestive of Flash Gordon and Salvador Dali. On stage, the Arkestra wore shimmering sequined robes and elaborate space hats, lights suggesting space vehicles bathed the musicians, and the typical set included a handful of Ra's "space chants" — catchy and upbeat futuristic cousins to the sea shanty and, as Lock persuasively argues, closely linked to the tradition of the spiritual (35).

In addition to the costumes and space chants, Sun Ra's recorded works typically bore titles that reflected Ra's debt to science fiction. To name just a handful: *We Travel the Spaceways* (1956), *Sun Ra Visits Planet Earth* (1956), *Cosmic Tones for Mental Therapy* (1962), *The Heliocentric Worlds of Sun Ra* (1965), *Outer Spaceways Incorporated* (1966), and *Monorails and Satellites* (1966). In 1972, Ra collaborated with director John Coney on *Space Is the Place*, a film, starring Sun Ra and the Arkestra as themselves, which owed much visually, sonically and thematically to the B science fiction films of the 1950s. Ra's work in the '60s and '70s was likewise infused with science fiction elements, and for a brief period in the '70s Arkestra performances featured a light saber duel and a little person dressed as Darth Vader (Szwed 348). Ra and the Arkestra continued to record and perform his unique brand of "space music" until Ra's death in 1993.

Unfortunately, many mainstream jazz critics continue to treat Ra's space mysticism and references to ancient Egypt as, at best, relatively benign eccentricities; at worst, Ra's importance as a jazz composer, performer, and visionary artist have been overlooked entirely, as in Ken Burns' popular documentary series *Jazz*. This is a trap that it is all too easy to fall into. Encountering Ra for the first time can be a disorienting experience. As much of his output was self-released on the El Saturn (later Saturn) and other independent labels, the Ra discography is extraordinarily untidy. Additionally, Ra's body of work is multifaceted in style, sometimes overburdened with philosophical portentousness, and often deliberately, albeit humorously, mystifying. Most notoriously, Ra claimed that he was himself of extraterrestrial origin (he was from Saturn), and occasionally recounted a visionary experience involving travel to outer space that bears many similarities to classic alien abduction narratives. In the late 90s, a reassessment of Ra was initiated by scholars and critics such as John Corbett, John Szwed, and Graham Lock. In particular, Szwed's *Space Is the Place* (1997) and Lock's *Blutopia* (1999) take Sun Ra's philosophy and spirituality with the seriousness they deserve, and are welcome correctives to the dismissive attitudes just alluded to.

Ra's Comic-Sublime Aesthetic

As many commentators have noted, Sun Ra's aesthetic is an aesthetic of the *sublime* in that his music, poetry, and philosophy are animated by the ideas of infinity and the impossible. The sublime, in the sense defined by Edmund Burke and Immanuel Kant in the eighteenth century, is an aesthetic response of awe and fascination that has as its object the immensity and power of nature and, especially for Kant, the idea of the infinite.

It is tantalizing to suppose that Ra was familiar with the eighteenth century literature on the sublime. As Szwed's biography makes plain, Ra was a voracious reader who often referenced literary and philosophical works in conversation. In his introduction to *The Immeasurable Equation*, Harmut Geerken claims that Sun Ra was familiar with Kant's philosophy, and that Ra's poem "Thing in Itself" is a meditation on Kant (Introduction xxiv).

Geerken speculates that Ra's appropriation of Kant was done in a playful spirit, "not in an analytical way, word by word, note by note but spontaneously, freely, intuitively and lightheartedly with regards to keeping to the original and without worrying that the original might have been meant in a different way" (xxiv).

One eighteenth century philosopher Ra did know well was C.F. Volney, whose work *The Ruins, or, Meditations on the Revolutions of Empire and the Law of Nature* (1790) argued for the African origins of civilization (Szwed 67). Szwed relates that *The Ruins* had also been read by "William Blake, Thomas Jefferson, Percy Shelley, Tom Paine, and Walt Whitman," and had the distinction of being the first book read by the creature in Mary Shelley's *Frankenstein* (67). In addition to being an important source and inspiration for many of Ra's historical and philosophical views, Volney's *Ruins* is extraordinarily rich in sublime imagery, and surely this aspect of the work would have impressed Ra. In the opening of the second chapter of *The Ruins*, for example, the author relates a visionary narrative set in the ruins of Palmyra in which he is visited by the spirit of the ancient world. In a detail that must have delighted Sun Ra, the appearance of the phantom is announced by a startling sound:

> A sound struck my ear, like the agitation of a flowing robe, or that of slow foot-
> steps on dry and rustling grass. Startled, I opened my mantle, and looking
> about with fear and trembling, suddenly, on my left, by the glimmering light of
> the moon, through the columns and ruins of a neighboring temple, I thought I
> saw an apparition, pale, clothed in large and flowing robes, such as spectres are
> painted rising from their tombs [Volney 47].

Volney here marshals the standard eighteenth century repertory of sublime imagery; ruins, the moon, a ghostly apparition, the tombs of an ancient civilization, and a mood of fear and agitation. This mood of sublimity persists throughout *The Ruins*, and though Szwed's discussion of Ra's use of Volney understandably focuses on the latter's thesis concerning the black origins of "civilization, religion, law, literature, science, and art," it seems likely that Volney's use of sublime imagery in the service of a visionary message to humanity deeply appealed to Sun Ra (Szwed 68).

A sense of the sublime pervades Ra's music and art throughout his career, and Ra often chooses to express sublimity through the familiar iconography of low budget science fiction films. The music of Ra's craft in *Space Is the Place*, for example, is sublime in the traditional sense in its utilization of sounds and musical structures that disorient and disrupt with jarring force. Similarly, Ra's dialogues in the film, written by him and reflective of his philosophy in general, suggest the sublime by continually referring to unknown worlds and impossible myths.

The sublime as traditionally understood is an emotion of profound seriousness, and it is invariably tinged with outright terror. In Kant's early essay *Observations of the Feeling of the Beautiful and Sublime*, for example, he differentiates the feeling of the sublime from that of the beautiful in terms of the gravity of sublime feeling. The sublime precludes cheerfulness and concerns very deep and grave matters, whereas the beautiful can be evoked by the small and the delicate (Kant 48–9).

But Sun Ra's use of sublime soundworlds does not preclude cheerfulness, and is indeed often found intermingled with it. Whereas the sublime is usually taken, as in Kant, to be a feeling of almost unbearable angst or dread, Sun Ra frequently and characteristically combines the sublime with a palpable sense of the ridiculous. Humor is a strikingly consistent feature of Sun Ra's art and persona, as is the dramatic juxtaposition of forbiddingly intense sounds and complex musical structures with more accessible music presented in cheerful and welcoming manner. One moment we are assaulted by the shrieking tones of one of Marshall Allen's blazing alto saxophone statements, the next we are being gently serenaded by singer June Tyson as she sings a space lullaby or leads the Arkestra in one of Ra's rousing and upbeat "space chants," as in 1973's live recording *Celebration for the Comet Kohoutek*, in which the frightening Ra Moog workout "Outer Space Emergency" abruptly morphs into a jaunty reading of "Space is the Place." Ra's chants themselves, as well as his poems, also frequently combine the apocalyptic and visionary with the humorous.

The combination in Sun Ra's music of the accessible and the experimental has not always been understood or accepted, even by those with obvious affinities with Ra's musical and philosophical ambitions. Many works that champion Ra's aesthetic, such as Kodwo Eshun's stunning aesthetic manifesto *More Brilliant Than the Sun*, seem to emphasize the shocking and disruptive aspects of Ra's art at the expense of its humor. In focusing on the sublime, countercultural, and difficult in Ra's music, Ra's disciples often downplay his humorous and accessible side. Zuberi, for example, writes that "noise annoys and destroys. Sun Ra brings the noise," and compares Ra's art to that of the Italian futurist Luigi Russolo (86).

And this is undeniably true, but what is suppressed or ignored here is that Sun Ra also brings the playful, the traditionally beautiful, the romantic and the uproariously comic. Indeed, it is precisely the combination of these elements that I would argue lies at the heart of Sun Ra's aesthetic. As Szwed rightly observes, Sun Ra's sensibility was "too inclusive to settle for art-shock for art-shock's sake" (382). Critic Martha Bayles agrees, and she praises Sun Ra for sidestepping what she calls the "perverse modernism" characteristic of much avant-garde art and music (276). Bayles regards Ra's music as celebratory and permeated with joy, whereas, for her, most avant-garde art aims solely to shock and disgust its audience (277). Whether or not one agrees with Bayles about the aims of the avant-garde in general, it seems true that Sun Ra's form of sublime expression is a uniquely cheerful, humorous, and inviting one.

Ra himself claimed on numerous occasions that the central purpose of his art was to "help people" and to promote beauty and happiness, a sentiment which again serves to distinguish Ra rather sharply from the shock and awe aesthetic of some segments of the avant-garde. Szwed records that when asked in 1970 how Sun Ra thought that his music could be beneficial to people, Ra emphasized the importance of humor:

> First of all I express sincerity. There's also that sense of humor, by which people sometimes learn to laugh about themselves. I mean, the situation is so serious that the people could go crazy because of it. They need to smile and realize how ridiculous everything is. A race without a sense of humor is in bad shape. A race needs clowns. ... I believe that nations too should have jesters, in the congress, near the president, everywhere.... You could call me the jester of the Creator. The whole world, all the disease and misery, it's all ridiculous [236].

Similarly, when some Arkestra members complained that the disco rhythms Ra was asking them to play during the recording of 1979's *On Jupiter* were "some corny shit," Ra retorted that the music represented "someone's hopes and dreams" and that they should stop trying "to be so hip" (Szwed 131).

It is plausible to suppose, then, that part of what appealed to Sun Ra in popular science fiction was the genre's free spirited blend of the sublime and the ridiculous, the fact that it was in most cases it too was not trying very hard to be hip. Szwed reports that Ra was attracted to science fiction from a very early age, "reading early comic books and seeing the movie serials of Buck Rogers and Flash Gordon; learning its language, incorporating its themes and motifs into his performances" (131).

Ra's interest in science fiction continued unabated throughout his career, though he was critical of science fiction films in which space was portrayed as a "strange and horrible place" (Szwed 131). Ra's enthusiasm for *Star Wars*, which as noted earlier led to a choreographed light-saber battle with a little person portraying Darth Vader being incorporated into a handful of Arkestra performances in 1978, makes sense in light of his comic-sublime sensibility (Szwed 348). George Lucas's film was of course in large part an homage to the science fiction serials popular during Ra's youth, and the film shares Ra's preference for mythmaking over the attempted verisimilitude of hard science fiction.

Perhaps the best place to look in order to shed light on Ra's appropriation of science fiction material is the 1974 science fiction film *Space Is the*

Place, directed by John Coney. *Space Is the Place* was filmed in 1972 while Sun Ra and his Arkestra were living in Oakland, California. Ra was a visiting lecturer at the University of California, Berkeley, teaching a course entitled "The Black Man in the Cosmos" (Zuberi 77). According to producer Jim Newman, the original idea had been to film a documentary about Sun Ra and the Arkestra that would prominently feature a full Arkestra performance (Szwed 330). That plan never materialized, and it was decided instead to pursue a feature film that would both capture the Arkestra in performance and reflect the philosophical worldview of Sun Ra. The plot of *Space Is the Place*, as John Szwed has noted, is fairly straightforward even if the meaning of the film remains somewhat baffling (330). Sun Ra, who is traveling in a spacecraft powered by the sound of the Intergalactic Solar Myth Arkestra in full force, locates a planet of great beauty and mystery that he deems an appropriate future home for oppressed African Americans. Ra will bring them there, he intones, through "isotope teleportation, transmolecularization, or, better still, transport the whole planet here through music." Ra and the Arkestra then return to Earth, apparently in order to save African Americans from the debilitating realities of racist and materialist American culture. Once on Earth, Ra fights a kind of metaphysical pimp known as the Overseer, while at the same time he is interfered with by the FBI (and possibly NASA as well). In what appears to be a nod to Bergman's *The Seventh Seal*, the scenes in which Ra puts his rescue operation into place are interspersed with shots of a cosmic card game between Ra and the Overseer. In the Earth scenes, Ra sets up an operation called the "Outer Spaceways Incorporated Employment Agency" designed to help people to realize their "alter-destiny," is kidnapped by the FBI and tortured with a recording of "Dixie," and, after his subsequent rescue and a shooting at an Arkestra concert, successfully rescues at least a handful of people before returning to space. As the Arkestra's craft disembarks, the Earth is blown apart as the band, led by singer June Tyson, perform "Space is the Place," one of Ra's most memorable space chants.

Interpreting *Space Is the Place*, and articulating its significance for an understanding of Ra's art, is a somewhat daunting task for numerous reasons. Szwed suggests a cautious approach, noting that director John Coney, producer Jim Newman, and Ra were all contributors to the film's aesthetic, and that, according to Newman, in the end "no one was sure" exactly what the film meant (Szwed 331). Ra himself expressed dissatisfaction with the project in its final form, his main criticism being that the film had too little real beauty in it (332). According to Szwed, Ra's misgivings about the film were in large part responsible for the two-year gap between the completion of the film and its eventual release, during which period Ra repeatedly asked that the film be made more beautiful (332).

I think that Szwed is right that, given Ra's misgivings as to its final form, *Space Is the Place* is problematic as a reflection of Ra's art and philosophy. At the same time, the film is an ideal place to glean some insights into Ra's fascination with the science fiction genre, and in particular the new meanings he suggests for the familiar iconography of science fiction. One prevalent reading of *Space Is the Place* is that it is best understood as an example, and indeed a foundational work, of Afrofuturism. Zuberi summarizes Afrofuturism as follows:

> Transcending musical genres, Afrofuturism draws upon the feeling of alienation inherited from the slavery of American blacks, which it sublimates. In this conception, certain elements of Afro-American culture ... are re-imagined and transposed into a new cosmic and legendary perspective, where the alienated becomes extraterrestrial [79].

Afrofuturism employs the alien civilizations and creatures familiar to us from science fiction as a metaphor for cultural alienation. The black experience of alienation, which is connected with slavery, racist oppression and exclusion, is transposed metaphorically so that it becomes the keynote in a visionary art form that proposes an alternate history (or myth) and an elevated destiny (Ra's "alter-destiny") for African Americans. As John Corbett explains, Sun Ra "builds his mythology on an image of disorientation that becomes a metaphor for social marginalization, an experience familiar to many African-Americans though alien to most of the terrestrial, dominant white center" (18).

Eshun similarly contends that Ra's strategy in *Space Is the Place,* and indeed in his philosophy and art generally, was precisely to "assemble countermythologies"; that is, to propose a re-visioning of black history along with an "alter-destiny" promising a future of heightened beauty and harmony (Eshun 158). In *Space Is the Place,* the Afrofuturist countermythology alluded to by Eshun is central to the narrative of the film. Ra and the Arkestra have located a planet of great beauty and harmony, a place in space where the "musical vibrations" are both natural and spiritually nourishing, and are attempting to rescue African Americans from their oppressive physical, social, aesthetic and spiritual conditions on Earth. In one of the film's most powerful and effective scenes, Sun Ra is confronted by a group of African American teens at the Oakland Youth Development Center who question his authenticity and intentions, demanding an explanation for Ra's eccentric dress and odd pronouncements. When asked to explain why a person dressed like him and talking about space should be taken seriously, Ra calls their bluff:

> How do you know I'm real? I'm not real, I'm just like you. You don't exist in this society. If you did, your people wouldn't be seeking equal rights. You're not real. If you were you'd have some status among the nations of the world. So we're both myths. I do not come to you as reality. I come to you as the myth because that's what's black [Zuberi 88].

This is a revealing bit of dialogue, and it provides some insight into Ra's own form of Afrofuturism at the time of the filming of *Space Is the Place*. To be black in contemporary American society, Ra observes, is to be nonexistent, a myth. But Ra and the Arkestra represent another kind of myth: a myth predicated on beauty, higher spiritual values, and one that is transmitted through music. Throughout the film, Ra contrasts the space music of the Arkestra with the morally damaging, and ugly, music of Earth. "Earth music" is, for Ra, a derogatory term. The music of Earth is out of tune with the "nature" of its inhabitants, and especially African Americans who, for Ra, "have no music to call their own." Ra's rescue operation in *Space Is the Place* is thus a kind of allegory of spiritual ascent not unlike Plato's famous cave allegory in *The Republic,* but an allegory which in this case substitutes the beauty of art and music for Plato's reason and the philosophical life. The alien Sun Ra in the film is represented as a "higher order of being." The Arkestra's spacecraft is powered by music and art rather than futuristic technology. Thus, Zuberi claims that "the central message of *Space Is the Place* is ... that music is *the* special effect that can transport black people into a higher state of consciousness and being" (92).

The Afrofuturist reading of *Space Is the Place* adduced so far would suggest that the film is primarily an allegory addressing the social and spiritual condition of African Americans, and much of the film does focus on these issues — as did Ra's contemporaneous Berkley course on "The Black Man in the Cosmos." This reading of *Space Is the Place* pretty well captures the film that director John Coney and producer Jim Newman released. The problem is that the relationship between Ra's ideas and ambitions and Coney's and Newman's realization of them, was strained at best.

Ra himself thought of the film as a "spiritual blueprint" for the future of humanity, and felt that it needed more beauty (Szwed 332). Ra also believed that science fiction as a whole suffered from a tendency to emphasize fear and ugliness at the expense of beauty. Ra's criticism here was twofold: science fiction films were both deficient in real beauty and wrongheaded in their portrayal of interspecies relationships across interplanetary and galactic divides. For Ra, space was an image of beauty and enlightenment rather than terror, and alien civilizations were likely to be more advanced than human cultures both technologically and morally. In a late interview cited by Szwed, Ra makes the source of his dissatisfaction with contemporary science fiction plain:

> They make strange and horrible ones [films], and I don't see any reason why space is horrible. I believe, rather, that people who make these movies show a sort of portrait of the Earth. Moreover, in these movies you often see people from space who are doing something worthwhile, are conquered by Earthlings. I believe that someday Earth will be invaded by beings from outer space. It will

be necessary that people from space and Earthlings teach each other, or else it will be general destruction for us all [Szwed 131].

This comment might also help to explain Ra's remark to critic Francis Davis regarding George Lucas's *Star Wars*, which Ra praised as being "very accurate." While this might at first seem an ironic putdown of *Star Wars* or simply a joke, I think it is likely that Ra was in this case expressing his sincere admiration for the film. It is plausible to suppose that Ra's attraction to *Star Wars* refers to the visual splendor of the film and to its narrative of cooperation and allegiance between various cultures, what Ra might have termed its "cosmopolitanism." For Ra, science fiction is valuable, in part, for its potential to express an emancipatory countermyth opposed to the ugliness and banality of the "real." When Ra praises *Star Wars* for its "accuracy," then, he is knowingly and playfully upending our assumptions about both science fiction and art. *Star Wars*, of course, is pure fantasy. The film is resolutely unhip, and makes absolutely no attempt to explain the science behind its technology. It is, on the whole, simplistic in its portrayal of good and evil, and centrally features characters who display magical powers and/or are fantastical beings. It is in many ways the last work of art that we would expect an important avant-garde artist to champion. But to conclude that Sun Ra was being ironic in lauding *Star Wars*, or that his taste lacked sophistication, would be to miss part of what makes Ra's work and his personality so distinctive. Ra is challenging our pretensions, encouraging us to embrace a sense of humor and lightness and, perhaps above all, recognize the connection between humor and a higher kind of wisdom and happiness derived from myth. Ra thought of *Space Is the Place* as a "spiritual film; a blueprint for a better world" (Szwed 132). Ra also apparently believed that the film was never properly finished, and decided simply to move on to other projects rather than continue with *Space Is the Place*.

Space Is the Place, then, is perhaps most interesting for what it might have been. Ra felt that the film was lacking in beauty and that his hopes for it had not been realized. Ra's heartfelt enthusiasm for *Star Wars*, as well as *Close Encounters of the Third Kind*, might provide a clue as to the kind of film Ra has hoped *Space Is the Place* would be. Given Ra's criticism of science fiction that portrays space as horrible, and his own admonition to add more beauty to *Space Is the Place*, it seems likely that the qualities Ra admired in *Star Wars* and *Close Encounters* were their visual beauty, sense of wonder, and optimism. *Star Wars* especially must have appealed to Ra for some of the same reasons that led him to incorporate science fiction into his own work. The familiar iconography of the B science fiction films, serials, and comics was an ideal vehicle for Ra's comic-sublime spiritual allegorizing. It is precisely the genre's unselfconscious blend of the traditional sublime with outwardly ridiculous characters and situations that makes this form of science fiction useful for pursuing Ra's overarching aesthetic goals of cheerful enlightenment and higher beauty. The fact that Ra appropriated the light-saber battles and characters of *Star Wars* into his live shows suggests that he thought of Lucas's film in the same way. Ra claimed that art that fails to assist people spiritually, to help them out of the malaise and boredom of contemporary life, is "useless" even when it was technically accomplished and sophisticated (Szwed 236).

Ra's Cosmopolitanism

I have argued that Sun Ra's use of the science fiction themes and space metaphors is best understood within a framework of the "comic-sublime," and that *Space Is the Place*, in addition to being an inaugural work in the Afrofuturist mode, is important for what it suggests about Ra's penchant for combining lofty seriousness with the ridiculous. The aspect of Ra's aesthetic framework that remains to be explored is his cosmopolitanism, an aspect which on the face of it seems to be in tension with the Afrofuturist interpretation of *Space Is the Place* offered earlier.

Commentators have sometimes made the case that Ra's Afrofuturism in *Space Is the Place* contradicts the cosmopolitanism that many of his remarks about art and its purpose suggest. Zuberi, for example, points out that in *Space Is the Place* "only black men go to outer space," suggesting that Ra's form of emancipation ignores women and other oppressed groups and is best seen as opposed to the broader "humanism" and cosmopolitanism suggested in other aspects of Ra's philosophy and art (95). Interestingly, Szwed reports that one of the scenes cut from the film *did* involve some white people being saved, but Ra indicated that it had been removed because "the NAACP will be after us" (332). Ra's opening monologue in *Space Is the Place* similarly specified that the planet of art and beauty he has discovered will be a colony for black people "without any white people there."

It is unclear from Szwed's account whether it was Ra or one of his collaborators who deleted the scene alluded to above, but Ra's comment about the NAACP intriguingly echoes the content of one of his 1950s polemical broadsheet sermons entitled "what must negroes do to be saved," and may be helpful in attempting to sort out the issue of Ra's cosmopolitanism (126). In that work, a transcription of a street corner sermon, Ra writes:

> If the Negroes of America insist on an organization that advances Negroes only, then the white people of America has a perfect right to insist on an organization which advances white people only. After all the name of the NAACP is

National Association for the Advancement of Colored People, It does not mention white people who need advancement just as much as Negroes [127].

Later in the same sermon, Ra articulates a vision that anticipates his later view that a higher spiritual state is possible only by way of an art of beauty and discipline:

> ... I myself have approached them [black leaders] for help in developing an art form for the purpose of instilling beauty in the hearts of the people of the world, but I have met silence and antagonism. I know that any man or nation which refuses to recognize beauty is more beast than human. The love of beauty is the beginning of wisdom, the appreciation of beauty is an absolute necessity for the survival of the higher instincts. You have heard it said that the white people are going to be destroyed, but I say unto you that it is your duty to teach white people the meaning of love and you can do this through propagating and sponsoring beauty [128].

Strikingly, the example Ra chooses of an ideally beautiful artwork is "a movie that would be recognized by the whole world as a thing of beauty because art knows no color line in its higher forms" (128).

It is of course impossible to say whether Ra intended *Space Is the Place* to be that film, but the existence of this sermon at least establishes that Ra thought of his art as of significance for the "whole planet" as early as the 1950s. It also helps to establish that Ra was committed to an inclusive and cosmopolitan philosophy already in the Arkestra's formative years in Chicago, whereas it is usually argued that Ra gradually "toned down" his message by deemphasizing its Afrofuturist themes in the late '60s and '70s so as not to alienate his "crossover" audience (Corbett, Introduction 6).

It is undeniably the case that Ra's art and music is conflicted with respect to the question of whether Afrofuturism is compatible with cosmopolitanism. *Space Is the Place* itself, as we have seen, seems to suggest that in order for African Americans to assume their "alter-destiny" they require a new planet of their own. However, given Ra's insistence that the film in its final form was not beautiful enough, and his early thought that the beauty of art in its highest form speaks, as Kant argued, with "a universal voice," it seems plausible that this was part of what Ra found lacking in *Space Is the Place*.

Ra's cosmopolitanism is also intimately linked to his version of the sublime, what I have been calling the "comic-sublime," in order to distinguish it from an aesthetic of sublimity that emphasizes fear and confusion. For Sun Ra, the sublime and the beautiful must ultimately support rather than oppose one another. Thus, it is a mistake to conclude from Ra's use of sublime sounds and images that his primary aesthetic goal was "shock and awe," as both Zuberi and Eshun seem to do. Zuberi remarks in the conclusion of his interpretation of *Space Is the Place* that "given *SITP*'s place at the intersection of black nationalism, blaxploitation and Sun Ra's musical theatre of alienation, the film's 'cult' and camp status risks us not taking its humour and other elements seriously" (94). But this leaves the question of what taking seriously Ra's humor, and his message amounts to. For Eshun, the message is one of "antisocial surrealism," and Ra is best understood as proposing an African American version of Russolo's futurism which confronts the listener with a "post-human" vision (Zuberi 94). Zuberi is more circumspect about Ra's alleged "post-humanism," recognizing that for Ra "the human might still be a useful category," but he seems to endorse Eshun's interpretation of Ra's use of the sublime (94).

Both Zuberi and Eshun assume that Ra's sublime sounds and visuals are at odds with traditional criteria of beauty and suggest a "Dionysian impetus for entropy" as an animating principle of Ra's art (Zuberi 86). Ra's combination of the comic and the sublime, along with his cosmopolitanism, supports an aesthetic that is far less forbidding and exclusionary, and more Apollonian in character. It is one in which Ra welcomes anyone who will listen to "laugh about themselves" in order to pave the way for a more beautiful mode of existence. Ra's use of humor combined with spectacle did not rule out beauty as an aesthetic goal, and despite what is often assumed about him, Ra valued both accessibility and humor in music. Commenting on avantgarde jazz in a 1970 interview with Bert Vuijsje, Ra distanced himself from what he took to be its guiding aesthetic:

> The musicians don't know how to connect with the people. They play music, and are very good at that, but what they are doing has nothing to do with the people. They have no sense of humor.... There's humor in all my music. It always has rhythm. No matter how far out it may be, you can always dance to it [Szwed 236].

All of which is not to deny that Ra's body of work includes much music that is just as intense and forbidding as Zuberi and Eshun claim, or that Ra is a central figure in avant-garde jazz. My claim is simply that Ra's imaginative transposition of traditional science fiction sounds and imagery is best understood in light of an overarching aesthetic in which the sublime, the comic, and the accessible are intertwined in the service of an optimistic philosophy of universal enlightenment. Ra held that the "spirits of the people of Earth are starved for beauty" (Szwed 298). The iconography of B science fiction provided Ra with an ideally accessible, and even cheerful, vehicle for his message of spiritual enlightenment through beauty. And although he may have failed to make *Space Is the Place* the movie "the whole world would recognize as a thing of beauty" he had earlier envisioned, his vast body of science-fiction themed recordings and poetry testifies to the enduring appeal of his aesthetic and spiritual vision. Ra's creative work was so infused with science fiction imagery and tropes that, in the end, it became difficult to think of Ra as anything other than what he consistently claimed to be: an alien being attempting to awaken a benighted humanity through the power and beauty of sound. Indeed, in some ways Ra's entire artistic output seems, in retrospect, like an open-ended science fiction work with the Arkestra and Ra himself as the central characters.

WORKS CITED

Bayles, Martha. *Hole in Our Soul: The Loss of Beauty and Meaning in American Popular Music.* New York: The Free Press, 1994.

Corbett, John. *Extended Play: Sounding Off from John Cage to Dr. Funkenstein.* Durham: Duke University Press, 1994.

Eshun, Kodwo. *More Brilliant Than the Sun: Adventures in Sonic Fiction.* London: Quartet Books, 1998.

Kant, Immanuel. *Observations on the Feeling of the Beauty and the Sublime.* Trans. John T. Goldthwait. Berkley: The University of California Press, 1960.

Lock, Graham. *Blutopia: Visions of the Future and Revisions of the Past in the Work of Sun Ra, Duke Ellington, and Anthony Braxton.* Durham: Duke University Press, 1999.

Ra, Sun. *The Wisdom of Sun Ra: Sun Ra's Polemical Broadsheets and Streetcorner Leaflets.* Ed. John Corbett. Chicago: Whitewalls, 2006.

Szwed, John. *Space Is the Place: The Lives and Times of Sun Ra.* New York: Da Capo, 1997.

Volney, C.F. *The Ruins or Meditations on the Ruins of Empires: And the Laws of Nature.* 1792. Trans. Peter Eckler. Charleston: Bibliobazaar, 2006.

Zuberi, Nabeel. "The Transmolecularization of Black Folk." *Off the Planet: Music, Sound and Science Fiction Cinema.* London: John Libbey, 2004.

PART V

"ALL THOSE MOMENTS": INSTANCES THAT SHAPED OUR AUDITORY FUTURE

10

Suspended Motion in the Title Scene from *The Day the Earth Stood Still*

Stephen Husarik

Bernard Herrmann's soundtrack for *The Day the Earth Stood Still* (1950) is widely celebrated among film historians, yet Herrmann's landmark musical composition remains almost unnoticed among histories of electronic music.[1] The situation is curious because, with the exception of Edgar Varése's *Ecuatorial* (1934), few electronic music compositions of this scope and magnitude appeared anywhere before 1950, and the music also pre-dates mainstream electronic compositions performed on the First International Electronic Music concert and other venues of the early 1950s.[2] Although the soundtrack of this film is routinely cited for its conspicuous use of theremins, instrumentation alone can't explain its artistic allure. At least as striking as the novel instrumentation are the composer's sophisticated musical structures that take this score to a level beyond mere solo instrument display. Herrmann understood how acoustical sounds (Earthlings) can be controlled by electronic sounds (aliens) in order to dramatize the conflict in a plot, and this becomes a critical feature in the title sequence of the film, entitled "The Magnetic Pull." The sounds Herrmann produced by combining and manipulating bands of electric, electronic and acoustic instruments are so unique they may never again be duplicated.

The Day the Earth Stood Still originates in a story called "Return of the Master" by Harry Bates. It tells about a robot trying to rebuild a murdered alien visitor to Earth (Klaatu) whom everyone in the story assumes to be the robot's master (Bates). Immoveable and frozen during the day, the robot wakes up at night and goes about trying to locate recordings of Klaatu's voice in an

164

attempt to reconstruct him, but to no avail. A punch line comes at the end of the story when a person apologizes to the robot for the death of his "master" and the robot answers, "You misunderstand, I am the master."

Screenwriter Edmund H. North took this story and rewrote it with cold war features (1951). In fact the entire film can be interpreted as a study in cold war history — with main characters and events running parallel to political events of the 1950s. While the film doesn't actually refer to a conflict between the Soviet Union and America, it played upon the expectations of the audience at the time and suggested that nations who acquire nuclear power are prone to use it to achieve political gain. In such a scenario all nations, including extraterrestrial ones, are subject to common nuclear threat. Alien representative Klaatu comes to warn Earthlings about their warring ways and his appearance in an oval spacecraft adds to the then-popular notion of alien flying saucers.

Already popular as a pulp fiction genre in the 1930s and 1940s, science fiction was becoming increasingly popular in film because it provided an outlet for imaginative special effects. Movie audiences were primed for this genre in Saturday afternoon matinees that included weekly serial features such as Gene Autry in *The Phantom Empire* (1935), or Buster Crabbe in *Flash Gordon* (1936, 1938 and 1940). With few other forms of mass entertainment available, 20th century audiences waited expectantly each week to see the next segment of a serial adventure. Music for these films had to be otherworldly, imaginative and full of action and drama.

The limitations on special effects — which are always very expensive to produce — forced audiences to accept suspended disbelief when viewing some scenes in science fiction films. *The Day the Earth Stood Still* was exceptional in this regard because it received a serious budget for background matting effects and second unit shots that placed it on a level far above contemporary low-budget science fiction films. Scenes such as the flight of the alien saucer over Washington, D.C., or its descent onto the National Mall are impressive even by today's standards. The fact that it was produced in black-and-white format (not unusual in the early years of color) may have enhanced the film's effectiveness because then modern materials such as clear acrylic plastic and aluminum look especially alien under fluorescent lighting — with their simplified core shadows and smooth textures.

The music for *The Day the Earth Stood Still* was equally modern in its musical instrumentation. Herrmann had used the eerie-sounding theremin in his earlier films (e.g., *A Portrait of Jennie*, 1948), but the music of *The Day the Earth Stood Still* was the first of its kind to present a total orchestral complement of acoustic/ electric/ electronic instruments (and multiple theremins) that were subjected to intricate mixing, and tape-cutting techniques. It may turn out that future audiences are drawn to this film more because of its unique musical colors and structures than its film techniques, which have now become dated.

E. Todd Fiegel produced an outstanding article on the timbral qualities of the music in *The Day the Earth Stood Still*; however, he did not discuss music for the title sequence of the film at length — thus leaving an important gap in the understanding of the main idea of this film music. Fiegel quotes Herrmann as saying that "film music must supply what actors cannot say ... music can give to an audience their feelings. [But] It must really convey what the word cannot do" (25). In this remarkable statement, Herrmann reveals his understanding that film music has the capacity to become an actor-narrator and create musical diegesis. The scenes in films where music becomes a narrator are familiar to all film-goers: the gain level goes up and we hear with our ears that which cannot be presented adequately with dramatic dialog. It occurs regularly in old westerns from the 1950s and 1960s where music conveys the viewing audience across grand landscapes in cattle drives. A scene from Herrmann's music for Alfred Hitchcock's *Psycho* illustrates his application of musical diegesis quite well.

Those familiar with the film will remember how the gain level rises during Marion's highway escape and how Herrmann's highly pulsating "Rainstorm" music accompanies her to the site of her demise at the Bates Motel. Shown driving her car after she has stolen $40,000 from her boss, Marion is thinking about what people will say when they return to work and find out that she hasn't deposited the money in the bank. Step-by-step, tension builds as the camera closes in on her face and we hear the agitated voices of the people she has robbed. A rainstorm begins, Marion turns on the windshield wipers, and music takes over the action. As if to emphasize the sense of her desperate escape, the windshield wipers pick up the beat of the music and start to swing synchronously with it. With music in the lead, Hermann's dramatic soundscape accomplishes what words simply cannot express at this point in the film — the frenetic escape and delivery of Marion to the site of her demise at the Bates Motel.

Music also becomes an actor-narrator in the title sequence of *The Day the Earth Stood Still* where Herrmann enhances some rather boring black-and-white footage of stopped vehicles and frozen machinery in Washington, Paris, and Moscow with music that depicts stopped action. His score for the title sequence is labeled "The Magnetic Pull." Since this music comes at the very crux of the drama from which there is no turning back, let us briefly place it within a dramatic context before considering its relation to other musical structures in the film.

Klaatu, an alien ambassador, has come to inform Earthlings that they must stop their warring ways because other heavenly civilizations don't care for the waste of war and they have the power to protect themselves from it. Unable to communicate this warning, Klaatu gives a demonstration of power to Earth's people so that they will take notice, and (except for emergency services) everything mechanical and electrical is halted for a period of a half hour.

Klaatu's demonstration aggravates existing political powers and he is subsequently killed. Mrs. Benson, the protagonist of the film, believes in his message and carries it to the robot Gort — thus saving it for Earthlings to consider. Like any main character in a drama, Mrs. Benson learns the "truth"— the true reason why the alien has come to Earth — and she acts upon it. Klaatu is resurrected by Gort, and the alien informs a group of influential Earth people what is at stake and asks them to consider changing their ways. There is an indirect moral message to contemporary viewers of the film that the acquisition of power — nuclear or other — involves both privilege and responsibility.

The aliens demonstrate their superior power through invisible means to temporarily defeat Earthly mechanics and electricity with electronic force. Herrmann's music for "The Magnetic Pull" demonstrates this both in literal and figurative terms. Audience members can't see "The Magnetic Pull" in the film, nor hear it as a sound effect, but Herrmann allows it to be heard in the form of electronic music that becomes an actor-narrator in the drama.

The first effects of the "The Magnetic Pull" are heard at the end of the cue called "The Elevator." Standing in an elevator, the conversation between Mrs. Benson and Klaatu is interrupted when the lights go off and a strangely ambiguous electronic polychord[3] is heard. Klaatu tells Mrs. Benson that Earthly activities will be frozen for a period of a half hour. Viewers then see examples of what is happening around the world. Herrmann's musical score follows the story in a series of accented sequential steps corresponding to the following images: Washington, D.C., Times Square/London, Paris/Moscow, a factory, a stopped locomotive/boat, in a barn/roller coaster, auto plant/diesel train, and Dr. Barnhardt's study.

The visuals in the title sequence of *The Day the Earth Stood Still* are not particularly unusual. Second unit shots of street scenes in Washington, D.C. (e.g., a motorcycle that that is stopped in traffic) are followed by matted street scenes of stopped traffic from Paris and London to Moscow. Thereafter, stock footage of scenes from factories, homes, and a stopped train are linked with very common film techniques such as wipe lines and jump cuts. These scenes are not at all outstanding for the time, especially if one considers that both *Gone with the Wind* and *Fantasia* were produced almost a decade earlier. Whatever the audience learns about the impact of the alien "Magnetic Pull" at this point must come from the music because even the very limited dialog in this sequence merely serves to identify cultural locations (e.g., Paris: "Oh, mon Dieu").

Herrmann's job was to illustrate the power of the "Magnetic Pull" to suspend mechanical and electrical motion through musical means. This is an awkward assignment because music itself is an art of motion, and it would seem contradictory to represent stopped motion in an art of continuous change. A film director can use freeze frames or one-camera shots, as director Robert Wise does at this point in the film, but how does a composer freeze music?

Suspended motion in this one-minute cue is achieved through various compositional means derived from harmonic nullification, rhythmic confusion and acoustical cancellation. Herrmann accomplishes these ends by employing polychords, polyrhythms, and using electronic music procedures that include tape splicing and multiple recording techniques. The attention to detail in this musical cue probably exceeds the camera work and editing applied to the same segment of the film.

One of the ways to create stasis in music is to cancel the forward motion of harmony. Traditional 19th century harmony creates a sense of motion and movement through the alternation of dissonant and consonant chords such as one would find in a traditional church hymnal. Dissonant (or harsh-sounding) chords are followed by consonant (relaxed-sounding) ones. Dissonant chords, harsh to the ear, are resolved with consonant ones. But the ear gets so quickly tired of consonant chords that a composer must provide a new dissonant chord in just a few seconds to keep up musical interest. The continual pulsation from dissonance (on) to consonance (off) drives the listener forward — on, off, on, off — somewhat like the peristaltic waves that push food through the human gut.

Peristaltic harmonic motion is canceled in the title sequence from *The Day the Earth Stood Still* because dissonant strings of polychords follow one another without regard for their dissonance or resolution. As these polychords ascend scale steps sequentially, they are repeated and re-shuffled so as to retain their harsh dissonance. What carries the listener forward is that the chords are constructed around a chromatic melodic figure heard earlier in the film (from "Space Control," see Example 1). When Klaatu communicates to his fellow aliens that a show of force is needed, a short musical figure emerges in

Example 1. Melodic figure from "Space Control."

the electronic theremin part. This chromatic figure is presented in augmentation (lengthened) in "The Magnetic Pull" and slowly carries the listener forward while stacked polychords simultaneously inhibit harmonic progress. Herrmann combines his polychordal style with electronic instrumentation to achieve a highly original result. One can look to Charles Ives as the source of this harmonic style not only because Herrmann championed the works of Ives in his writings, but also because he conducted Ives' music in public.[4] But it is also interesting to note the similarity between Herrmann's polytonal style and Stravinsky's — whose music Herrmann also conducted. Stravinsky was once allegedly pleased after discovering the sounds of two stacked major triads a tritone apart (C major and F sharp major) when he created the famous "Petrushka Chord" in 1911.[5] Herrmann does him one better in this music — stacking two minor triads — sometimes a tritone apart and sometimes a whole or half-step apart in this music. The difference is that Stravinsky used popular folk melodies to drive his polytonal music forward; Herrmann used short melodic devises such as scale fragments, figures and motifs.[6]

The first chord heard in *The Day the Earth Stood Still* is an unresolved polychord consisting of a D minor triad stacked upon an E flat triad. With this stridently unresolved polychord we are warned at the outset of the film that unresolved dissonances and harmonic nullification may permeate the entire film. The audience soon realizes that these polychords are not merely a coloristic effect, but serve a structural purpose in the drama.

Suspension of motion begins in the cue just before "The Magnetic Pull" labeled "The Elevator." Two stacked minor triads — A flat minor and D minor — signal the halt of both harmonic progress and Earthly machinery. If music is to become an actor-narrator on *The Day the Earth Stood Still*, it has to solve the paradox that changing music can depict suspended motion in an ongoing narrative. The associational parallel between harmonic inaction and dramatic stasis is aroused in the listener's mind at this point in the drama and acts as preparation for the subsequent inaction.

The title sequence of *The Day the Earth Stood Still*, "The Magnetic Pull," consists of three recorded channels that are combined (Herrmann). Channel 1 is ten measures in length, stretches across the entire cue of "The Magnetic Pull" and fades out in "The Study." It is orchestrated with theremins, Hammond organs, a reed organ, trumpets, trombones, tubas, and electric bass and is assigned a very soft dynamic designation (see Example 2).

Channel 2 consists of eight block chords marked "sfforzando" played by chimes, pianos and cymbals that sharply accent the change of screen images. The instrumentation consists of 2 theremins, 2 studio (Hammond) organs, 3 trumpets, 3 trombones, 4 tubas, 1 electric bass, 6 chimes, 2 pianos, 1 cymbals (see Example 3). Herrmann writes in his manuscript that "Lyn" [Mur-

Example 2. Channel 1, "The Magnetic Pull," harmonic reduction (Herrmann).

Example 3. Channel 2, "The Magnetic Pull" (Herrmann).

ray] should "[use a] 3rd channel Theremin ... to taste."[7] Let us review these channels separately in order to determine their combined effect upon suspended motion.

Channel 1 (Example 2) is a recording of instruments performing in metrical rhythm for ten measures, or 138 seconds of clock time. This music forms a background to the changing images of the title sequence and continues up to the cue of "The Study," where it fades out. The harmony of Channel 1 is represented as ten measures of dense, unresolved polychords that reflect the design of Example 3. These polychords ascend a chromatic scale and ultimately outline a variant of the musical figure shown in Example 1. The whole chord pattern can be simplified even further as given in Example 4.

It might seem that merely stacking triads upon one another would not affect harmonic motion. However, progress in traditional triadic harmony is accomplished by alternating consonance and dissonance. Progress stops if there is no alternation of consonance and dissonance, and this passage contains continuous dissonance — even when the chords change.

On screen, the audience sees various shots of stopped machinery around the world while in the music, streams of unresolved chords push forward slowly. When one triad moves up, its octave neighbor moves down to reoccupy the same position, thus retaining the same level of dissonance and nullifying forward harmonic motion. Chords are reshuffled and repeated so that the ear can detect them canceling out each other as they pretend to move forward. This harmonic nullification slows down the perception of motion and is a principal contributor to suspended motion in the title sequence.

Channel 2 (Example 3) is made of eight block chords that the editor matched to shots of frozen machinery around the world using clock-time (in seconds). Since these attacks were matched to the entry point and clock-time length of the changing visuals, there is a polyrhythmic relation between Channel 1 and Channel 2 that prevents the listener from identifying a steady pulsebeat. Without a steady pulsebeat — which listeners usually rely upon to reckon how consonances and dissonances are arranged — the listener has no rhythmic landmarks. Rhythmic ambiguity also impedes progress and accounts for the second aspect of suspended motion in the film.

Earth's residents are referenced with acoustic instruments (trumpets, pianos, etc.) and traditional melodic figures throughout this film music (e.g. the trumpet figure in "Arlington" and "Lincoln Memorial"). When the alien ship first approaches the planet, Earthlings are depicted as musical primitives, pounding on pianos (like gongs or drums) in additive rhythms with traditional harmonic tuning. Since the music of the Earthlings is associated with strong accents and harmonic motion, the removal of harmonic direction and rhythmic coordination is symbolic of the stoppage of earthmoving machinery in the film.

The chords in Channel 2 are an echo of Channel 1 but they, too, move up a chromatic scale and outline the musical figure shown in Example 1. Once again, the entire passage can be reduced to a series of polychords to illustrate how the chords are arranged as shown in Example 4.

The chords of Channel 2 are played by gong-like instruments (pianos and chimes) that are sharply accented as if to emphasize the sudden stoppage

Example 4. Channels 1 and 2 reduced to a polychord stream.

of mechanical equipment in each visual cut. However, Herrmann's music also illustrates that the machinery is being modified by an external force, so he alters these sounds electronically with yet another sound technique — tape manipulation and splicing.

Channel 2 went through several stages of recording. The first stage sounded like the explosive clanging of pianos and cymbals (hit with steel mallets), followed by a long decay. But Herrmann wrote in his manuscript that "all attacks should be cut off" (Herrmann). So, the editor trimmed off the attack of each piano/chime chord on the tape recording with a razor blade (perhaps a half inch or so of tape) and then reassembled the pieces. The resulting playback gave these acoustical instruments a strange otherworldly sound because the ear hears only the residual ambience of each note. Removal of the attacks sacrifices the identity of individual instruments, but it retains the original decay character of each note. Acoustical instruments are heard playing, but they are converted into electronic notes because of these tiny editorial modifications. Each accented chord was then allowed to decay about seven seconds and the recording was cut, spliced and re-attached as a retrograde (reverse), and played backwards in anticipation of the next explosive chord. The final stage of the recording thus sounds like a strange hammer hitting an anvil, followed by a wavering crescendo into the next accent (Herrmann). The fact that each polychord is recorded forwards and then played backwards has important implications for the acoustics of this passage because the harmonics (overtones) are effectively frozen.

In addition to pianos and chimes, the cymbals of Channel 2 afford an otherworldly sound (like radio static, called "white noise") that fades away and then rises again into the next attack. Coupled with the chimes and pianos, this sounds like static superimposed upon instruments that were never invented and never before heard. The final sound mass is modified, fades away and grows into the next attack as stopped machinery is shown on screen.[8] All of this electronic manipulation is a metaphor for the stoppage of mechanics by electronics.

Each channel is recorded separately, so the harmonics (overtones) of the acoustic instruments (pianos, chimes, cymbals) are unable to resonate with each other as they would in a natural setting. Acoustical instruments interact with everything around them in nature — even other instruments. They "hear" each other, adjust to each other, and tune up.[9] Electronic instruments, on the other hand, defiantly ignore each other and do not adjust to sounds around them. Herrmann uses this subtle distinction to distinguish between music of the Earthlings and music of the aliens in *The Day the Earth Stood Still*. He also uses it to show the influence of alien electronic technology over Earthly mechanical power. Once the acoustic instruments are recorded, they are frozen and can no longer interact with their surroundings; they become as defiant as electronic instruments. It doesn't matter how loud the pianos pound or the chimes ring in Channel 2, they have been absorbed into the electronic world. Deprivation of acoustical interaction creates a third aspect of stasis in *The Day the Earth Stood Still*— nullification of acoustical color, or denial of the interaction between overtones.

Acoustical nullification has both a dramatic and musical advantage in that it enables the composer both to slow down the action and to improve the aural clarity when these channels are combined. Such dense musical tracks would ordinarily create a muddy sound; it would be difficult to hear everything if they were allowed to resonate with each other. By recording the tracks separately, the dense texture of each channel remains clear to the ear when they are combined.

There is a third track in which Herrmann instructs "Lyn" (Murray) to add a theremin part "to taste."[10] This track does not acoustically interact with the others because it, too, is pre-recorded. The theremin performances are considerably off-pitch in the original film performances, but that oddity only adds to the alien feel of the music. With their off-pitched melodic figures wafting in and out of the musical texture, the microtonal inflections of these unreliable performers sound as if aliens had joined the traditional orchestra pit. Serendipity gave the original film performance a unique acoustical quality.

Hermann's music is a metaphor for the idea that electronic control is far more efficient than electrical and mechanical control. When we hear the title sequence of this film, we hear only electronic music; even the acoustical instruments are electronically altered. Earlier episodes in the film were accompanied by music consisting of a mix of electronic and/or acoustical sounds. At the scene of the Arlington cemetery, for example, sounds are exclusively acoustical. But in the title sequence, where everything is under the control of aliens, Herrmann scores only electronic or electronically-manipulated music. Even though there are acoustical instruments playing, they have been absorbed into the electronic world through multiple recording techniques and tape manipulations. Nothing purely acoustical is allowed to thrive in the electronically controlled environment on *The Day the Earth Stood Still.*

Herrmann's music of "The Magnetic Pull" achieves suspended motion in the following ways: 1) nullification of harmony through the use of polytonal structures 2) nullification of rhythmic pulse beat through polyrhythms and 3) nullification of acoustical resonance through the use of electronic instruments and manipulated tape recordings. On *The Day the Earth Stood Still* everything became electronic; acoustical sounds disappeared, and only electronic instruments or electronically recorded acoustical instruments were heard. This is a musical metaphor designed to illustrate the superiority of electronic power over electric and mechanical power; it explains how music became an actor-narrator in the film. The sound of the future in *The Day the Earth Stood Still* is polychordal, polyrhythmic, and acoustically defiant in the title sequence of this film.

Notwithstanding its esteemed position in film history, *The Day the Earth Stood Still* should rank as one of the important steps in the development of electronic music for several reasons. It brought new electronic music techniques into the awareness of a popular audience and, although there were previous uses of electronic instruments and techniques in film history, this was the first time these techniques came together in a large, coherent musical composition that took on the task of defining a drama. The title sequence alone illustrates the extent to which the composer understood and manipulated acoustical and electronic sounds for his dramatic purposes. Far exceeding the contemporaneous experiments of Henry, Schaeffer, and others in the 1950s, the sophisticated orchestration of this film music occurred well before electronic music composers consciously attempted to write major programmatic works (e.g., Berio, Stockhausen, etc.). Few electronic music compositions of the 1950s reached a mass audience, but the music of *The Day the Earth Stood Still* stands unchallenged today as a natural sounding accompaniment to the events of its film-drama. The composition deserves recognition as a landmark in the history of electronic music because it is the first large, coherent electronic music composition in history.[11]

NOTES

1. This film music is barely mentioned in the online sites devoted to electronic music history and it receives only a token reference in works such as *The Cambridge Companion to Electronic Music* (edited by Nick Collins and Julio d' Escrivan [Cambridge University Press, 2007]). Louis and Beebe Baron's contribution to *Forbidden Planet*, produced five years after *The Day the Earth Stood Still*, receives more references in electronic music publications.

2. First International Music Concerts, including works of American and French *musique concrète* composers, presented by John Cage in Paris, New York and in Urbana, Illinois, 1952–3.

3. Polychords are traditional three-note triads stacked upon one another without regard for the resulting dissonance.

4. From his earliest compositional years Bernard Herrmann was experimenting with polytonality as in a piece called "Dawn," from *Forest*. His association with Charles Ives is well known through his essay on the composer where he wrote: "Ives was developing twenty years ago a musical technique which today[']s moderns declare are their innovations...." Herrmann also conducted Stravinsky's works with the composer present on a number of occasions.

5. Stravinsky is alleged to have been pleased when he discovered two chords simultaneously (F sharp and C) as the "Petrushka" chords. What makes Bernard Herrmann special in this style is his ability to assign these dissonances to appropriate visual images. In the film *Psycho*, for example, he give us a perfectly tonal melody to represent the psychotic

main character ("The Psycho Theme") and then disassembles it to show the disintegration of the main character — as I showed in my paper "Transformation of 'The Psycho Theme' in Bernard Herrmann's Music for *Psycho*," AMS-MTO Mega-Conference, University of Georgia, Athens, March 16, 2007.

6. Like Beethoven, Herrmann's musical style is about process rather than melody. One can easily recall the melodies of Max Steiner (*Gone with the Wind*) or Maurice Jarre (*Lawrence of Arabia*), but one would be hard pressed to sing back a tune by Herrmann. Like the short motif from Beethoven's *Symphony No. 5*, Herrmann's most famous motif is an iconic squeal from the murder scene in *Psycho*. He is clearly interested in figures, motifs and the process of composition rather than song-writing.

7. Murray was a family friend of Bernard Herrmann and audio-engineer associate. Herrmann gave him advice on many of his musical compositions and he should be considered one of the joint authors of this passage in view of its polydynamic character. Although Herrmann's input into the actual changes during the final mix is unknown, it is probably Murray's taste that we hear when all of the notes, instruments, recordings and recording levels are adjusted in this sequence.

8. If one wishes to imagine how traditional piano notes or gongs sound in reverse, just imagine the beginning of the popular song from the 1970s by Queen, "Another One Bites the Dust," where a piano note is played backwards.

9. Acoustic instruments are unique in that they hear each other. Try the following demonstration: play a note on the piano and hold the finger on it; then play other notes in its overtone series above. That note will start to resonate or ring sympathetically — and get louder. This happens in live performances. Electronic instruments defiantly ignore each other and also the acoustic instruments around them, and this is what gives them their alien sound.

10. The issue of mixing and sound board control is perhaps the least examined aspect of film music. The person who controls the gain level on each part is a joint composer of film music. It explains why there can be such a dramatic difference between what was recorded in the early fifties and what is re-recorded today in the modern studio. Even though the recording is excellent, the recent re-recording of "The Magnetic Pull" (*The Day The Earth Stood Still*, conducted by Joel McNeely, produced by Robert Townson, 2002, Varese/Sarabande Film Classics sound recording, No. 302 066 314 2) with Joel McNeely conducting is strikingly different from the original 1950s recording. Herrmann's manuscript indicates that a dynamic curve applies not only to the cymbals, but also to the pianos and chimes — as heard in the original recording of *The Day the Earth Stood Still*, but that effect is not heard in the McNeely re-recording.

11. Special thanks are due librarian Carolyn Filippelli for help in locating scores and related materials, Professor Tim Wall for reviewing portions of the manuscript, and Darren Rainey for transcribing my handwritten musical reductions into finished notation.

WORKS CITED

Bates, Harry. "Farewell to the Master." *Astounding Science Fiction*, October 1, 1940. Available in *Real Pulp Fiction*. Online. 27 July 2009. <http://www.unexploredworlds.com/RealPulp/htm/rpulp17.htm>

Fiegel, E. Todd. "Bernard Herrmann as Musical Colorist: A Musico-Dramatic Analysis of His Score for *The Day the Earth Stood Still.*" *Journal of Film Music* 1/2–3 (Fall/Winter 2003). <http://www.ifms-jfm.org/Fiegel.pdf>

Herrmann, Bernard. "The Magnetic Pull," from *The Day the Earth Stood Still* (1950), holograph. Viewed by permission, Alfred Publications (2009).

Murray, Lyn. *Musician: A Hollywood Journal.* Secaucus, NJ: Lyle Stuart, 1987.

North, Edmund H. *The Day The Earth Stood Still,* screenplay, 1951.

11

Strauss, Kubrick and Nietzsche: Recurrence and Reactivity in the Dance of Becoming That Is *2001: A Space Odyssey*

Gregg Redner

This essay grows out of a life long frustration with the form that much film music analysis takes. It is not so much that traditional film music is bad per say, but rather that it rarely helps us to understand what is happening when the score interacts with the mise-en-scène. As a general rule film music analysis takes one of three forms: employing either the vocabulary of musical analysis, the language of film theory or the economic language of commodification. Each of these approaches is perfectly acceptable in and of its own right, but none of them really gets to the core of what a film score actually does when it enters the filmic universe. It is my opinion that the traditional musical and filmic approaches rely too heavily on describing how the music imitates the image visually or underscores it emotionally. In this essay I would like to explore a different path; one which attempts a deeper reading of how one brief cue from Stanley Kubrick's 1968 film *2001: A Space Odyssey* functions to create meaning in the scene. The cue I will be examining is one of the most recognizable cues in the film music repertoire: the film's majestic title cue, which is a segment drawn from Richard Strauss' tone-poem, *Also Sprach Zarathustra*.

Before we begin our analysis, it is important to say a word about the score. The origins of the score for *2001* are famous in film music lore. Kubrick had originally engaged veteran film music composer Alex North to compose the score for the film. North was living in New York when Kubrick approached him about composing the score for the film. Kubrick had previously worked with North on *Spartacus* (1960) and had great respect for him. North flew over to London for two days of meetings with Kubrick in early December 1967, during which time the director was honest about his desire to retain a portion of the "temp" track he had been working with for the past year. North was uncomfortable with the idea of having his new score interpolated with music by other composers and felt that he could compose a score which would give Kubrick what he wanted, without relying on the music of others. He began composing the score in late December of that year, but always had the nagging feeling that his score would never replace Kubrick's "temp" score. North realized that it would be nearly impossible to break Kubrick's attachment to the use of Strauss' tone-poem for the title sequence even if he followed the same structure and only updated the harmonic language and style. North continues:

> After having composed and recorded over forty minutes of music in those two weeks, I waited around for the opportunity to look at the balance of the film, spot the music, etc. During that period I was rewriting some of the stuff that I was not completely satisfied with, and Kubrick even suggested over the phone certain changes that I could make in the subsequent recording. After eleven tense days of waiting to see more film in order to record in early February, I received word from Kubrick that no more score was necessary, that he was going to use breathing effects for the remainder of the film. It was all very strange, and I thought perhaps I would still be called upon to compose more music; I even suggested to Kubrick that I could do whatever necessary back in L.A. at the M-G-M studios. Nothing happened. I went to a screening in New York, and there were most of the "temporary" tracks [Agel 198–9].

What is shocking is of course it that Kubrick did not inform North in advance that he was not going to use his music in the finished film. The explosion that followed the premiere is certainly the stuff of film music legend.

Ultimately, I believe that Kubrick made the right choice by not using North's score. What North was ultimately attempting to do in at least several cases was to write cues that imitated and updated the music which Kubrick had used on his temp track. One can see this most clearly in the cue under consideration in this essay. The cue North wrote to replace Strauss' music goes so far as to begin with the same initial low pedal point, and appoggiatura laden arpeggiated chords, which were clearly patterned after Strauss' tone-poem. Perhaps where North failed in Kubrick's eyes was in sticking so closely to the syntax of the original. Certainly, while thrilling, North's cue for the Main Titles is nothing more than an imitation of the original. Those interested in hearing what North composed for the film can hear his complete score on a 1993 Varese Sarabande recording with the National Orchestra under the baton of Jerry Goldsmith.

Strauss, Kubrick and *2001*

As we mentioned above the use of the opening of Richard Strauss' famous tone-poem for the title sequence of *2001: A Space Odyssey* has made it one of the famous and recognizable film cues of the last forty years. In fact the composition/cue is so firmly fixed in the public's collective cultural memory that it has been used as entrance music by performers like singer Elvis Presley and professional wrestler Ric Flair. It has been set in popular music arrangements by Deodato (1973 Grammy Award for Best Pop Instrumental Performance), the Australian band Powderfinger (as their introduction music during the 2001 Big Day Out music festival) and by the Dave Matthews Band. Filmic usages, beyond that of Kubrick's *2001*, include *Toy Story 2* (1999), *Charlie and the Chocolate Factory* (2005), *The Simpsons Movie* (2007), *WALL-E* (2008) and the "Monolith" cartoons from the *Electric Company* TV show.

Yet in some respects the cultural familiarity with which we experience the opening of Strauss' *Also Sprach Zarathustra* (referred to from here on in as the *2001 Theme*) makes our ability to understand it all the more complicated. This is not just an example of the use of a pre-existing classical composition; this is an example of a pre-existing composition which has taken on a life of its own, beyond the film, beyond its original context. This fact creates a number of serious challenges for anyone who attempts to analyze the cue's interaction with the mise-en-scène and narrative. Let's examine why.

First, the fact that this cue was not composed for the film but, existed previously means that it carries with it the weight and associations of the composer's original intentions, as well as the listener's now manifold previous experiences of it. Whatever the cue does, it does not do what it was originally intended to do, and as such cannot innocently reflect the director's intention. Secondly, because the appropriated cue was not written in response to the screenplay or mise-en-scène, it becomes very difficult to speak about how it reflects and inflects either the narrative or mise-en-scène.

Similarly, traditional musical analysis reveals nothing except what is going on musically and because of the brevity of the cue this is very little. A traditional analysis would sound something like this: Strauss has chosen the key of C for his tone-poem because it is often used to represent strength, simplicity and brilliance. The cue begins with a long C pedal point played on the organ. This followed by a series of tonally ambiguous open fifths which are accumulated through ascending arpeggiation. An added element of tonal ambiguity comes from the vacillation between the major and minor third of the arpeggiated chords, perhaps representing the state of flux at the film's beginning. We could of course also go on to describe the fact that the cue seems to underscore the barbarity of its first two incarnations, but we would run into trouble if we attempted to extrapolate this out to the third use of the cue, where it is quite clearly not the case.

Kubrick chose to use only the first twenty-one measures of Strauss's fifty minute tone-poem for the *2001 Theme*. He employs the cue on three different occasions in the film. The first instance happens during the opening title sequence as the camera draws out from the darkness of an eclipse to reveal Jupiter rising behind the Earth. Here light is dawning on the Earth both figuratively and physically. The second instance occurs at the conclusion of the narrative's opening section, following the appearance of the strange black monolith to the apes. The final occurrence happens at the conclusion of the film, following the famous "star-gate" sequence preceding the appearance of the star child. As we mentioned above, these three applications are diverse and while the first two can be tenuously connected, the third application remains an anomaly: the first example is devoid of living creatures; the second is barbaric and evolutionary; and the final is an example of pure scientific fantasy.

While one could argue that the brute force of the *2001 Theme* is perfectly appropriate for the first two applications Kubrick made — the cosmic vastness of the first and the evolutionary brutality of the second — one is still left to puzzle over why Kubrick chose to use this cue in its third incarnation. The appeal may have been a sonic one and while Strauss' tone-poem would not have been as popular in 1967 as it is today, it would have been far from unknown in classical music circles. Certainly of those who were familiar with it, many would have associated it not only with Strauss, but perhaps more importantly with Nietzsche. However, what appears to be a seemingly promising connection to Nietzsche leads to an almost immediate dead end. Strauss was clear in his writings that the tone-poem was composed freely "after Nietzsche," and that one should not attempt to read a program into it. He seems to have avoided a strict program and instead limited his application of Nietzsche to the titles he drew from the book of the same name, which he subsequently applied to the various larger sections of the work. The title given by Strauss to the section that Kubrick uses in *2001* is "Sunrise." This of course beautifully ties the *2001 Theme* into the film's opening images, but beyond this any meta-textual properties attached to the work can only be intuited in a very abstract way. Indeed, Kubrick himself denied any meta-textual allusions to the philosophy of Nietzsche when commenting on his choice to use the cue. In his monograph on the film, Michel Chion even goes so far as to suggest that it is this ambiguity that drew Kubrick to the opening of Strauss' tone-poem. Chion writes, "The music ... wordlessly narrates all the ambivalence Kubrick wished to convey; for him, in this tableau of evolution, the exaltation of life and joy of destruction are inexorably linked" (Chion 92).

The next logical place to turn our insight would be to Arthur C. Clarke's book of the same name. Clarke's book is an expansion of an earlier short story entitled "The Sentinel." However, this too turns out to be a dead end, because Clarke wrote the book at Kubrick's request as a sort of pre-text for the screenplay. As such the book doesn't occupy its traditional place as inspiration for the film, but rather acts as a vehicle to substantiate and develop ideas which would remain unrepresented in the subsequent film.

Of course we might be tempted to fall back on the standard vehicle of film music analysis which is to suggest that on a purely affective level Kubrick was attracted to the barbarous power of Strauss's work, which seemed well-suited to establishing the rawness and nebulous quality of the film's beginning. However, this leads us to the rather disappointing dead end, suggesting that Kubrick ultimately chose the music because he liked how it sounded. Somehow this doesn't satisfy. It may indeed be true, but it leaves hanging the deeper question of just how the score interacts and engages with the mise-en-scène. If we are to understand the score on a deeper level we will need to find some way to take this to some further level of abstraction.

Ultimately, the closest tie we can find between image and cue can be found during the first eighteen minutes of the film. Here, Kubrick follows a group of apes as they evolve from agrarian mammals to aggressive carnivores. The climactic evolutionary moment occurs when the dominant ape realizes that he can use a bone from a nearby carcass as a weapon to kill and destroy. One can intuit a somewhat tenuous relationship here between Nietzsche's theory of the *Übermensch*, Strauss's tone-poem and Kubrick's mise-en-scène. However, this promising connection is soon thwarted by the fact that there is little or no way to follow this through to the final two sequences that also use the cue.

Thus, following standard analytical methodologies leaves us with a tangled mass of unresolved threads. We have a pre-existing, pre-composed cue which was influenced by, but does not literally represent the philosophy of one of the nineteenth-century's greatest thinkers. The film's director chose to use this segment drawn from a larger composition to accompany three wildly disparate and seemingly disconnected scenes in a film which bears no connection to the philosophy represented indirectly by the composition. Lastly, the film's origins exist in a book which itself served as the pre-text for the eventual screenplay, which bears no connection to either the philosophy in question or the original tone-poem.

At this point standard methodologies let us down and there seems to be little else that can be intuited by pursuing them. We seem left to puzzle about just how we might write and theorize about the cue's integration into the filmic universe, and it is this very question that gets directly to the core of why so much film music scholarship is less than completely successful. We can learn much about the music, we can learn much about the film, but we seem relegated to learn very little about how the score and mise-en-scène interact on a deeper level. Does Strauss' cue simply underscore or does it in fact engage with the image and create meaning? What is needed here is some type of methodological bridge to aid us in fording the chasm that exists between music and film theories. I would like to argue that we can find just such a bridge by reading the philosophy of Nietzsche through the conceptual lens of Gilles Deleuze.

Deleuze, Nietzsche, Strauss, Kubrick and the Dance of "Becoming"

Constructing a methodological bridge between film and music theories which makes use of a Deleuzian philosophical base is not as extreme as it might at first seem. Throughout his long career Deleuze was actively engaged with both film and music. He wrote two important discussions on film and even developed, one might say, one of the more original film theories of the twentieth century. Perhaps even most important for our purposes, Deleuze wrote a study of the philosophy of Friedrich Nietzsche, analyzing philosophical concepts which will be valuable for our discussion of Strauss' cue for *2001*.

Deleuze suggested that philosophy might be viewed as a toolkit, a collection of concepts which might be employed to solve conceptual problems. He does not suggest that these problems need necessarily be philosophical, but instead suggests that his philosophical concepts are designed to be used as part of a creative process intended to solve problems. As John Rajchman suggests, Deleuze "turned philosophy into an inquiry about what we may legitimately infer from such constructions of impressions, replacing the problem of certainty with that of probable belief and the question interests and contracts with that of the particularities of passions..." (Rajchman 3). Thus, the various concepts can be employed anew and related to the individual circumstances and challenges in each score. This results in a flexible toolkit which is adaptable to the situation rather than applicable to the whole. As such, the possibilities for analysis are limitless and unconstrained by process.

In this essay I would like to draw on two Nietzschean concepts as translated by Deleuze to form the foundation of my analysis of the *2001 Theme*. The first concept I will employ is that of the Eternal Return and its related sub-area of "becoming." I will use this concept to consider the reasons for the theme's three returns during the film. The second concept I will employ is that of active/reactive force, which I will use to discuss the role that the score plays in realizing the intent of the narrative.

Let us begin by examining the individual concepts we will employ. For Deleuze this concept of the eternal recurrence becomes an answer "to the problem of *passage*," and as such it should not be interpreted as the return of something that already is, something that is the "same." He suggests that we misinterpret the concept if we understand it as the "return of the same." It is not the pre-existent that returns but rather the returning itself that constitutes being because it is affirmed of becoming and of that which passes. In other words, Deleuze does not suggest that identity in the eternal return describes the nature of that which returns but instead the mere fact of returning for that which differs (Deleuze 48). It is for this reason that the eternal return can only be understood as the expression of a principle that serves as an explanation of difference and its repetition (Deleuze 49). The eternal return serves as the fundamental axiom of a philosophy of forces in which active force separates itself from and supplants reactive force and ultimately locates itself as the motor principle of becoming (Spinks 83).

Deleuze draws his concept of the eternal return from the teachings of Friedrich Nietzsche. Nietzsche based the concept on the fact that he believed that the universe contained a limited amount of matter and was finite by extension. In contrast he understood time to be infinite. Because Nietzsche believed that time had no beginning or ending, but the physical and metaphysical matter of the universe was limited, he intuited that eventually the same state would recur. The Eternal Return was crucial to Deleuze's radical extension of a philosophy of immanence and univocity (Spinks 82–3). Deleuze suggested that Nietzsche directed the aim of his philosophy towards the freeing of thought from the constraints of nihilism and its various forms. For Deleuze this implied a new way of thinking, a veritable overturning of the principle on which pre–Nietzschean thought had depended (Deleuze 35). Deleuze suggested that for Nietzsche the eternal return is not a form of the identical, but instead was a form of synthesis (Deleuze 47).

This is very helpful, because it opens the possibility of understanding Kubrick's film not as a series of component parts — the image, the sound, the narrative, the score — but rather as a synthesis of various but equal sensei. Deleuze first advanced the concept of sensation in his discussion of the painter Francis Bacon, where he suggested that in its purest form a work of art exists first and foremost as pure sensation. He carries the conceptualizing of this aesthetic plane of composition further by suggesting that what is preserved in an artwork "is a *bloc of sensations, that is to say, a compound of percepts and affects*" (authors' stress) (Deleuze & Guattari, 1994: 164). In other words, we perceive the sensation before we are able to feel it. Light from the movie screen reaches our eyes and we translate what we experience, or sense into an affective response on which the work of art is formed. What is helpful here is that by conceiving of a film in this way we are free to relate each element of it to the other elements on an equal playing field. The reason for this is that each sensation, whether visual, aural or intellectual is perceived in exactly the same fashion. From this we can conclude that at its most basic, the art work is a self-supporting, free standing assemblage of construction. In a musical sense we can understand this as a collection, an assemblage if you will, of vibrations and frequencies, a bloc of sensation that is self-contained and self-supporting.

Such a proposition is exciting because it allows us to relate any element of the filmic universe to any other on an equal playing field. Because we respond to each element in a film first as percept and then as affect it means that we can reconcile the perception of sound as represented in Strauss' cue and Kubrick's mise-en-scène first, and then respond to the combined affect that they create in the viewer. As such we perceive that both the cue and the image as sensory perceptions first of all. What does this result in? It results in the cue becoming first sensation and then a percept. The key here is the act of becoming which results first in the individual elements becoming sensation and then becoming percept. Thus, the very act of becoming results in producing the eventual bringing together of the unrelated aspects of the mise-en-scène to produce a becoming which results in affect.

The concept of becoming is essential to the entirety of Deleuze's philosophy. His philosophy is often called a philosophy of immanence because of his concern with the possibilities of becomings as they relate to life or the body, rather than predetermined subjects and transcendent values (Sotirin 101). The concept of becoming was developed by Deleuze and Guattari in order to help envision the definition of a world presented anew, and as such it is a foundational concept in their work. Deleuze's initial understanding of the concept is drawn from Friedrich Nietzsche, with Deleuze understanding becoming as "the continual production (or 'return') of difference immanent within the constitution of events, whether physical or otherwise. Becoming is the pure movement evident in changes *between* particular events" as instances (Stagoll 21). This suggests that becoming is not an evolution in the sense of a descent or progression (Deleuze & Guattari, 1987: 238), but rather represents "the moment of arrest in the roll of the dice, is always open to, and traversed by, becomings that are more than simple transformations of an existing real" (Conley 21).

Thus the very act of "becoming affect" in this instance, of eliciting an effective response, results in the pure movement evident in the bringing together of two previously unrelated elements: the *2001 Theme* and the three manifestations of Kubrick's mise-en-scène that it accompanies. In both cases the separate elements have returned as something new, something that retains the elements of its "original matter" but now returns not as a copy, but as new manifestation of the same separate affective sensation. They have in their recurrence "become" an assemblage of perceptive and affective sensation.

So what are the individual elements of this recurrence? First of all, in the individual elements of the film and cue we experience separate instances of becoming or recurrence: Nietzsche's philosophy returns as Strauss' tone-poem, which returns as Kubrick's cue. Secondly, in a separate stream of becoming we experience Arthur C. Clarke's book returning as Kubrick's screenplay and then subsequent film. Finally, we experience Kubrick's choice to use the *2001 Theme* as something new within the context of each of its three recurrences within the film. The result of this is that we experience *Also Sprach Zarathustra* becoming the *2001 Theme*, but in each of its recurrences the theme becomes again something new. The act of becoming which results through these individual recurrences creates a rich framework which allows for us to assemble a solid framework. With this we are able to relate the individual instances of the Strauss cue to Kubrick's mise-en-scène.

Having established this tapestry of interconnections between the various elements of the filmic and musical universe we must now find a way to relate the three diverse recurrences of the *2001 Theme* to each other. The problem, as we observed above, stems from the fact that each of these three sequences makes use of different and seemingly unrelated narrative materials. On the surface what binds these three instances together is the seemingly random return of our cue. However, things are not quite as simple as they first appear.

Each of the instances of return above also shares an element of becoming which relates the individual recurrences to each other and to the Strauss cue. The first example — The title sequence — is the only of the three not drawn from Clarke's book and on the surface appears to be a seemingly innocuous example of astronomical occurrence. Yet it is neither simple nor usual. The scene in question represents the rising of Jupiter and not the Moon over the Earth. This is a rare occurrence and one that would have signaled that something remarkable was about to happen to ancient astronomers. This is a point of great change, a sunrise of sorts. While it is true that Strauss subtitled this section of his tone-poem "Sunrise," the cue does not represent a literal dawning of time, for in a Deleuzian sense, time does not have a beginning or a terminal point. What it does represent is a point of immanence, a moment of becoming. We will see this same image recur again in the sequence with the apes, but there the rising will occur over the black monolith, which in Clarke's text represents a vehicle for change and evolution.

The second instance of the cue represents a moment of change and evolution. The apes have learned to kill, they have learned to use tools, and they
have begun an evolution towards thinking and rationality. They have become
something new. In the Deleuzian sense they have become-animal. "Becoming animal does not consist in playing animal or imitating animal, and the
human being does not really become an animal ... what is real is the becoming itself" (Deleuze & Guattari, 1987: 238). Instead, the element of becoming-animal implies the adoption of characteristics that represent aspects of
the animal, insect or bird. Thus one adopts an aspect of "bee-ness," or "bird-
ness." "You do not become a barking molar dog, but by barking, if it is done
with enough feeling, with enough necessity and composition, you emit a
molecular dog" (Deleuze & Guattari, 1987: 275). What is unusual about this
instance of "becoming-animal" is that the becoming-animal involves the adoption of human characteristics, a fact which draws the interconnectedness of
primate and Homo sapien to the forefront. The discovery of the ability to
kill and destroy, in essence the becoming-animal of this scene allows the evolution of the species, setting in place a process which will culminate in the
spectacular graphic match which ends this section, as the tossed bone becomes
the space craft.

The third instance takes place after the famous star-gate scene. Dave
Bowman has passed through the star-gate and has emerged on the other as a
rapidly aging man. These images are followed by the image of a baby cradled
in the celestial womb of space. What appears here to be a flight of science
fiction fantasy is in fact another immanent moment of becoming. Here the
implication is that man has progressed beyond the need for a physical becoming, whether becoming-animal, becoming-woman or becoming-human.
Instead, his corporeal body has been transcended and Bowman no longer has
any use for it. He has become pure consciousness.

What does each of these sequences have in common? Each marks the
beginning of some new becoming. Each marks a moment of recurrence, a
becoming, which as Deleuze reminds us in his reading of Nietzsche, "is the
pure movement evident in changes *between* particular events as instances."
Thus rather than serving as just an arbitrary choice made because of personal
preference, it is now possible to read the role of Kubrick's choice as a sonic
marker for the key instances of becoming animal, becoming man, and becoming new within the film. In so doing, we can relate the cue to the image, the
image to the philosophy, the philosophy to the book and the screenplay to
the cue in such a way that the filmic universe is revealed as both perfectly
integrated and artistically whole. Yet such a reading only provides us with a
function and does not allow us to differentiate between the three distinct
applications of mise-en-scène which are employed in each usage of the cue.

For this we will need to turn to a new Deleuzian concept, one which is again drawn from the philosophy of Friedrich Nietzsche.

Active and Reactive Forces as a Vehicle for Interpretation

The current conundrum facing our analysis of the *2001* cue is the fact that while we can account for the function of the cue, which through its application of the eternal return represents various manifestations of becoming, we do not have a solid footing on which to analyze the meaning of these cues as they relate individually to the mise-en-scène. However, Nietzsche via Deleuze can be of great assistance to us through the concept of active and reactive forces. Deleuze draws his concept of active/reactive forces directly from Nietzsche's *Will to Power*. The concept was seminal to Nietzsche's reevaluation of the idea of being and it enabled him to re-imagine the very process of being as "the distinction between active and reactive forces" (Spinks 7). By virtue of this, becoming is made an active process in which each force is related to each other force, with the distinction that some forces are active and some are reactive. What is key here is the distinction that all forces are related, but do not necessarily perform the same function. What defines them is "the relative difference in their quality of power" (Spinks 7).

Thus, the relationship between the three instances of the *2001* cue can be understood as different and yet related to each other. What is different is not the cue, i.e., the musical affect or compositional syntax, but rather the manner in which the cue engages with, or exerts its force on the mise-en-scène. As Lee Spinks suggests, according to Deleuze: "Forces are dominant, or dominated, depending upon their relative difference in quality. Once the relation has been established the quality of forces — dominant or dominated — produces an active power (that commands the relation) and a reactive power (defined by the relation)" (Spinks 8). This is very valuable to our analysis of the *2001* cue because it allows us to position the cue in two distinct and unique relationships to the image, positionings which will allow us to explain exactly what the cue does when it enters into a relationship with the image. Let's examine how.

The first statement of the theme occurs during the title sequence of the film. The image of celestial eclipse and occurrence is massive in its visual grandeur and one is left to question whether the image represents what is already — making the entire film a flashback — or what will be — making the entire film a conventional narrative. What is interesting here is that in spite of its sonic power, the *2001* cue cannot compete with the overwhelming nature of the image. The grandness of the universe, here represented by the planetary concordance on the screen and the collected energy and intelligence projected by the narrative, dwarf the cue, making it seem almost inconsequential by degree. In essence the activity represented by Strauss' original tone-poem becomes reactive here as it is divorced from its ability to dominate the mise-en-scène. Yet as Spinks suggests, "The remarkable feature of the becoming reactive of active forces is that historically [they] have managed to form the basis of an entire vision of life" (Spinks 8). In essence that is what is happening here, for the cue has in fact become reactive, stripped of its power and ability to dominate, it embodies the same future expectation of becoming which is embodied in the becoming-man in the narrative. The active force of the image has separated the force of the *2001* cue from what it is capable of doing, dominating the filmic universe. It is not that the cue is not sonically impressive, but that in reacting to the image it becomes a force which attempts to subvert and overcome rather than to dominate. In essence, the cue here contains the entirety of the narrative in itself by embodying the future: the future becoming of man.

The second use of the cue in the scene with the apes represents a very different engagement between forces. Here the passivity of the apes, the minuteness of the image field, and the static slowness of narrative allow the interpolation of the cue to eventually overwhelm the image, rendering it reactive rather than active in this case. Therefore, in its second incarnation the *2001* cue dominates the image. Certainly, a portion of this can be explained by the fact that a large segment of this section of the film is presented without music, which helps to underscore the barrenness and primitiveness of the early development of the primates. The cue underscores and establishes the reality of the evolutionary change in the apes, a fact which coincides with the arrival of the black monolith. Because of this, we can understand the result of the cue's interpolation here to be very different from that of the first example discussed above. Here, the cue allows us to understand the gravitas of the moment. As Spinks suggests, Deleuze's concept of active force suggests that its "characteristics are dominating, possessing, subjugating, and commanding" (Spinks 8). That is certainly, the role of the cue in this scene, for it announces that the apes have made an evolutionary advancement which has taken them from the position of the hunted to the hunter. They now take the dominant position in their ecosystem, and as such it is the role of the cue to represent and assert this dominance. Had the cue been introduced earlier its use would have suggested the dominance of nature or of the monolith over the ape's nature. Its introduction here allows us to read confidently that both the cue and the primates are active forces in their respective worlds.

The third and final instance of the cue comes in the final scene in the film. After passing through the star-gate, Dave Bowman ends his journey in what appears to be an oddly cold, unwelcoming, and yet comfortable French baroque style bedroom. Here his needs are met as he ages, perhaps more quickly than usual. Indeed, one has the sense that Bowman is not aging but transforming and evolving. He constantly sees himself in his next incarnation before he dismisses his former. The final time we see Bowman in a corporeal form he is lying in bed as a very old man, seemingly incapable of movement. The black monolith is again present at the foot of his bed and here once again appears to serve a transformative purpose. It is during this sequence that we hear the final instance of the *2001 Theme*. Bowman's body has now been replaced by a fetus in a womblike enclosure and he will subsequently be reborn as the star-child whose image ends the film. What has happened in this scene? According to Clarke's book, Bowman is freed from his physical body and is replaced by an intelligent and conscious being which no longer has the physical need for a corporeal body to contain and support it. As such Bowman has been freed to exist in consciousness and it is this representation of his transformation that is captured in the film's final image as the star-child is shown protected in the womb of space.

While not passive, such transformation does not contain the physical intensity of the earlier scene with the primates. As such, the role of the *2001* cue in this case is to represent the active translation of Bowman in time, space, and consciousness. This is very different than the active position of the cue as the representation of physical evolutionary change, expressed in the preceding example. There the cue represented the acquisition of physical prowess and acuity which allowed the apes to dominate their milieu. By virtue of this, the cue represents the savagery of the image and the situation's dominance. In this instance however, the cue although active, establishes an intensity which would be impossible to represent visually, the becoming-pure-consciousness of the human. This cannot be depicted cinematically without being expressed here by the cue, which we have come to understand as representing recurrence and becoming, a process which is always immanent. The cue, in this third and final instance, allows the significance of this translation of state to be realized visually and as such the image becomes reactive to the activity of the cue.

Conclusion

We began this essay by posing a theoretical and analytical question: how does one discuss a piece of film music that was not composed for the particular bit of the mise-en-scène which it accompanies? Certainly, this is not an unusual question in film music analysis, especially with the preponderance of appropriated scores in use today. Normal theoretical procedures quickly lead to a dead end, as does the desire to connect the cue to its original philosophical underpinnings.

With this realization we came to the conclusion that current analytical methodologies would not suffice. We decided that what was needed was a type of methodological bridge which would allow us to engage the interaction between the mise-en-scène and the score on a deeper level than previously thought possible. We found this platform in the philosophy of Gilles Deleuze. Deleuze's concept of the eternal return which he drew from Nietzsche allowed us to relate Nietzsche's philosophy to Strauss' tone-poem and via this through to Kubrick's mise-en-scène. Yet, this understanding of the various elements of the film as a form of an eternal recurrence did not allow us to do anything other than interrelate the various filmic components in a cohesive fashion, which left us still unable to account for the variations in mise-en-scène in which the cue was employed.

A further level of abstraction was necessary in order to overcome this issue and this was found in the application of Deleuze's concept of active and reactive force. By approaching the way in which each of the three statements of the theme relate to the mise-en-scène and attempting to discern whether the cue or the image was the dominant active force within the totality of the filmic universe, we were able to understand the role that the cue plays as different and distinct in each case. The application of the Deleuzian activity/reactivity to this level of abstraction allowed us to view the cue as a distinct musico/filmic entity overcoming the stilted passivity of our earlier attempts.

Throughout this essay we have encountered a series of theoretical roadblocks which would have hampered a traditional film musical analysis of the cue under consideration. Through the application of Deleuzian philosophical concepts we were able to understand the cue as occupying a much deeper relationship to the mise-en-scène than we had a first thought. Instead of being a mere reflection of the mood of the film, the cue has instead been rightly placed as an establisher of meaning, occupying a distinct, rich and productive relationship to the entirety of the filmic universe in each of its incarnations.

WORKS CITED

Agel, James. *The Making of Kubrick's 2001.* New York: New American Library, 1970.

Chion, Michel. *Kubrick's Cinema Odyssey.* London: BFI, 2001.

Conley, Tom. "Space." *The Deleuze Dictionary.* Ed. Adrian Parr. New York: Columbia University Press, 2005. 257–59.

Deleuze, Gilles. *Nietzsche & Philosophy.* Trans. Hugh Tomlinson. New York: Columbia University Press, 2006.

Deleuze, Gilles, and Felix Guattari. *A Thousand Plateaus: Capitalism and Schizophrenia.* Trans. Brian Massumi. Minneapolis: University of Minnesota Press, 1987.

_____. *What Is Philosophy?* Trans. Hugh Tomlinson and Graham Burchell. New York: Columbia University Press, 1994.

Rajchman, John. *Constructions.* Cambridge: MIT Press, 1998.

Sotirin, Patty. "Becoming-woman." *Gilles Deleuze: Key Concepts.* Ed. Charles J. Stivale. Montreal: McGill-Queens' University Press, 2005. 98–109.

Spinks, Lee. "Eternal Return." *The Deleuze Dictionary.* Ed. Adrian Parr. New York: Columbia University Press, 2005. 82–84.

Stagoll, Cliff. "Becoming." *The Deleuze Dictionary.* Ed. Adrian Parr. New York: Columbia University Press, 2005. 21–22.

PART VI

"SETTING THE CONTROLS FOR THE HEART OF THE SUN": COMPOSERS AND COMPOSITIONS IN SCIENCE FICTION FILM

12

Rocketship X-M: The Sounds of a Martian Breeze

John C. Tibbetts

"Music can even make *silence* speak."
— Rousseau, *Dictionnaire de musique*

"I feel the wind of another planet," sang the soprano soloist in Arnold Schönberg's Second Quartet.[1] Since this musical evocation of a "Martian breeze" was first heard in 1908, many composers for concert platform, radio, and screen have made their own journeys to and from the Red Planet.[2] Not the least of these musical planetary voyages was the score written by composer Ferde Grofé for *Rocketship X-M*, released in 1950 at the dawn of the space age. While the film itself has garnered its fair share of acclaim — even cult status — from legions of enthusiasts and buffs, the score itself deserves our special attention. It proclaimed the main title, propelled rocket and crew into space, floated free in deep space, landed on Mars, evoked nuclear holocaust, sang a beautiful love song, and tragically lamented a doomed return. Above all, it gave *music* to the vast silences of Deep Space. How that music came to be, and what it contributed to the flight of the RXM is the subject of this essay. Part of that story is a series of happy accidents that allow us now to watch and listen to a film whose images and music once seemed consigned to oblivion. As will be seen, thanks to a Kansas City producer, Wade Williams, both prophetic film and its weirdly *outré* music escaped oblivion and are now available to new generations of viewers.

Long before Steven Spielberg's wedding-cake monstrosities and Stanley Kubrick's warehouse-proportioned freighters lumbered across the galaxies, the sleek RXM navigated the spaceways bound for the moon and beyond. The film's release in 1950 echoed post-war anxieties regarding the Cold War and nuclear energy. Just a few months before, on 17 December 1949, Col. Charles A. Lindbergh had predicted moon flight when he addressed the Aero Club of Washington, D.C.: "We talk about flying to the Moon as freely as people talked about flying from one city to another before that December day at Kitty Hawk."[3] According to Dennis Fischer in his *Science Fiction Film Directors*, "It was the success of *Rocketship X-M* that launched a vogue for many subsequent films which defined science fiction for the mass audience" (476). Budgeted at a mere $94,000, and playing in only two hundred theaters (many of them independents), its first-year box office gross brought in a hefty $495,000.[4] Sure enough, soon after the release of *Rocketship X-M*, the cinematic heavens swarmed with more celestial bodies than were stabled at MGM. During the next three or four years, expeditions rocketed to the Moon (*Destination Moon, Project Moonbase*); targeted Mars (*RXM, Flight to Mars, Conquest of Space*); and blasted beyond the solar system (*When Worlds Collide* and television's *Tom Corbett, Captain Video,* and *Space Patrol*).

Robert Lippert's *RXM* and its nearest contemporary rival, George Pal's *Destination Moon* (also 1950), exemplified, respectively, what Judith Merrill once defined as the polarities of science fiction, "whirling wheels and soft footfalls of thought." While *Destination Moon* provided the whirling wheels, an array of expert rocketry advisors, special effects technicians, *RXM* sounded the soft footfalls of thought in its dystopian meditations on humanity's future. The Technicolor *Moon* rolled off the Universal assembly line with all the prestige of a customized, top-of-the line car; the black-and-white *RXM* tottered out from the used car lot of Poverty Row. *Moon* proudly boasted a budget three times that of *RXM* and the (then) impeccable credentials of science advisor Hermann Oberth and ace science fiction writer Robert A. Heinlein. *RXM* guiltily concealed its blacklisted writer, Dalton Trumbo, beneath a pseudonym, "I.A. Block."[5] *Moon* won an Oscar for its special effects and studio-designed lunar landscapes inspired by famed painter Chesley Bonestell. *RXM* relied on a chalk-board lecture and desert locations for its Martian terrain. *Moon* depicted a successful round trip to the Moon. *RXM* missed the Moon, crashed on Mars instead, and burned to a cinder on its re-entry to Earth. What *RXM did* have, and its rival did not, however, was a romantic core, interesting characters, and a tragic nobility to its cautionary message. More importantly, for our purposes, its composer, Ferde Grofé, by contrast to *Moon*'s composer, Leith Stevens, lent the picture his prestige as a famous composer of concert jazz and symphonic music.[6] These were the factors that, working in tandem, lifted *RXM* above the rest (as it were) and into the Hall of Fame of science fiction films.

A brief review is in order. *RXM* chronicled the story of the first manned expedition to the moon. Because of a fuel and equipment malfunction dur-

The screen's FIRST story of man's conquest of space!

ROCKETSHIP X-M

* EXPEDITION MOON

STARRING

LLOYD BRIDGES · OSA MASSEN · JOHN EMERY
NOAH BEERY, JR. · HUGH O'BRIAN WITH MORRIS ANKRUM

Written and Directed by KURT NEUMANN · Director of Photography KARL STRUSS, A.S.C.
Executive Producer MURRAY LERNER · Released by LIPPERT PICTURES, INC.

Original lobby card for *Rocketship X-M* (1950).

ing a meteor shower, it finds itself diverted on a trajectory for Mars. On board is a five-person crew, portrayed by Lloyd Bridges, John Emory, Hugh O'Brian, Noah Beery, Jr., and Osa Massen. Miss Massen finds herself the most misunderstood of the group as she alternately tries to defend her position on the crew (she *is* a woman in a man's world, after all), keep amorous swains like Lloyd Bridges at bay, and connect with her own awakening sense of romance and poetry (the film really is perhaps as much a story of her *inner* discovery as it is of the rocket's outer exploration). Upon landing on Mars, they find signs of a buried city and scattered artifacts scattered among the arid wastes. Evidence everywhere mutely attests to the holocaust that destroyed the planet. Suddenly the crew is attacked by the planet's only survivors, a tribe of savage, blind mutants. In scenes of mounting terror, two of the crew are killed while the others stagger back to the ship and hurriedly liftoff back to Earth. But there is not enough of the precious fuel left for a safe reentry. In the emotional highlight of the film, as Massen and Bridges embrace in their new-found love, they transmit a radio message describing the conditions and the message of the tragedy of Mars.[7] The ship plunges into Earth's atmosphere and is burned to a cinder.

Production

The film's original title, *Journey into the Unknown*, was later changed to *None Came Back*, then *Rocketship to the Moon*, and finally released as *Rocketship X-M*. Budgetary constraints demanded a quick shoot and a hasty post-production wrap. In a letter to Wade Williams, the legendary cinematographer Karl Struss (*Sunrise*, 1927, *Dr. Jekyll and Mr. Hyde*, 1931, *Island of Lost Souls*, 1932) confirmed that *RXM* was largely shot in Red Rock Canyon, and "was made in 4–5 weeks — quickly — in order to be released prior to [the] Technicolor Color science fiction film produced and directed by George Pal [*Destination Moon*]."[8]

Immediately, contemporary reviews took notice of the music. "Ferde Grofé's musical score fits the eerie mood of the story," wrote *The Hollywood Reporter* (25 April 1950). *Variety*'s "Brog" praised "the eerie music that builds mood" as "among the calculated means used to thrill" (3 May 1950). And Ezra Goodman, in the *Daily News*, specifically cited the "eerie theremin" music (29 May 1950). But it was the critic for *Downbeat* who delivered the fullest and most prescient commentary:

> [Here is] something rare in the movie business — a picture in which the underscore is an important box office factor. Without the music ... *Rocketship X-M* wouldn't intrigue even comic book readers.... Many critics refuse to take unpretentious Ferde Grofé seriously as a composer, but most agree that he has a gift for expressing concrete ideas in music. There should be a more important place for him scoring pictures [Emge 9].

He was born Ferdinand Rudolph von Grof to Emil and Elsa von Grof in New York City on 27 March 1892. He came by his instincts for music naturally, as his father was a baritone singer and his mother was a cellist and music teacher. When the family relocated to Los Angeles, Grofé began studying violin and piano when he was not taking on an assortment of odd jobs. In 1915, his arrangements and jazz improvisations came to the attention of popular bandleader Paul Whiteman, who invited him to join his orchestra two years later. Grofé made several notable arrangements for Whiteman, including the 1924 premiere of George Gershwin's *Rhapsody in Blue* (with Gershwin at the piano), several subsequent arrangements for chamber for a variety of ensemble groupings, an abridged version of Gershwin's *Concerto in F*, and the soundtrack scoring of the John Murray Anderson Universal film, *King of Jazz* (1930).[9] As historian John Warthen Struble notes, Grofé's "intimate knowledge of the individual capabilities of Whiteman's players" made him White-man's arranger of choice (106).

As a composer on his own, in the next two decades he wrote many successful compositions, including a tone-poem, *Broadway at Night* and the first of his many successful concert suites, the *Mississippi Suite*, which was followed in 1931 by the enormously popular *Grand Canyon Suite*. His humor and whimsy are revealed in several oddities, such as *Theme and Variations on Noises from a Garage* and *The Hudson River Suite*, for which he scored parts for bowling balls and ten pins. Other works further reveal his eclectic sensibilities to the American scene including: *Symphony in Steel, Tabloid Suite, Henry Ford, Death Valley Suite*.

Meanwhile, on the fringes of Hollywood's Glitter Gulch, he was scoring a handful of films from the 1930s through the 1950s. He is credited with *Diamond Jim* (1935), a 1944 documentary, *Minstrel Man* (for which he won an Academy Award), *Rocketship X-M* (1950), and *The Return of Jesse James* (1950).[10] Yet, as his son Ferde explains, Grofé's prestige as a jazz and symphonic arranger and composer failed to carry over into his Hollywood years:

> Even though my father had already been Academy-nominated for his score of *Minstrel Man*, with Benny Fields and Blossom Seely just a few years earlier, he had been largely ignored by the Hollywood community. The years before, during and after WWII in some quarters of the film industry were uncomfortable for someone like my father, whose full name was Ferdinand Rudolph von Grofé. A "von" anything in Hollywood could be a disadvantage. My dad was grateful that wasn't a problem for independent producer Robert Lippert. Lippert contracted with my father in 1950 to write the music for *RXM*— at a very modest price, I might add. For my father's side, he was pleased to get some work.[11]

Unable to lift himself out of the B-movie morass, Grofé by now had developed a distaste for the practice of film scoring. As someone who had occupied center stage as an arranger and composer, he suffered from the loss of control in the collaborative nature of filmmaking. All too often, he lamented, the music underlying dialogue scenes was muted to the point where it was virtually inaudible. This, as we shall see, became a particular problem in *RXM*. And there was the issue of mediocre assignments. "If Grofé remains a minor figure in film music," writes historian Ross Care, "it is merely because of the type of films which came his way.... Grofé's more well-known concert music could easily be taken for film music in search of a film...." (40–41).

Lippert Production's contract with Grofé was dated 31 March 1950 for a fee of $1250,00. He began work on the score on 10 April. At this point the unsung hero behind *RXM*'s music, Lippert's arranger/composer Albert Glasser, literally comes into the picture. According to Glasser, Grofé expressed reluctance to write the score when first approached. "Finally, after taking him to dinner several times, he agreed, but he never felt comfortable with the project. I still had to do the orchestrating and conducting since Ferde was only paid less than $1500 for the score" (quoted in Lipscomb 35). Glasser had served as a copyist in the 1930s at Warner Bros. for Erich Wolfgang Korngold, and had begun composing for low-budget films, beginning with the *Monster Maker* in 1944. Thus, Glasser, like Grofé, was thoroughly versed in orchestral scoring. Unlike Grofé, he was more familiar with the technicalities of timings between image and the music cues. During the post production, he took Grofé's sketches and orchestrated them for a 35-piece orchestra modeled after the instrumentations customarily used by Grofé in his concert suites. In particular, the choice of instruments evoking the textures of the dry, arid Martian terrain recall Grofé's use of winds and strings for portions of the *Death Valley Suite*. The effect is masterful and always in line with Grofé's intentions. (See the illustrations here comparing Grofé's penciled sketch with Glasser's finished product.) Elsewhere, brash Straussian declamations surmount winding, contrapuntally intersecting chromatic lines. Romantic melodies emerge from tonally ambivalent soundscapes. The nontraditional "effects" instruments include the Novachord, an electric organ notable for its "echo" resonances, and the theremin (played by Samuel Hoffman), an electronic device controlled by the performer's hand movements in front of two radio frequency oscillators.[12] The full vibrato of its reedy, rather "stringing" sound creates indeed an unearthly effect.

The theremin had been deployed earlier in avant-garde music performances by Edgar Varèse and in the movies in Alfred Hitchcock's *Spellbound* (1945). Within just a year after *RXM* it would be deployed extensively by Bernard Herrmann in *The Day the Earth Stood Still* and Dmitri Tiomkin in *The Thing*. Unfortunately, its subsequent overuse in Grade-B horror movies quickly became a cliché. In *RXM*, however, the interplay of the theremin's vibrato and the Novachord organ's echoing resonance achieves an innovative, unearthly effect.[13]

Glasser himself went on to score more than 100 films, including more fantasy and horror films, notably *The Amazing Colossal Man* in 1957. It is interesting to compare these scores to the work he did with Grofé. Unlike *RXM*, which uses music for atmospheric effects and emotional charge, Glasser's other films more closely follow the action with the traditional "Mickey-Mousing" technique characteristic of Hollywood masters Max Steiner and Dmitri Tiomkin.

In order to examine the function and effect of Grofé's music, we must turn to two sources, the soundtrack of the film and the music released in 1973 by Starlog Records. The latter contains the *complete* score, as recorded for the film. "While 'mixing' movie soundtracks," explains producer Kerry O'Quinn,

Glasser arrangement on three staves of Grofé's "Main Title" (courtesy Irv Lipscomb and Wade Williams Productions).

Grofé sketches the "Main Title" of *Rocketship X-M* (courtesy Irv Lipscomb and Wade Williams Productions).

"the music will often end up 'dipped under' the dialogue and effects; and in some cases may be eliminated entirely at the director's discretion. (We recall Grofé's fears of just such an occurrence.) The Starlog album contained *all* the music that was originally recorded by Glasser and the orchestra."[14] My notes represent a confluence of both, as noted.

Main Title: A trumpeting fanfare leads to the Main Title theme, a vaulting two-octave leap in the brass complemented by a descending chromatic figure. The counterpoint of the rising and falling figures forecast the film's story of man's first Olympian leap into space and the subsequent fatal return to Earth's gravity. With shots of the launch site, the music lapses into silence.

Countdown: Launch: Press conference scene: Professor Fleming (Morris Ankrum) tells newsmen: "Forever, Man has dreamed of visiting the nearest of heavenly bodies — some, for adventurous fantastic reasons; others, like ourselves, because they visualize the successful lunar expedition as a first step toward practical interplanetary travel." As the crew members climb into their bunks, a faint ostinato figure in the strings is heard under a winding figure, the Ascent Theme. This propulsive figure consists of chains of a rising, scalar figure in two-and-three-note groups. Higher and higher it goes, increasing in tempo and volume as the rocket blasts off and leaves orbit. The music, which shares an affinity with the rising crescendo of the "Sunrise" portion of *The Grand Canyon Suite*, is full of textured dissonances and creates tremendous suspense. The theremin is faintly heard for the first time.

Floating Free: The booster section is jettisoned, the rocket achieves escape velocity, and the last radio contact is made. For the first time the crew experiences weightlessness. The music hovers "weightlessly," as it were, between tonalities, as the brass, strings, and winds wind in and out in a delicious transparency of textures. The Novachord floats in and out. A sudden blast of brass in a minor-key variant on the Main Title theme proclaims news of an engine problem. (Cuts in the film's soundtrack are restored in the Starlog recording.)

Interrupted Mission: A fuel problem causes the ship to lose its trajectory. The Main Title theme is heard against a shot of the observatory tracking the mission.

Romance in Space: Crewman Floyd Graham (Lloyd Bridges) banters flirtatiously with Lisa Van Horne (Osa Massen). The romantic music of "Lisa's Theme" is scored for solo violin, harp, strings, and horn. Unfortunately, it is almost inaudible on the film's soundtrack. This is a great loss to the movie viewer; and one must turn to the soundtrack recording for the full effect of the music. The six-note legato romance for violin (and later for cello) is the emotional core of the music. It recurs later — again, heard only faintly on the soundtrack — scored for cello, during the dramatic moments before the rocket's return to Earth.

Approaching Mars: As the rockets careen out of control and the crew lapses into unconsciousness, the rising scalar figures of the Ascent Theme return, this time accompanied by the eerie sound of the theremin and the high, keening sounds of strings. Upon reviving, the crew discover their new trajectory is the planet Mars. In moments of intense silence, they adjust their

A tender moment between Osa Masson and Lloyd Bridges by moonlight, the setting for Grofé's "Lisa's Theme" (courtesy Wade Williams Productions).

retrorockets to slow their descent. Upon landing, a thunderstorm breaks out — "Mars extending us a welcome!" exclaims Dr. Eckstrom.

Theremin Solo: A track that was recorded for the film but never used. This is a variation on the theme heard in "Floating Free."

Exploring the Red Planet: The planet has thin, but breathable oxygen. While exploring the Martian terrain, the crew discovers a ruined city and evidence of planetary holocaust. "This is definitely blast effect coupled with intense heat," explains Eckstrom, noting the high degree of radioactive activity. "Ironic, isn't it, the highest attainment of intellect, always diverted to self destruction. What a lesson for our world. One blast and an entire civilization is wiped out. I should hate to think that any survived." The full orchestra erupts in a discordant blast of sound that lapses into the complex, muted interplay of double basses, Novachord, strings, and theremin. The effect beautifully complements the arid, sandy contours of the Red Planet.

The Martian Mutants: In the distance a horde of strange figures is seen. A six-note ostinato pattern in the double basses coupled with a rapidly repeating three-note figure is heard briefly. The figures disappear. Silence. Minutes later the strange figures reappear and the ostinato pattern is repeated. Counterpointing this now is an obsessively repeating chromatic figure in the strings that creates a painful, wailing effect. This is a highly complex sequence, scoring the ostinato figure against a complex interplay of double basses, Novachord, strings, and theremin. The pattern rises and falls, in a series of gradually accelerating accelerandos and ritardandos, by turn, underscoring the attacks of the mutants and the retreats of the astronauts. "We must get back to Earth, and tell them what we've found," says the dying Eckstrom.

None Came Back: Escaping in the rocket ship, Lisa and Floyd set a course for Earth. Realizing they have insufficient fuel to return safely to Earth, they send out a broadcast that warns Earth of what they have seen. Back home, Professor Fleming strides to the radio receiver as a variant in the winds of the "Ascent Theme" is repeated. As Fleming receives the news of the disaster, a tight closeup of his face is complemented by the gradually accelerating and intensifying Ascent Theme. Lisa and Floyd bravely embrace in their new-found love. A recapitulation of the Love Theme culminates in a discordant crash of descending brass and harp figures as the rocket hurtles to its doom.

End Title: Despite the tragedy of the RXM, Professor Fleming declares to the press that attempts at space flight will continue with the help of Providence: "There are times when a mere scientist has gone as far as he can — he must pause and observe respectfully while something infinitely greater assumes control." Fleming walks out to the empty launch site as the music swells in a last, brief triumphal variant of the Ascent Theme. Plans are afoot for an RXM2.

With the exception of "Lisa's Theme," Grofé's score is notable for its avoidance of the "big tunes" that were standard to the Hollywood "middle–European" style. Moreover, there is little of the aforementioned "mickey-mousing" strategy. Rather, Grofé seems to have inherited the more modernist models of Edgar Varése's Futurist-inflected works, which utilized the new theremin synthesizer and other electro-acoustic effects in creating what might best be described as "soundscapes." Varese, writes historian John Warthen Struble, "began to emphasize the need for new instruments to encompass a vastly wider variety of sound than those available to traditional ensembles, and to refine his conception of the composer's role in shaping organized sound structures" (270). Similarly, I refer here particularly to Grofé's unusual instrumental textures and ambiguous tonalities for the weightless, free-floating scenes in space and the crashing discords of the liftoff and crash sequences.

As if attentive to the film's prophecy of an RXM-2, the movie and its score, once consigned to oblivion after its initial runs in theaters and on television, found new life in the restoration efforts by its foremost fan, Kansas

A whimsical break between takes on the set of *Rocketship X-M* with Osa Masson catching up on her reading (courtesy Wade Williams Productions).

City–based entrepreneur Wade Williams. His determination to restore both to new generations of viewers is in itself a fantastic voyage of remarkable implications. After its theatrical run, the film was syndicated and 16mm prints sold to television in 1955, where they were cut and shortened for commercials and, in the process, lost their magenta tints in the Martian sequences. Williams spent six years in the early 1970s tracking down the rights to distributor Adrian Weiss, who owned Western Hemisphere rights to the Lippert pictures. Upon learning of his decease, Williams next turned to writer and director Kurt Neumann. A trip to Hollywood brought the news that Neumann had also passed away, and the original negative had deteriorated and had been destroyed. Undaunted, further investigation unearthed a fine-grain positive 35mm composite print, which was stored in the Warner Bros vaults (Warners owned the foreign rights to many Lippert films). Williams bought and restored the print. "In another six months or a year," Williams recalls, "*RXM* would have been lost forever in its 35mm theatrical format."[15] In 1979 Williams, who was likewise a fan of Grofé's music score, accompanied the film's theatrical re-release with a soundtrack album on the Starlog Records imprint.

When asked at the time about the possible disapproval of *RXM*'s fans to its refurbishing, Williams says, "If we hadn't given a facelift to this picture, it probably wouldn't have gotten any new bookings. It's a film with a good story and which develops characters, and today very few action films do that. For the most part, today's films are done by television directors who have to develop a climax every seven or eight minutes. *RXM* builds throughout the whole film. I don't know if today's audiences will find this dull by comparison with what they see today. But we have not changed the mood and pacing; I don't think there will be any complaints" (Tibbetts 12).

Finally, there is no question that Grofé's remarkable score is a vital component in the unusual dramatic power and seriousness of purpose that is *Rocketship X-M*. That both music and image conspired to deliver a powerful cautionary tale of nuclear holocaust we know. Perhaps more significantly, however, Grofé's music raises a very intriguing question: What will be the function and effect of music and performance in an Interplanetary Age? It's an intriguing question. Scores heard for space operas like the *Star Trek* and *Star Wars* series skirted the issue. They anchored their futuristic sagas securely backward into the quaint world of late 19th century music. More to the point, perhaps, were the examples of the all-electronic scores utilized in *Forbidden Planet* (1954) by Louis and Bebe Barron, former collaborators with John Cage, and by Gil Mellé for *The Andromeda Strain* (1971); and the experimental polytonal clusters of Krzysztof Penderecki in *The Exorcist* (1973) and Gyorgy Ligeti in *2001: A Space Odyssey* (1968).

Visionaries in the early Romantic age in Germany such as Novalis and Wackenroder, and the philosopher Schopenhauer, had long since predicted a kinship of music, machine, philosophy, and science that speaks in its own cosmic language.[16] A few decades later composer Hector Berlioz envisioned in his "A Description of Euphonia," a city far in the distant future that was one vast musical instrument operated by devoted citizens who gave their time, wrote Berlioz, "to acoustical research and to the study of that branch of physics which relates to the production of sound" (283). Remarkably, a similar conception of the wedding of music and physics appeared in Kim Stanley Robinson's 1985 novel, *The Memory of Whiteness*. Set in the 31st century, a brilliant physicist creates a strange, beautiful musical instrument called "The Orchestra," a kind of super-synthesizer, which contains within itself hundreds of instruments operating according to mathematics and newly discovered laws of physics. Performer and performance are joined in a perfect sensuous, psychological, and mechanical symbiosis in the creation of a galactic identity. As a result, writes Robinson, "the universe was a sort of music of ideas" (225).

An anxious moment as the rocket's trajectory has been deflected away from the moon (left to right: Hugh O'Brien, Osa Massen, Lloyd Bridges, John Emery and Noah Beery, Jr.) (courtesy Wade Williams Productions).

Grofé's music for *RXM*, with its modest orchestra of just 35 members, can hardly embody the vast scope of those prophecies. It would be preposterous to make such claims. But I do think it's no mere whimsy to suggest that it at least hints in its own humble way at a futuristic art form that will kick away altogether the "gravity" of performers and performance, systems of tonality and notation, and conventional instrumentation toward the creation of a new aural consciousness, a "music of the spheres." Meanwhile, at the very least, like the adaptable life forms in Clifford Simak's classic "City" stories, the sights and sounds of the restored *RXM* will seek out and lay claim to new audiences and new environments, some perhaps not even of this world....

NOTES

Author's Note: This essay could not have been written without the generous assistance of those stalwart custodians of the *Rocketship X-M* legacy, Irv Lipscomb and Wade Williams. This essay is dedicated to them. Mr. Lipscomb invites *RXM* enthusiasts to correspond with him (*ilipscomb@cfl.rr.com*).

1. In the final two movements of Schoenberg's Second Quartet (1908), a soprano voice joins the string players to declaim two poems by Stefan George, "Litany" and "Rapture." The latter poem's lines suggest a profound estrangement from the world. "This Martian breeze is mimicked in soft, sinister streams of notes," writes Alex Ross, "recalling the episode in *Salome* when Herod hallucinates a chilly wind. Special effects on the strings (mutes, harmonics, bowing at the bridge) heighten the sense of otherness, as singing tones become whispers and high cries" (51). This work appeared four years before the Earthling John Carter succumbs to the lure of the "Martian breeze" in Edgar Rice Burroughs' *A Princess of Mars* (1912).

2. Just a few examples of "Martian music" include Gustav Holst's famous "Mars," from *The Planets*, Bernard Herrmann's score for Orson Welles' radio broadcast of *War of the Worlds*, and contemporaneous with *RXM*, film scores by Mahlon Merrick for *Red Planet Mars* (1952), Raoul Krashaar for *Invaders from Mars* (1953), and Van Cleave for *Conquest of Space* (1956).

3. Pressbook, *Destination Moon*, Wade Williams files.

4. Financial report dated 31 March 1951, Lippert Papers in the Wade Williams Archives, Kansas City, MO. This is an impressive statistic, considering that the average ticket price at the time was just 35 cents. Other statistics regarding the film and its composer, unless otherwise indicated, are from these papers.

5. Irv Lipscomb reports that extant copies of the screenplay "officially" credit director Kurt Neumann as the author. However, in an undated letter from Glenn Erickson to Wade Williams, the subject of Dalton Trumbo's authorship is broached: "The information about Dalton Trumbo's writing of *RXM* came out in the 1980s. It apparently had been fairly common knowledge. A web search comes up with the Writers Guild page on 'Corrections.'" Lipscomb reveals that "I.A. Block" was Irving Block, who was on the *RXM* production staff. The IMDB lists Block as a "matte artist" for *RXM* and *Invaders from Mars*, and the writer of the story for *Forbidden Planet*. The question of Block's authorship of *RXM* requires further research.

6. By contrast to Grofé, who scored only one fantasy film, Leith Stevens made a name for himself scoring other fantasy films, including George Pal's *When Worlds Collide* (1951) and *War of the Worlds* (1953). He also contributed to the television series *The Twilight Zone* and *Lost in Space* (1953). See the tribute to Stevens in Larson, 76–80.

7. Dennis Fischer reports that Lloyd Bridges strenuously objected to shooting this love scene. "I begged [director Neumann] not to shoot that love scene," Bridges is quoted, "when we're plummeting to the Earth and we pour our hearts to one another. I told him, 'You know, at a time like that, it just doesn't make sense!' It seemed so *wrong* to me to destroy the illusion. I was sure people would laugh at it. But he insisted...." Happily, Bridges was wrong. That scene as it stands is the greatest emotional impact of the film. See Fischer, 475.

8. Letter from Karl Struss to Wade Williams, 8 October 1975. The *RXM* shooting schedule reports additional locations of Death Valley and the Nassour Studios (Irv Lipscomb letter of 24 May 2009).

9. In Howard Pollack's *George Gershwin: His Life and Work*, it is alleged that Gershwin objected to Grofé's "lean" scoring, because it "accentuated the music's connection with Milhaud and Copland" (355).

10. For further information on a number of Grofé's aborted film projects, see James Farrington's unpublished Master's thesis, "Ferde Grofé: An Investigation into his Musical Activities and Works."

11. Letter from Ferde Grofé, Jr., to the author, 3 February 2009.

12. The theremin uses the heterodyne principle to generate an audio signal. The instrument's circuitry includes two radio frequency oscillators. One oscillator operates at a fixed

frequency. The frequency of the other oscillator is controlled by the performer's distance from the pitch control antenna. The hand then acts as the grounded plate (the performer's body as the connection to the found) of a variable capacitor in an inductance-capacitance circuit. The difference between the frequencies of the two oscillators at each moment allows the creation of a difference tone in the audio frequency range, resulting in audio signals that are amplified and sent to a loudspeaker.

13. According to Randall Larson, in his history of music in the fantastic cinema, it was Glasser's idea to use the theremin (80).

14. Author's telephone interview with Kerry O'Quinn, 23 April 2009. The album was released on LP and to date has not been re-released on compact disc.

15. Author's interview with Wade Williams, Kansas City, MO, 21 April 2009. Aware that some of *RXM*'s scenes and special effects inserts needed to be re-made for his new release print, Williams trekked to the Mojave Desert in 1979 with a crew of *RXM* stalwarts who, like him, treasured the film that had inspired them in their youth. They included Bob Burns ("Major Mars"), production Manager and Supervising Editor; Technical Consultant Dennis Muren, who had just finished work on the starship for *Close Encounters*; Mike Minor, moonlighting while working as Production Designer on *Star Trek: The Movie*; and Irv Lipscomb. They all determined what new scenes would be shot — the rocket's liftoffs from Earth and the landing on Mars to replace the stock V-2 footage, scenes of the rocket under acceleration in space, and shots of the crew exploring the Martian terrain around the rocket. They worked on locations close to the original site of Red Rock Canyon (a highway now runs through the area). In 1979 Williams, who was a fan of Grofé's music score, accompanied the film's re-release with a soundtrack album on the Starlog Records imprint. For detailed accounts of the film's restoration, see Naha, Tibbetts, and Lipscomb.

16. The status of music as a "transfiguring power" in the Romantic sensibility cannot be overestimated. There is no better overview of this complex subject than John Daverio's *Nineteenth-Century Music and the German Romantic Ideology* (New York: Schirmer Books, 1993).

WORKS CITED

Berlioz, Hector. *Evenings with the Orchestra*. Trans. Jacques Barzun. New York: Alfred A. Knopf, 1957.

Care, Ross, "Into Orbit: The Scores of Ferde Grofé." *Take One*, January 1979, 40–41.

Emge, Charles. "Movie Music Reviews — Rocketship X-M." *Downbeat* Col. XVII, No. 15, 28 July 1950, p. 9.

Fischer, Dennis. *Science Fiction Film Directors, 1895–1998*. Jefferson, NC: McFarland. 2000.

Larson, Randall D. *Musique Fantastique: A Survey of Film Music in the Fantastic Cinema*. Metuchen, NJ: Scarecrow, 1985.

Lipscomb, Irv. "*Rocketship X-M* Lives Again!" *Space Wars* Vol. 3, No. 5 (November 1979), 32–37.

Naha, Ed. "*Rocketship X-M*: From the Brink of Oblivion." *Starlog* No. 7 (August 1977), 54–59.

Pollack, Howard. *George Gershwin: His Life and Music*. Berkeley: University of California Press, 1966.

Robinson, Kim Stanley. *A Memory of Whiteness*. New York: Tor Books, 1985.

Ross, Alex. *The Rest Is Noise: Listening to the Twentieth Century*. New York: Farrar, Straus and Giroux, 2007.

Struble, John Warthen. *The History of American Classical Music: MacDowell through Minimalism*. New York: Facts on File, 1995.

Tibbetts, John C. "Project RXM." *American Classic Screen* Vol. 3, No. 6 (July-August 1979), 8–12, 25.

13

Seeing Beyond His Own Time: The Sounds of Jerry Goldsmith

Cynthia J. Miller

Each person, who tries to see beyond his own time,
must face questions to which there cannot yet be absolute answers.
—The Illustrated Man, *1969*

It would be easy to suggest that if our cinematic imaginings of the future have a common thread, that thread was spun by Jerry Goldsmith. From the deception of rebirth, to the promise of first contact, Goldsmith's sweeping motion picture and televised soundtracks have brought universes to life, fueled voyages to distant planets, and animated fantastic beings in both the present and the future. For over forty years, his cinematic scores have shaped both our brightest fantasies and our darkest nightmares, creating a backdrop for frontiers, explorations, and encounters, and bringing music to the vast expanses of space that gave context to them all. However, to suggest that there was a "Goldsmith sound" available to the untrained ear — an absolute answer to the future that carried us from film to film, through narratives of aborted launches, alien menaces, and life-altering technology — would diminish the range and depth of Goldsmith's soundtracks, and place limits on the imaginings he sought to create. If anything, Goldsmith used sound in unanticipated ways, in order to interrogate our assumptions and invert our expectations of exactly how the "future" should sound.

With eighteen Academy Award nominations, including a 1976 win for Best Original Score for *The Omen*, five Emmys, nine Golden Globe nominations, and six Grammy nominations, Jerry Goldsmith was one of the film industry's most prolific, eclectic, and innovative film score composers. His soundtrack credits range from *The Sand Pebbles* (1966), to *Patton* (1970), to the *Rambo* series, to *Hoosiers* (1986), to *Along Came a Spider* (2002), with countless films in between. While these credits testify to Goldsmith's ease at composing scores across genres, his notable work in science fiction has helped to create enduring images of the future for generations of moviegoers. From his earliest futuristic work — *Planet of the Apes* (1968) and *The Illustrated Man* (1969) — to his latest — *Hollow Man* (2000) and *Star Trek Nemesis* (2002) — Goldsmith called upon orchestras and synthesizers, poems and motifs, to draw audiences into worlds far, far from their own.

As a composer, Goldsmith was noted for his innovation and adaptation to the changing face of sound production over the many decades of his career. Having begun scoring films in the twilight years of the "classical period" of the studio system (with the 1957 Warner Bros. release of *Black Patch*), Goldsmith entered the industry at a time when "a consistent system of production and consumption, a set of formalized creative practices and constraints, and thus a body of work with a uniform style, a standard way of telling stories, from camera work and cutting to plot structure and thematics" was well-established and maintained (Schatz 8–9). A look at his futuristic films will demonstrate the ways in which his compositions often stepped away from standard orchestral writing and performance, evoking contrasting images of time and space, and creating tension between the strange and the familiar. Familiar instruments, used in uncommon ways, created sounds that were otherworldly and unidentifiable; unfamiliar instruments, wrested from their contexts, added dimension to alien soundscapes.

As the music industry moved into the digital era in the 1980s, Goldsmith remained on the cutting edge, experimenting with Musical Instrument Digital Interface (MIDI) technologies and a range of synthesized sounds and effects, but still held that these new developments required perspective: "I don't look at it as a technology. I look at it as the improved means of expressing oneself" (Tibbetts). While agreeing that contemporary films provide a cutting edge environment for composers to experiment with music, he remained critical about the use of technology in film, however, and of the industry's emphasis on digital sound as an end in itself, rather than a means to achieve a larger narrative end, commenting that "a sound by itself doesn't mean anything. It's got to be put into a musical context. Then it means something" (Tibbetts). He states, "I'm not at all convinced about the musical validity of sounds. While I'm very impressed with some of the experiments I've heard, it's difficult to make music out of it. Music should be primary — it should make the effects, and not the other way around" (Mulhall 1).

Even though creating the sounds of the future, Goldsmith saw the use of digital technologies, such as synthesizers, not as a means of imitating or replacing "traditional" orchestral and acoustic sound, but as opening up new possibilities for expression in his scores: "It's not a matter of trying to disguise the sound of an orchestra, it's trying to expand the range and color. It's like having a new color in the color spectrum" (Tibbetts). Thus, even his most futuristic scores were hybrids — past and present, creating the future.

The Sounds of Future-Primitive

> "The question is not so much where we are, as when we are."
> — Charlton Heston, as Taylor in *Planet of the Apes*

Goldsmith's earliest full-fledged encounter with the future was actually an encounter with what might well be termed "future-primitive": Franklin J. Schaffner's *Planet of the Apes*, which was loosely based on the novel *La planete de singes* by Pierre Boulle (1963). Three astronauts in the year 3978 survive a crash landing, emerging from hibernation to find themselves on an unknown planet, where apes are the higher life forms, and humans, the primitive species. When one of the astronauts is killed, and the other lobotomized, George Taylor (Charlton Heston) becomes the central character, negotiating his captivity, release, and status as a sentient being, with ape scientist Zira (Kim Hunter) and archaeologist Cornelius (Roddy McDowall). Set in a world reminiscent of 20th century Earth, the *Planet of the Apes* finally unveils its darkest secret, that Taylor and his crew did not crash land on a planet in some unknown galaxy, but in fact returned to Earth, over 2000 years after their launch, to a world where the dominance of species had been reordered, and the "truth" about ape-human relations was hidden, and ultimately, destroyed.

Ranked in the American Film Institute's "100 Years of Film Scores" as the 18th best film score in American cinema, Goldsmith's work on this futuristic drama in a hostile world netted an Academy Award nomination (his fourth) in 1968, for Best Original Score in a Motion Picture (not a musical). The film's groundbreaking avant-garde score was influenced, as producer and music historian, Jon Burlingame, notes, by both Bartók ("A New Mate") and Stravinsky ("The Hunt"), but was "utterly original" (Burlingame). Goldsmith draws audiences into a primitivized future through sounds that seem drawn from an earlier, primordial time — the battle call of a ram's horn, as the gorillas on horseback first become visible; the gentle clatter of a vibraslap, resembling the rapid beating of metallic wings[1]; the hooting of the Brazilian cuica,[2] traditionally used by samba schools, is drawn on to create the apes' haunting calls; and the clamor of stainless steel mixing bowls, repurposed to add to the percussive effects of the soundtrack — a kind of *musique concrete* (Brown 178). Conventional instrumentation is subject to its own repurposing and inversion, as French horn players reverse their mouthpieces, string players bow with wood on strings, and clarinetists focus their attention on the clicking of keys, rather than the utterance of notes. While these odd and unrecognizable sounds evoked, for some, curiosity about the composer's use of synthesized music, the only technological enhancement used by Goldsmith for the *Planet of the Apes* score was the echoplex, typically in conjunction with pizzicato strings, creating multiple echoes and causing the notes from the plucked strings to combine and recombine. As Randall Larson notes, "This was an especially deft approach in a period when most science fiction films were characterized by the burgeoning electronic sounds then being developed" (Larson 245). For Goldsmith, this was a deliberate shift in representational strategies, which emerged from not only the soundscape he sought to create, but from the desire to grow — to challenge existing conventions in instrumentation[3]:

> There was a great deal of thought on my part on how to approach it.... The obvious way would be to use electronic and all sorts of synthetic means of reproducing the music, and I feel, without trying to sound pretentious, that the resources of the orchestra had just barely begun to be tapped, and I felt it was an exercise for myself to see what I could do to make some strange sounds and yet try to make them musically rather than effect wise [Larson 245].

These exotic, decontextualized sounds are complemented with more identifiable orchestral strains throughout the score: brass that blares and swaggers; the tension of high-pitched strings; woodwinds, alternately playful and fierce. The "Main Title," edgy and dissonant, with its echoplexed percussion and eerie bass slide whistle, warns of the randomness and tension inherent in the vastness of space, adding a new layer of discomfort to Taylor's stoic pre-hibernation reflection in his recorded log: "Seen from out here, everything is different. Time bends. Space is ... boundless. It squashes a man's ego. I feel lonely." The tension and inscrutability of vastness continues on the harsh, post-apocalyptic terrain of the planet's surface, and is given sonic expression in desperate percussive "chirps" in "The Searchers" and "The Search Continues." Taylor's team treks for miles across desert and over vast hills of rock, in search of water and signs of life. Hope dwindles, worldviews are challenged, and relationships become frayed, as the astronauts' bodies begin to falter from heat, exhaustion, and dehydration. Raw and primitive, Goldsmith's score uses complex combinations of percussion to move the characters through the landscape, but more significantly, as an intensifier for emotion: "The function of a score is to enlarge the scope of a film. I try for emotional penetration, not complementing the action" (Thomas 286). With the joyous discovery of water in abundance, comes the discovery of sentient life with "The Clothes Snatch- ers," as primitive, apparently mute humans make off with the team's belong- ings while they swim. The fraught percussion of the astronaut's search gives way to the dance of an impish xylophone, juxtaposed against low bass, broad brass and strings overlaid with playful percussive clacking ... and motion, always motion ... in fleeting progressive motifs, as clothes and the primitive inhabitants disappear in the overgrowth of the veldt.

The soundtrack's most acclaimed element, the soul-splitting call of the ram's horn, heralds the impending descent of the gorilla soldiers on horse- back in "The Hunt." Taylor's team and the primitive humans scatter in ter- ror, as the frenzy of capture and execution begins. Dodge (Jeff Burton) is killed; Taylor and Landon (Robert Gunner) are captured and imprisoned sep- arately in Ape City, leaving Taylor, wounded in the hunt, alone. The con- straint of Taylor's captivity is reflected in the sparse score, which bursts forth again in a frenzy of percussion, brass and strings as he flees through streets and over rooftops in "No Escape." From the distinct sound of water drop bars punctuating the foreboding strings in "The Trial," where the fate of both Taylor and the "truth" hang in the balance, through the rage and chaos of angry brass and clamoring strings in "A New Identity," where he discovers that Landon has been lobotomized, to the menacing high-pitched strings and cuica that signal the return of the gorilla soldiers in "The Intruders," Gold- smith's score contrasts and combines the future and the primitive in both the score's instrumentation and its disposition of sound, speaking to both the imaginative and instinctive worlds of its listeners (Bond 3). As musicologist Kathryn Kalinak notes, "The power of rhythm has frequently been traced to primitive origins, music 'borrowing' from human physiological processes — heartbeat, pulse, breathing — their rhythmic construction" (17). Goldsmith's use of a vast range of percussive sounds in *Planet of the Apes*, both rhythmic and decidedly arrhythmic, appear designed to harness not only the futuris- tic imagination, but the evocative power of the body's sympathetic tone and most basic, primitive responses — apprehension, panic, flight, anger — as well.

The film closes with the rounded, foreboding tones of horns and per- cussion in "Revelation Part II." A series of arpeggiated chords from guitar- like strings mark the threshold of bitter revelation, as Taylor and his "mate," Nova (Linda Harrison), released to discover their "destiny," discover the past instead — the half-buried form of the Statue of Liberty — and Taylor realizes that he has returned to an Earth that has fallen victim to the greed and hatred he lamented prior to his hibernation. These are the same selfish, destructive passions Cornelius read to him from the Apes' Sacred Scrolls:

Beware the beast, Man, for he is the Devil's pawn.
Alone among God's primates, he kills for sport or lust or greed.

Yea, he will murder his brother to possess his brother's land.
Let him not breed in great numbers,
for he will make a desert of his home, and yours.
Shun him; drive him back into his jungle lair,
for he is the harbinger of death [29th Scroll, 6th verse].

As Taylor falls to his knees, pounding his fist into the sand, the bellowing of his fury is accompanied only by the sound of the rushing wind, and waves, crashing on the shore. Goldsmith's soundtrack falls away, leaving Taylor's rage at the past, naked, on the beach of his species' future.

The Voice of Technology

> "Sanctuary is a pre-catastrophe code word, used for a place of munity."[4]
> — The Computer, *Logan's Run*

The post-apocalyptic warning voiced in *Planet of the Apes'* final revelation was reiterated in several of the futuristic films for which Goldsmith composed. Catastrophic thinking has always been a mainstay of science fiction, and advances in cinematic sound and visual technology elaborated those thoughts in ways not previously possible. Goldsmith's score to *The Illustrated Man* (1969) uses some of the same serial techniques found in *Planet of the Apes*, but here he focused the soundtrack on a combination of sterile, emotionless atonal electronics and an earthy, impressionistic theme with fragile, wordless soprano vocals to match the disquieting tone of Ray Bradbury's story collection, from which the film was adapted.[5] These contrasting elements weave together the main narrative — focusing on Rod Steiger's Karl, and his hypnotic, sensual relationship with the timeless witch, Felicia (played by Claire Bloom), who covers him in "skin illustrations" — and the three deadly, futuristic vignettes that mystically spring to life from her art. Adapting a more lyrical form of the serialist techniques that had been popularized in the 1950s,[6] Goldsmith's score is low-key and chamber-like (Dalkin 2001). The warm, round-toned score is heavily dominated by woodwinds and French horns. The orchestration includes minimal strings, and is absent trumpets, but adds celesta and sitar to the orchestra's percussive voices (Bond and Kendall 3). Featuring the first all-electronic cues of his career, the score to *The Illustrated Man*, with its atonality and tape delay effects, foreshadows a future where the awful reality of technology would be realized, both in the present film, and in the composer's later futuristic work, *Logan's Run* (1976). Here, Goldsmith uses the combination of technology (in the form of electronic effects) and melodic orchestra scoring (in the form of tone poem and fantasy) to narrate the dominance, deception, and death that the privileging of a different sort of technology can bring.

In *Logan's Run* the survivors of a holocaust now live in a domed city, sealed off from the rest of the world. Life within the dome is controlled by the Computer; all needs are met, all pleasures within easy reach. In order to control the density of this hedonistic population and safeguard scarce resources, however, life must end at thirty — a kind of sacred technological population ecology. At that time, birth cohorts enter a ceremony called "Carrousel" with the promise of "renewal" or rebirth. Non-believers, or those who simply choose not to relinquish life, attempt to escape outside the domed city. Known as "Runners," they are hunted and "terminated," by elite enforcement agents called "Sandmen."

Based on the 1966 novel by William F. Nolan, the film's narrative focuses on Sandmen Logan 5 (Michael York), and Francis 7 (Richard Jordan), and Logan's object of desire, Jessica 6 (Jenny Agutter), a member of a secret collective that aids runners in their search for a hideaway known only as "Sanctuary." Reigning as the cutting edge in futuristic soundtracks in the year before the debut of John Williams' score for *Star Wars*, the soundtrack to *Logan's Run* may be seen as the culmination of Goldsmith's innovation and experimentation with electronic sound through the 1960s and '70s. The composer's early electronic cues in *The Illustrated Man* have expanded and evolved into full-blown commentary on two key interlocking themes — the threat of the unreflexive privileging of technology, and the tension between society and the individual.[7] The score provides a passionate contradiction to dogmatic dialogue, such as Francis 7's comment to Logan, when early in the narrative, the latter questions the former's uncritical acceptance of Carrousel's "one is terminated, one is born" ideology:

> L: But you don't know. You just assume — one for one. What everyone's been taught to believe — one for one.
> F: Well, why not? That's exactly how everything works. It keeps everything in balance: one is terminated, one is born. Simple, logical, perfect. You have a better system?
> L: Of course not. At least I wonder about it sometimes.... Not like you with your automatic one-for-one routine....
> F: Logan, leave it alone. It's perfect. You wonder a lot; too much for a Sandman.... You know, when you question, it slows you down.

In much the same way as was previously seen in *2001: A Space Odyssey* (1968) and *Dark Star* (1975), computers are the agents of dehumanization, the nemesis of emotion, intuition, community, and hope for the future (Cumbow 72–73). While the film's score is noted for its traditional symphonic elements (Mulhall 1), it is, in fact, the duality of the soundtrack — the evocative, flowing melodies of the full orchestra associated, with Logan and Jessica's emotional relationship and the natural world outside the dome ("On the Circuit," "Love Theme," "Sun"), and the stark, three-note chromatic motive, on strings, keyboards, and atonal electronics associated with the City and life under its dome — that truly interrogates the future (Screen Archives).

Beginning with a slow, electronic drone in "The Dome," the first segment of a three-part opening, Goldsmith's three-note motif is introduced, and slowly builds into a sweeping orchestral statement, before giving way to the brief, efficient electronic tones of "The City," which function to create a propulsive ostinato as futuristic vehicles traverse transparent tubular roadways. The trilogy resolves with a celesta-based lullaby in "The Nursery," as Logan and Francis gaze at Logan's new descendant, Logan 6 — a child he has spawned, but, by custom, will not rear — a suggestion, perhaps, of a "renewal" other than the one offered by technology (a theme that re-emerges much later in the narrative, in the "natural" world outside the city's dome). That early three-note motif may be heard in virtually every piece in the score, from coarse synthetic sound invoked at the voice of the Computer, to the imaginative set pieces, reminiscent of Stravinsky ("Little Muscle") and Copland ("Monument").[8]

Throughout the soundtrack, Goldsmith's electronic cues each serve to highlight a de-centering of humanity: the ritual of imposed death, in both the frenzied coliseum spectacle of Carrousel and the fatal, taunting hunt of a desperate runner, are given emotional shape and form in the electronic cues "Flameout" and "Fatal Game"; the disorientation and fear of "The Assignment/Lost Years," frames Logan's forced metamorphosis into a runner, as he is stripped of four years on his life clock, and ordered to find and destroy "Sanctuary"; the "Love Shop" cue gives context to surreal, swirling visuals of smoke, erotic lighting, and anonymous writhing bodies in the City's pleasure palace; and the menacing force of the Computer's attempt to break Logan's will and extract information via holographic "surrogates."

Unlike the delayed post-apocalyptic despair found in the final scenes of *Planet of the Apes*, or the final horrors of the internal vignettes of *The Illustrated Man*, *Logan's Run* closes on the joy and optimism of the film's love theme, celebrating the triumph of humanity and the reunion with nature (embodied by Peter Ustinov as the Old Man). Goldsmith's work would continue to celebrate the retention and triumph of humanity in the next year, with the exuberant tonal resolutions of both *Alien* (1979) and *Star Trek: The Motion Picture* (1979).

The Final Frontier

"To explore strange new worlds. To seek out new life and new civilizations.
To boldly go where no man has gone before."
— Gene Roddenberry

No discussion of Jerry Goldsmith's soundtracks to the future would be complete without the sounds of those two spacecraft — the tow-ship and the starship — that dominated movie screens and imaginations in 1979. Differing dramatically in their missions and their narratives, *Alien* and *Star Trek* have each played a significant role in our imaginings of space, and of the future. Individually, their soundtracks each highlight the best of their genres; taken together, the two scores hint at Goldsmith's vast and diverse reach as a composer. The former, directed by Ridley Scott, is a terrifying masterwork about an alien creature that terrorizes and kills the crew of the towing vessel, *Nostromo,* the first space film featuring working-class characters (Peary 295). The latter, directed by Robert Wise, and produced by its creator, Gene Roddenberry, was the initial cinematic voyage of the starship Enterprise, and was the first motion picture based on a television series. The cinematic legacies of both films extend into the present day, through sequels, merchandizing spin-offs, fan culture, and of course, their soundtracks. The three *Alien* sequels (1986, 1992, 1997), and cross-over franchise, *Alien v. Predator* (2004, 2007), were scored by other composers, while Goldsmith remained a strong presence in the *Star Trek* franchise, scoring *The Final Frontier* (1989), *First Contact* (1996),[9] *Insurrection* (1998), *Nemesis* (2002), and the theme for the television spin-off series, *Voyager* (1995). Roddenberry was so taken with Goldsmith's opening theme, that he later insisted that it also be used for the new television series, *Star Trek: The Next Generation.* And for his part, Goldsmith was enthusiastic about his work with Roddenberry:

> I loved doing *Star Trek*! It's sort of a broad romantic canvas. *Star Trek* is very operatic, as far as I'm concerned. It's one of the few things that's bigger than life. The whole story is about a better world, a peaceful world, a better life.... The whole moral of it is really quite uplifting. There's that quality in the music, and they're just fun to do [Burlingame].

Goldsmith's expansive main title, so well-liked by Roddenberry, displays an elegant use of strings, percussion, and brass.[10] As it progresses, the broad, majestic theme conveys not only the vastness of space, but movement, and a sense of journey. The work transforms into a bold fanfare that builds to a heralding crescendo, as it ushers in the first appearance of the Klingons. This title theme presented two distinct challenges for the composer: first, to rewrite the theme of an already popular television franchise, and second, to create a unique main title that would rival John Williams' highly popular theme for George Lucas's *Star Wars*, which had debuted two years earlier. Film scholar Royal Brown credits Williams' score with almost "single-filmedly" reviving the popularity of the heroic, fantasy-driven romantic score — a genre of film music that had its heyday in the 1930s and early '40s — thereby changing the face of action and science fiction film music in the 1970s (Brown 118). From within this context, Goldsmith crafted one of the most acclaimed and well-recognized themes in the history of science fiction film. With its secondary theme, the romantic strings-over-woodwind "Ilsa's Theme," the film would also become the only *Star Trek* film to boast an overture.

The sweeping soundtrack for *Star Trek*, while privileging acoustic — and large-scale orchestral[11]— sound, defies its 1970s origins, making significant use of electronics in its sonic expression of V'ger's character, and in Goldsmith's acclaimed crafting of the soundscape for the Klingon battle. The introduction of the Blaster Beam, heard first in the Klingon battle, and again in V'ger's cues, is a key element in the composer's innovations for the film. The Blaster, an enormous metal beam with a scaling magnet, can be played with a variety of objects, to create dark, unnatural sounds. A fearsome noise in the bass regions, it is also used to add an air of menace to the V'ger cloud. "The Cloud," and other suspenseful cues, is enhanced by wind-and-surf effects that would resurface over a decade later, in *Total Recall* (1990) (Filmtracks).

In *Alien*, on the other hand, the composer returns to the all-acoustic strategy that proved so effective in *Planet of the Apes,* to create what Jon Burlingame cites as one of the composer's "most complex, eerie, and intense scores." With an echoplex as the only electronics, the composer once again turns to unfamiliar instruments in his sonic representation of the parasitic alien — the ram's horn, conch, didgeridoo, and serpent[12]— as well as revisiting unfamiliar performance techniques of innovative bowing and the clacking of keys in the brass. With few "romantic" cues at all, Goldsmith's strong atonal 12-tone composition and careful orchestration create one of cinema's most enduringly chilling scores, bleak and dissonant, as it moves past the main title and into swirling action cues. In a post-production interview, director Ridley Scott described the score as "seriously threatening, but beautiful. Has beauty, darkness, and seems to play the DNA of some distant society..." (*Alien*).

The *Alien* score, however, was fraught with controversy for Scott and Goldsmith. Though they would work together again years later, their disputes on this film have become the stuff of legend. Initially, the tension focused on the character of the main title, which Goldsmith would ultimately rewrite.

> I thought, well, let me play the whole opening very romantically and very lyrically, and then let the shock come as the story evolved. In other words, don't give it away in the main title. So, I wrote this very nice main title. There was

mystery, but it was lyrical mystery. It didn't go over too well. Ridley and I had major disagreements over that. So then, I subsequently wrote a new main title, which was the obvious thing, weird and strange, and which everybody loved, and I didn't love [*Alien*].

The "Hyper Sleep" cue was also a point of contention. Here, for the crew's emergence from the sleep pods, Scott employed a temporary track for use during production, taken from Goldsmith's earlier work on the film *Freud* (1962). Goldsmith's score replaced that borrowed track with a mysterious, impressionistic lullaby; Scott, however, bought the rights to the *Freud* cue, and it became part of the final score. Additionally, Scott replaced Goldsmith's end credits with Howard Hanson's "Symphony No. 2," a choice that Scott acknowledges angered the composer: "I don't think he ever forgave me for using Howard Hanson for the end of the film." In summing up their creative differences at the time, Goldsmith observed:

> Music cannot replicate the visuals; that's not what it's supposed to do. The message I was getting from him was that he wanted me to be visual with the music. I can't be visual with the music that's not what I'm supposed to do. Let the director and the cinematographer put the visuals on the screen, and let me do the emotional element [*Alien*].

Scott, the director, has also been criticized for his shredding of the score in the original soundtrack (which Goldsmith later recorded with the National Philharmonic Orchestra as a unified concert work), excising cues from the "craft and egg chamber" sequences on the planetoid's surface, which achieve some of Goldsmith's boldest experimentation (Drannon; Charleton). Here, the soundtrack crosses from underlying score to diegetic sound, as Goldsmith's music blurs boundaries to mimic, and become part of, the on-screen action.[13] These cues also introduce the complex, acutely precise *Alien* motif which recurs throughout the creature's reign of terror, until the chimes of the end title track herald the crossing of a narrative threshold and the soundtrack's tonal resolution (Charleton).

Sound, Vision, Memory ... Future

> "I always think of space as being the great unknown.
> Not as terrifying, but questioning...."
> — Jerry Goldsmith[14]

Goldsmith's forays into the time and space of the future continued into the new millennium, with films that probed more and more deeply at our collective understandings of what the unknown might hold. Some of these are discussed elsewhere in this volume, others remaining subjects for another day. In 1981, he revisited an earlier partnership with Peter Hyams, with whom he had worked on *Capricorn One* (1978), to create *Outland* (1981), a bleak science fiction remake of Fred Zinnemann's 1952 western, *High Noon*, that starred Sean Connery, as the new marshal of the mining colony on Jupiter's moon, Io. Written in the lyrical, dramatic style rejected by Scott for *Alien*, Goldsmith's opening credits to *Outland* recall the film version of *Alien*'s main titles. In 1990, Goldsmith's work on Paul Verhoeven's science fiction–action hybrid, *Total Recall*, would emphasize his uncanny abilities to construct emotional and psychological texture so tangible, it would function as another character in the narrative's unfolding. The composer would team with Verhoeven again in another futuristic genre-blending film, the 2000 science fiction–thriller *Hollow Man*. These films, along with his *Star Trek* sequels, join the over ninety films and television broadcasts scored in the last twenty years of Goldsmith's prolific career, many of which contained fantastic, time-bending, or futuristic elements, including *Supergirl* (1984), *Twilight Zone: The Movie* (1983), *Innerspace* (1987), and his unused score for *Timeline* (2003). With his focus always on enlarging the scope of the film, through innovation, adaptation, and his desire to constantly expand the range and expression of his music, Goldsmith's work has filled cinematic visions of the future with cherished majestic themes and uneasy atonal contrasts. By embracing and blending the full range of sound, and the possibilities for creating it, from lyric orchestral romanticism to the harshest of electronic effects, Goldsmith's music ushers the listener into the great unknown. He, like the witch in *The Illustrated Man*, creates space for questions about the nature of the future, and then, reminds that there cannot be absolute answers.

NOTES

1. A modernized version of the jawbone, consisting of a wooden ball, connected to a cowbell-shaped resonator box, by means of an L-shaped metal rod.

2. The cuica is a Brazilian friction drum.

3. In a similar spirit, Bernard Herrmann's experimental score for *The Day the Earth Stood Still* (1951) suggested electronic music without the use of electronic instruments.

4. "Munity," according to Webster's Revised Unabridged Dictionary (1913), indicates "freedom, security, immunity."

5. This adaptation of Ray Bradbury's collection of short stories led to the author's collaboration with Goldsmith the following year on the cantata *Christus Apollo*.

6. It should be noted here that composer Luigi Dallapiccola (1904–1975) began innovations with lyrical serialism as early as the 1930s.

7. The film's key themes remain the subject of debate in science fiction. Michael Crichton, author of *The Andromeda Strain* and *The Terminal Man*, disagrees with this position, arguing that the film is a statement about "contemporary America's preoccupation with youth" (Peary 250), while Kevin Mulhall limits his argument to "society versus the individual" (Mulhall 3).

8. Stravinsky's influence on Goldsmith, noted earlier in *Planet of the Apes*, would also be apparent in the composer's title theme for *The Omen* (1976).

9. Scored with his son, Joel Goldsmith.

10. The Main Title was initially a point of contention between Goldsmith and director Wise, who criticized an early version as "too nautical."

11. At its fullest, the score called on a 90-piece orchestra.

12. The serpent is an ancient wind instrument, related to the Euphonium and Baritone. When played loudly, it creates a sound reminiscent of a large animal in distress.

13. This synchronizing of musical and visual action is known as "Mickey-Mousing," due to its prevalent use in animated cartoons.

14. Commentary in "Future Tense: Music and Editing" from the post-production supplement to the director's cut of *Alien*.

WORKS CITED

Alien. "Future Tense: Music and Editing." Post-production interviews. Director's Cut. 2004.

Bond, Jeff. Liner notes, *Planet of the Apes*." Audio recording, Varese Sarabande, 2004.

_____, and Lucas Kendall. Liner notes, "The Illustrated Man." Audio recording, *Film Score Monthly*, 2001.

Brown, Royal. *Overtones and Undertones: Reading Film Music*. Berkeley and Los Angeles: University of California Press, 1984.

Burlingame, John. "A Jerry Goldsmith Retrospective." Audio recording featured on *L.A. Confidential* WKUSC, University of Southern California, February 22, 2009.

Charlton, Darren. "*Alien: The Complete Original Score* Soundtrack Review." 2008. <www.jerrygoldsmithonline.com>

Cumbow, Robert C. "Prometheus: The Scientist and His Creations." *Omni's Screen Flights, Screen Fantasies: The Future According to Science Fiction Cinema*. New York: Doubleday, 1984.

Dalkin, Gary S. "Jerry Goldsmith: The Illustrated Man." *Film Score Monthly* 42:01, 2001. <www.musicweb-international.com>

Drannon, Andrew. "*Alien* Soundtrack Review," 1999. <www.scoresheet.tripod.com>

Filmtracks. "*Star Trek: The Motion Picture*, Filmtracks Editorial Review." <www.filmtracks.com>

Kalinak, Kathryn. "The Language of Music: A Brief Analysis of Vertigo." *Movie Music, the Film Reader*. Kay Dickinson, ed. London: Routledge, 2003.

Larson, Randall. *Musique Fantastique: A Survey of Film Music in the Fantastic Cinema*. Metuchen, NJ: Scarecrow, 1985.

Mulhall, Kevin. Liner notes, "Jerry Goldsmith: Frontiers." Audio recording, Varese Saraband, 1997.

Peary, Danny. *Omni's Screen Flights, Screen Fantasies: The Future According to Science Fiction Cinema*. New York: Doubleday, 1984.

Schatz, Thomas. *The Genius of the System*. New York: Pantheon, 1988.

Screen Archives Entertainment. "Logan's Run." *Film Score Monthly* <www.screenarchives.com>

Thomas, Tony. *Music for the Movies*. Los Angeles: Silman-James Press, 1997.

Tibbetts, John. "Jerry Goldsmith." Videotaped interview, 1986.

About the Contributors

Mathew J. Bartkowiak is an assistant professor of English at the University of Wisconsin–Marshfield/Wood County. He is the author of *The MC5 and Social Change: A Study in Rock and Revolution* (McFarland, 2009). His research interests focus on popular culture studies, popular music, social change, and the 1960s counterculture.

Cara Marisa Deleon received her M.A. in film studies from the University of Iowa and her M.F.A in film and video production from Savannah College of Art and Design. She is an award-winning filmmaker and an assistant professor of media arts and mass communication design at California State University–Chico.

Kathryn A.T. Edney earned her Ph.D. at Michigan State University in American studies in 2009. She is an Editorial Advisory Board member for the *Journal of Popular Culture* and has published and presented on various aspects of American musical theater.

Kit Hughes received her M.A. in media studies from the University of Texas at Austin in 2009, where she served as a senior editor for FlowTV.org and a member of *Velvet Light Trap*. Her most recent project explores the representation of fictional psychic figures and the formal construction of their visions on American television.

Stephen Husarik is a professor of humanities/music and head carillonneur at the University of Arkansas–Fort Smith. He attended the School of the Art Institute (Chicago) and the universities of Illinois and Iowa. Dr. Husarik is co-editor of *Interdisciplinary Humanities* and has published numerous articles in music and humanities journals.

Matthias Konzett has taught at Yale and Tufts University. He is currently teaching at the University of New Hampshire in the areas of film studies, theory and modern literature and drama. He is the author of *Rhetoric of Dissent* and editor of *The Encyclopedia of German Literature*.

Jerome J. Langguth is an associate professor in the Philosophy Department at Thomas More College in Crestview Hills, Kentucky. His research interests include Kant's aesthetics, the philosophy of music, and the philosophy of film.

Cynthia J. Miller is a cultural anthropologist, specializing in popular culture and visual media. She is currently a scholar-in-residence at Emerson College in Boston and serves as associate editor of *Film & History: An Interdisciplinary Journal of Film and Television Studies*. She is currently at work on an edited volume, *Too Bold for the Box Office* (forthcoming, Wayne State University Press), and on *The Encyclopedia of B Westerns* (forthcoming, Scarecrow Press).

Seth Mulliken is a Ph.D. student in communication, rhetoric, and digital media at North Carolina State University. He holds an M.F.A. in filmmaking from Temple University and has taught audio and radio production at Villanova University. His research interests include aural subjectivity, sonic identities, and sound as a political force.

Gregg Redner holds a Ph.D. in film studies from the University of Exeter, where his dissertation applied the philosophy of Gilles Deleuze to the analysis of film music. He is a faculty member in the Film Studies Department at the University of Western Ontario. Gregg is also a graduate of the Juilliard School from which he holds a double master's degree in organ and harpsichord performance. His research on film music has been published in *Studies in French Cinema, Music, Sound and the Moving Image* and *Rhizomes,* as well as in various anthologies on film.

Lisa M. Schmidt is a Ph.D. candidate at the University of Texas at Austin. Her research interests encompass genre, phenomenology, sound, television and fandom. Her dissertation, titled "Sensational Genres: Experiencing Science Fiction, Fantasy and Horror," employs phenomenology to explore how embodied filmgoers experience contemporary fantastic genres.

Katherine Spring is an assistant professor of film studies at Wilfrid Laurier University. Her research interests include film sound and music, American film history, and theories of narration. Her essays and reviews have appeared in *Cinema Journal, Film International,* and *16:9.* She is currently at work on a book about the relationship between Hollywood and Tin Pan Alley during the film industry's transition to sound.

John C. Tibbetts is an associate professor in the Department of Theatre and Film at the University of Kansas. He is an author, educator and broadcaster as well as an artist and pianist. He holds a Ph.D. from the University of Kansas in multi-disciplinary studies. He has worked as a news reporter for CBS Television and National Public Radio; produced classical music programming for Kansas Public Radio; written (and illustrated) 14 books, more than 200 articles, and several short stories.

A. Bowdoin Van Riper is a historian specializing in the cultural relations of science and technology. He received his Ph.D. in the history of science from the University of Wisconsin–Madison and teaches at Southern Polytechnic State University in Marietta, Georgia. He is the author of four books as well as numerous articles on the history of nineteenth-century geology and archaeology, the history of aerospace technology, and images of science and technology in popular culture.

Index